The Seven Seals o

FIRST VISION

First Seal	Second Seal	Third Seal	Fourth Seal
White Horse	Red Horse	Black Horse	Pale Horse
Deception	War	Famine	Pestilence
Matthew 24: 4-5	Matthew 24: 6-8	Matthew 24: 7-8	Matthew 24: 7-8
Revelation 6: 1-2	Revelation 6: 3-4	Revelation 6: 5-6	Revelation 6: 7-8

Fifth Seal
Great Tribulation
Tribulation of Early Saints
Matthew 24: 9,21-22 Luke 21: 23-24
Revelation 6: 9-11

BIRTH OF JESUS CHRIST

B.C. 720 NATIONAL CAPTIVITY

1260 (DAYS OF YEARS)

THE 'WILDERNESS' PERIOD

A.D. A time, times, and half of time (1260 ye
540 THE NOURISHING PERIOD (in her pla

★ ★ ★
★ ISRAEL
★ GOD'S
★ TRUE
★ KINGDOM ★
★ ★ ★

Revelation 12: 1-6, 13-14

And there appeared a great wonder in heaven; a woman clothed with the sun and the moon under her feet, and upon her head A CROWN OF TWELVE STARS.

And there appeared another wonder in heaven; and behold a great red dragon, having seven heads and ten horns, and seven crowns upon his heads.

GOD'S CHOSEN WOMAN

"THE WOMAN FLED INTO THE WILDERNESS WHERE SHE HATH A PLACE PREPARED OF GOD"

SECOND VISION

554 — 554 -1814 = 1

In 1814, just 1260 years after "deadly wou

The ROMAN EMPIRE, 31 B.C.- A.D. 476, in 2 divisions West and East Fall of the ROMAN EMPIRE A.D. 476	
1st HORN The VANDALS (rooted up) A.D. 429-533	
2nd HORN The HERULI Odoacer's Government A.D. 476-493	
3rd HORN The OSTROGOTHS (rooted up) A.D. 493-554	
TWO HORNED "LAMB DRAGON" and "IMAGE"	

4th HORN DEADLY WOUND HEALED (to continue 1260 years)	"IMPERIAL RESTORATION of empire by Justinian A.D. 554 He recognized supremacy of the Pope in the West	1st HEAD of BEAST (healed) ridden by a woman in purple robes.
5th HORN	FRANKISH KINGDOM Began 774. Charlemagne crowned by Pope A.D. 800	2nd HEAD ridden by woman
6th HORN	HOLY ROMAN EMPIRE (German head) Otto the Great crowned by Pope. 962	3rd HEAD ridden by woman
7th HORN	HAPSBURG dynasty (Austrian head), Charles the Great crowned by Pope. 1520	4th HEAD ridden by woman

THE FALSE
GREAT RED D
HEADS,

T0102862

Sixth Seal

Heavenly Signs

Sealing of God's People

Revelation 7: 1-17

Matthew 24: 29-30

Joel 2: 30-31

Revelation 6: 12-17

Revelation 14: 1-5

REV chap 1 to 11

Seventh Seal

Silence in heaven

(Revelation 8: 1-6)

A.D. 2001

Seven Trumpet Plagues

First Trumpet	Second Trumpet	Third Trumpet	Fourth Trumpet	Fifth Trumpet	Sixth Trumpet	Seventh Trumpet
One third of trees and all grass burned	One third of sea becomes blood, one third of sea creatures die, one third of ships destroyed	A great 'star' falls upon earth. One third of rivers become wormwood	One third of moon, sun and stars darkened	Locusts and scorpions symbolic of atomic war of radiation	200 million horsemen see third of humanity killed, humanity refuses to repent war lasts 13 months	Great earthquake and hail Two prophets slain in Jerusalem Kingdom of God established
Revelation 8:7	Revelation 8:8-9	Revelation 8:10-11	Revelation 8:12	Revelation 9:1-12	Revelation 9:13-21	Revelation 11:15

ISRAEL'S DESTINY

AFTER TWO DAYS HE WILL REVIVE US: (HOSEA 6:2) IN THE THIRD DAY HE WILL RAISE US UP - AND WE SHALL LIVE IN HIS SIGHT.

The Dragon was wroth with the Woman and went to make war with the remnant of her seed. Revelation XII. 17

Angels with Seven Vials

First Plague	Second Plague	Third Plague	Fourth Plague	Fifth Plague	Sixth Plague	Seventh Plague
Sores on people who accepted mark of beast	Sea turns to blood, all sea creatures die	Rivers turn to blood	Sun scorches humanity with great heat, humanity blasphemes God	Beast's seat of government afflicted Great Tribulation	Euphrates dried up, world's armies gathered to Armageddon The three unclean spirits	Great earthquake and hail, the fall of Babylon, the Great Voice saying IT IS DONE
Revelation 16: 2	Revelation 16: 3	Revelation 16: 4-7	Revelation 16: 8-9	Revelation 16: 10-11	Revelation 16: 12-16	Revelation 16: 17-21

A.D. 1800

A.D. 1280

(0 years) 520 years

...place) THE REVIVAL PERIOD

RESTORATION PERIOD SEVEN TIMES PUNISHMENT ENDS

1 = 1260 YEARS BEAST CONTINUED → 1814

REV chap 12 to 22

wound" was healed, the "HOLY ROMAN EMPIRE" was dissolved

8th HORN	NAPOLEON'S KINGDOM (French Head), crowned by Pope, 1805	5th HEAD ridden by woman

"HOLY ROMAN EMPIRE" was dissolved

GOSPEL RESTORED 1820

9th HORN (One IS)	ITALY, united by Garibaldi, 1870 to 1945	6th HEAD ridden by woman

Beast ascends out of pit

(One yet to come) 10th HORN	Revived ROMAN EMPIRE, by 10 rulers under one leader	7th head and ten HORNS

★ ★ ★
SATAN'S
COUNTERFEIT
KINGDOM
★ ★ ★

The Ten HORNS

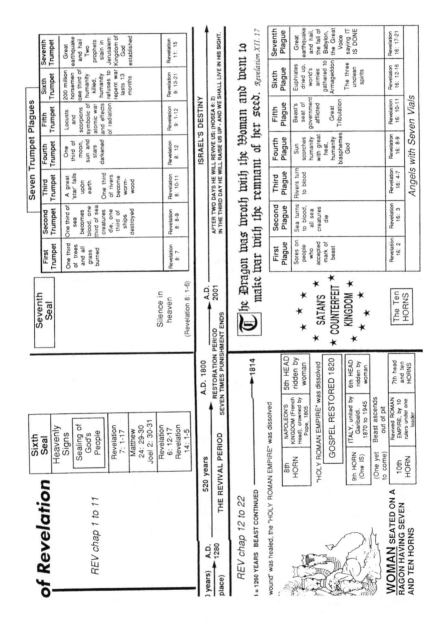

WOMAN SEATED ON A [D]RAGON HAVING SEVEN AND TEN HORNS

Order this book online at www.trafford.com
or email orders@trafford.com

Most Trafford titles are also available at major online book retailers.

Printed in Victoria, BC, Canada.

ISBN: 978-1-4269-2161-2 (sc)

ISBN: 978-1-4269-2298-5 (dj)

Library of Congress Control Number: 2009912302

Our mission is to efficiently provide the world's finest, most comprehensive book publishing service, enabling every author to experience success. To find out how to publish your book, your way, and have it available worldwide, visit us online at www.trafford.com

Trafford rev. 11/11/2009

www.trafford.com

North America & international
toll-free: 1 888 232 4444 (USA & Canada)
phone: 250 383 6864 ♦ fax: 812 355 4082

Photocopying of charts and diagrams

Permission is given to photocopy, and enlarge if necessary, any of the charts and diagrams in this book for closer study.

However permission is limited to singular copies for personal use only. Due to the length, the chart in the front of the book: THE SEVEN SEALS OF REVELATION had to be printed in two sections. Therefore, after copying the section on the right hand pages can be cut alongside the end bar; and the two sections pasted or glued together in the appropriate position to form a complete chart.

Unlocking
The Patmos Code

By William Walker

THE REVELATION
of
JESUS CHRIST
to
JOHN THE APOSTLE
on the
ISLE OF PATMOS – 96AD

The Revelation of Jesus Christ given to the apostle, John, on the Isle of Patmos in 96AD contained in what is known as the Book of Revelations, has been an enigma to bible students for generations.

BUT NOW THE CODE HAS BEEN CRACKED.

You can now read the
REAL, PLAIN, STRAIGHT FORWARD and EASY
interpretation only in this book;
UNLOCKING THE PATMOS CODE.

Be ready for some surprises.

Acknowledgements

To my Heavenly Father and His son Jesus Christ for their eternal love and inspiration.

To the pioneers and exponents of new ideas and truths in past ages who have challenged the traditions of men, suffering great hardships and persecution, and at times the cost of their lives, but whose spirit lives on in the legacy of their written word and testimony.

To my friend, Ron Larter, who assisted with artwork and graphics in the making of many charts and diagrams.

I am deeply indebted to my son Jörg, who spent many hours preparing the manuscript, and for his helpful comments.

To my family, who have given me their love, respect and encouragement at all times.

To my American friend Cory Brand without whose help this work would not have been possible.

Finally, words cannot express my gratitude to Freda, my eternal companion and devoted wife for her love, patience, constant support and encouragement at all times.

William Walker
Feburary 2006

esus answered and said unto them, this is the work of God, that Ye believe on Him whom He hath sent.

They said therefore unto Him, what sign shewest thou then, that we may see, and believe thee? What dost thou work?

Our fathers did eat manna in the desert; as it is written, He gave them bread from Heaven to eat.

Then Jesus said unto them, verily, verily, I say unto you, Moses gave you not that bread from Heaven; but my Father giveth you the true bread from Heaven.

For the bread of God is he which cometh down from Heaven, and giveth life unto the world.

Then said they unto Him, Lord, evermore give us this bread.

And Jesus said unto them, I am the bread of life: he that cometh to me shall never hunger; and he that believeth on me shall never thirst.

John 6:29-35

Introduction

There is a story of a man who traded blankets with an Indian for a pony. When the Indian returned to the Reservation, he found that the man had given him more than the agreed amount of blankets. The next day the Indian returned the surplus blankets and the man asked why he had done so. "I did not know I had given you too many." The Indian replied, pointing to his head, "I have two voices in here, one is a good man and one is a bad man; all night they argue, Good man say, 'Take blankets back', Bad man say, 'Keep blankets' and I get no sleep, so now I have returned blankets I can sleep with peace."

The moral of the story is that we all have two voices which we listen to. One which speaks the truth and encourages goodness, the other that leads us into error and evil. When we stop listening to the voice of truth we die spiritually and we retard our progress.

The Lord said, "I am the Way, the Truth, and the Life, no man cometh unto the Father but by me and ye shall know the Truth, and the Truth shall make you free." (John 14:6 – John 8:32)

When someone dies physically we take them to a cemetery and bury them. Each time we fail to heed the promptings of the spirit of truth, we die spiritually and we bury some part of ourselves – our character/talents/virtues/friendships.

Jesus said, "The Kingdom of God is within you"

> Within you is the power of LOVE
>
> Within you is the power of FORGIVENESS
>
> Within you is the power of REPENTANCE
>
> Within you is the power of FAITH

We may gain the whole world, but if we fail to find that which God had hidden within us, the rest is unimportant.

Paul said,

> *"For to be carnally minded is death; but to be spiritually*
> *minded is life and peace.*
> *Because the carnal mind is enmity against God: For it is*
> *not subject to the law of God, neither indeed can be.*
> *So then they that are in the flesh cannot please God.*
> *But ye are not in the flesh, but in the spirit, if so be that*
> *the spirit of God dwell in you."*

Romans 8:6-9

> *"And be not conformed to this world: But be ye*
> *transformed by the renewing of you mind, that ye may*
> *prove what is good, and acceptable, and perfect, will of*
> *God."*

Romans 12:2

In order to receive the 'Hidden Manna' of God's divine truths Paul says, one must shed the carnal mind, also the search for material things. In its place we must focus our minds on the spiritual things of life, that the spirit of truth may dwell in us. He goes on further to say that this would require "A RENEWING OF THE MIND". Yes, a complete change of direction, clearing out of the mind and heart the things of little consequences. Then, and only then, will we be able to prove that which is true and good and acceptable before God. May this book be received on these merits.

There is a beautiful illustration in a song called "The lost Chord". The organist said, "Seated one day at the organ, I was weary and ill at ease and my fingers wandered idly over the noisy keys." The organist struck a beautiful chord, but because of lack of concentration or some distraction, he lost it. He goes on to say, "I have sought but I seek it vainly that one lost chord divine which came from the soul of the organ and entered into mine." What a tragedy! What a tragedy to lose a beautiful truth, to lose faith, to lose a virtue, enthusiasm or a soul-satisfying conviction.

The last verse says, "It may be that death's bright angel will speak in that chord again, yet it may be that only in heaven I shall hear that great Amen."

However, it may be that even in Heaven we will not be able to recover the priceless riches of truth that we reject here on Earth.

What of Truth and Error?

Let us suppose that you have been taught a certain tradition either religious, historical, or even political. Then someone comes along and shows you quite factually, logically and categorically that it is incorrect. Would you be the kind of person to accept the New Truth? Do I hear you say you would?

What is the natural reaction? Well, no one or, very few, will accept that they are ever wrong, especially when the error has become a tradition. The general reaction is to defend the tradition. You may say, "Oh yes! But not me." However, it may be that the new truth sounds so incredible or unbelievable that it would mean a complete reversal of your beliefs so that instead of listening to the voice of Truth, you would defend the tradition. The Scribes and the Pharisees had this same problem.

Jesus said,

> *"For laying aside the commandments of God ye hold the tradition of men."*
>
> Mark 7:1-13

> *"And they were astonished at his doctrine: For he taught them as one that had authority, and not as the scribes."*
>
> Mark 1:22

> *"And it came to pass, when Jesus had ended these sayings, the people were astonished at his doctrine."*
>
> Matthew 7:28-29

> *"If I have told you earthly things, and ye believe not, how shall ye believe if I tell you of heavenly things?"*
>
> John 3:12

During the Feast of Tabernacles the Saviour went into the temple and taught;

*"And the Jews marvelled, saying, how knoweth this man
letters, having never learned?
Jesus answered them, and said, my doctrine is not mine,
but His that sent me.
If any man will do his will, he shall know of the doctrine,
whether if be of God, or whether I speak of myself."*

John 7:14-17

The Jews said, "How does this man know what he is talking about? He holds no theological degrees." "What college did he graduate from? He is only a carpenter's son." Is that not typical of our day?

*Then came the Jews around about him, and said unto
him, How long doest thou make us doubt? If thou be the
Christ tell us plainly.
Jesus answered them, I told you and ye believed not: The
works that I do in my father's name they bear witness of
me.
But ye believed not, because ye are not of my sheep, as I
said unto you.
My sheep hear my voice, and I know them, and they
follow me:
And I give unto them eternal life; and they shall never
perish, neither shall any man pluck them out of my hand.*

John 10:24-28

Only the true sheep will listen to and accept the voice of truth, they will not enquire into a man's background or education, they will only judge the words and works.

You are going to read in this book some new opinions in answer to God's revealed word. You will either have an open mind, or a closed mind. If you can overcome the prejudices and traditions of the fathers, then the words and ideas of this book will cast a new revelation upon your life, the windows of Heaven will be opened unto you and you will eat of THE HIDDEN MANNA (Rev 2:17). To eat of the Hidden Manna is to discover the hidden truths of God's divine plan and word, and when you also drink of the fountain of God's divine water, you will never thirst again.

> *"I will give unto him that is athirst of the fountain of the water of life freely."*
>
> *Revelation 21:6*

Yes, you have to be thirsty and ready to drink of that fountain. Thirsty for truth.

In the story 'Christmas Carol' Ebenezer Scrooge is visited by Marley's ghost. Scrooge asks Marley why he was dragging chains and fetters. Marley answers, "These are the fetters which I forged in my life."

However, we who are living do not have to wait until death to feel the weight of our fetters. In this life we shackle ourselves to traditions of men, error, ignorance, immorality, intolerance, ingratitude, unforgiveness and misunderstanding.

This book is written to assist you to unshackle yourself from the traditions of men. However, you and only you can break the fetters.

STATEMENTS BY PROMINENT LEADERS OF THE CHURCH OF JESUS CHRIST OF LATTER-DAY SAINTS

Wilford Woodruff said:

"Let us have truth; if any man has a truth that we have not, we say let us have it. I am willing to exchange all the errors and false notions I have for one truth, and should consider that I had made a good bargain. We are not afraid of Light and Truth, our religion embraces every truth in heaven, earth or hell. It embraces all Truth, the whole Gospel and plan of salvation, and the fulfilment of the whole volume of revelation that God has ever given."

Discourses

John Taylor said:
"We are after Truth. We commenced searching for it, and we are constantly in search of it, and so fast as we find any true principle

revealed by man, by God, or by holy angels, we embrace it and make it part of our religious creed."

Discourses

Joseph Smith said:
"This I believe,... if any man will prove to me, by one passage of holy writ, one item I believe to be false, I will renounce and disclaim it as far as I promulgated it."

Teachings of the Prophet Joseph Smith, page 137

May you read this book in the same spirit as words of these great men.

CONTENTS

This book is divided into four sections:

The Battle of Armageddon
The Angels with the Vials
The Great Misconception

SECTION 2: Israel's Eternal Destiny

Israel's National Awakening
Israel's Spiritual Awakening
A New and Everlasting Covenant
A New and Greater United Kingdom
One Supreme Monarch
A New Constitution
The Seventh Event
The Battle of Armageddon
George Washington's Vision
Modern Israel's Blindness removed
When the Towers Fall the Countdown Begins
The Jews Recognise their God
The Holy Festivals Restored

Table of Figures

SECTION ONE:

JOHN'S FIRST VISION:
THE BOOK WITH SEVEN SEALS

1
SETTING THE SCENE

To many the "Book of Revelation" is deemed to be one of the most difficult books in the Bible.

Students and Laymen alike are mystified by its symbols which speaks of Seals, Trumpets, Vials, Beasts with Seven Heads – and Ten Horns!; Beasts like a lion, a calf, a Flying Eagle – and even one with the face of a man!. Red Dragons, Scorpions, Earthquakes, Thunders and Lightening; and great woes: of unclean spirits which look like frogs. Of Olive Trees and candlesticks; Thrones, and people clothed in white garments. It speaks with rich contrast of the true and the false; of a TRUE WOMAN WITH A CROWN OF TWELVE STARS UPON HER HEAD; chased by a Serpent or Dragon. Of a FALSE WOMAN ARRAYED IN ROBES OF PURPLE and decked with gold, pearls and precious stones, RIDING A SCARLET COLOURED BEAST WITH SEVEN HEADS AND TEN HORNS – drunken with the blood of the Saints.

It speaks of a 'GREAT CITY' full of evil, and a 'BELOVED CITY', which one day will be full of glory.

Of a day of great rejoicing when the great deceiver and all that has deceived the earth is cast out.

Of a 'marriage' between Christ and the 'OVERCOMERS'.

And of a great day of judgement of a NEW HEAVEN and a NEW EARTH!

What do all these things mean? Can we unravel the story? Can we decipher the strange symbols? Or find a Key to unlock the hidden treasures of this Book?

The answer is Yes!

Once we have mastered the symbols – then the Book of Revelation reads like any other book.

John the Apostle

John, the apostle of Jesus Christ had experienced very hard times in his old age. He was over ninety years of age when he was banished by the Romans to the prison island of Patmos, on the coast Asia not far from Ephesus. Today Patmos can be located in the Aegean Sea off the west coast of Turkey, one of the Dodecanese islands.

The exact date on which the revelation was received by John is not known but is believed to be 96 AD. It was there on Patmos that the risen Christ appeared to him – disclosing the contents of the Book of Revelation (Revelation 1:17-19).

It was a pre-written history foretelling events from that time 96 AD and future, concerning in particular the true Church of Christ and also concerning Gods chosen twelve tribe nation of Israel which was by that time dispersed and scattered in various parts of the Earth (John 7:35) except for remnants of the House of Judah (Jews) and a few of the other tribes still residing in Judea.

It also foretold approaching developments in the great and powerful Empire of Rome which at that time was the ruling power over all the earth! However, this Pagan Empire was destined within two centuries to divide in two, and within three centuries to fall completely, making way for a revived system (Papal Rome) which would succeed it and hold temporal power in Europe for 1260 years.

John was given various revelatory experiences which comprised two main visions. As he received each of these individual revelations he recorded them in written word, whilst the experience was still clear in his mind.

Firstly he received seven individual messages to the seven existing branches of the Church in Asia (Revelation 1:11): EPHUSUS, SMYRNA, PERGAMOS, THYATIRA, SARDIS, PHILADELPHIA, and LAODICIA. These messages are recorded in chapters 1 – 2 – 3.

Commencing chapter 4 John was shown "things which must be hereafter". These revelations recorded a panorama of history from John's day until the end of this present age concluding with chapter eleven.

The Book with Seven Seals

In chapter 5 John sees a book in the hand of the personage in the vision which was written "within and on the backside" (i.e. written on both sides?!) sealed with Seven Seals. It seems from this account that the 'book' was not a book as we understand it to be, but a scroll, which, while being gradually unrolled revealed the sequence of events step by step between the first and second advents of the Lord Jesus. We are informed that only the Saviour himself was worthy to unlock or unseal the scroll.

Why Symbols?

Now the question may be asked: Why didn't the Saviour reveal the contents of this revelation in plain and simple language – why all the symbols and mystery? Surely this would have saved all the confusion there is today, and has been throughout previous generations, regarding the interpretation.

What we must remember is the political and social circumstances in which the revelation was given. In that day Rome was the most powerful and brutal Empire the world had seen. It crushed all opposition to its authority without question, whether it is military, political or social – by states, groups of individuals, by spoken or written word.

John was a political prisoner on a Roman prison island, he had been sent there because he was considered to be a political and religious threat to their pagan empire.

The island of Patmos was not just a place of exile, it was a penitentiary controlled by a cruel and brutal Roman administration.

Some of the prisoners, as in most penitentiaries, were trustees; those who were not considered a threat to the island authorities. John, due to his age, was seemingly a trustee and given certain privileges, i.e. freedom of movement about the island to a certain degree and materials for writing, however, his movements would have been monitored and his writings examined, had there been any evidence of subversion he would have been executed and his writings destroyed.

When the island Roman Governor read what John had written in what is now called the Book of Revelation he must have been as mystified by all the symbols as many have been since. And like many today considered it all to be a fairy tale; with Dragons and Beasts with seven heads and ten horns; coloured horses, frogs, etc. BUT IT WAS NO FAIRY TALE.

And so the truth was hidden in symbolism for its protection. The same can be said of the writings of Daniel and Ezekiel who were taken prisoners to Babylon about 604 BC, especially the visions received by Daniel; these are also full of symbolism. The punishment for subversion by the Babylonians was no less than that by the Romans, both were equally brutal.

Folklore

During the dark ages the seekers and promoters of truth found devious ways to promote the word of God. The most popular was in the imagery and symbolism of Folklore or Fairy Stories. The most popular are the Fairy Stories collected and recorded by the brothers JAKOB and WILHELM GRIMM. Except for the efforts of these two men more than 200 stories might have been lost forever.

Many of the stories are closely related to the stories of the Bible. They are particularly valuable to us for their preservation of the racial heritage which reaches back to the times of Abraham, Isaac and Jacob, the patriarchs of the Old Testament. They give evidences of the highly Christian character of the Anglo-Saxon-Celtic people, as these stories are saturated with Bible truths.

The symbolism of these tales can be compared with the symbols of the Bible. Indeed, many of the symbols of Revelation and Daniel are interchangeable. So immersed were the Saxon people with the Bible content that every fairy tale is flavoured with the message that the Holy Word holds.

Many suppose that the Grimm Brothers were the authors of the Fairy Stories, termed "The Household stories of the Brothers Grimm" but they did not create or originate any of the stories. They merely collected and recorded for posterity the 'old folk tales' that were passed on from generation to generation at family gatherings. They became increasingly aware of the values of these stories, both moral and religious, and began writing them down faithfully as they heard them. They never strayed from the oral tradition. Like Daniel of the Old Testament and John of the New they faithfully wrote down each story exactly as it was told to them, not knowing the full import of it all. The brothers were quite aware of the tale's magic attraction for children. "BUT THEY SENSED SOMETHING IN THEM OF A FAR DEEPER VALUE". The first volume was published 1812, the second volume of NURSERY and HOUSEHOLD TALES was published in 1814! It is obvious that the chief source of the tales is the Bible. There is the constantly recurring theme of JACOB or JACK who had twelve sons, as in JACK AND THE BEANSTALK, and THE TWELVE BROTHERS.

Another theme that is often used is the long trek taken by the children of Israel fleeing through the 'wilderness' or the 'forest' from their captivity in Assyria.

The most popular of the stories are SNOW WHITE, SLEEPING BEAUTY, CINDERELLA, HANSEL AND GRETEL, JACK AND THE BEANSTALK, LITTLE RED RIDING HOOD, SNOW WHITE AND ROSE RED, THE TWELVE BROTHERS, THE ENCHANTED STAG, THE FROG KING, THE SEVEN RAVENS, RAPUNZEL.

These all convey a biblical message – mainly concerning the history of Israel.

Symbolism of the Nursery Rhymes

In addition to the Fairy Tales there are the nursery rhymes – some of the original ones containing biblical symbolism, such as JACK (JACOB) and JILL, HUMPTY DUMPTY, LITTLE BO PEEP. All that one has to do is to work out the meaning of the symbols.

> Little Bo Peep has lost her sheep
> And doesn't know where to find them
> Ba-ba-ba
> But leave them alone – they will come home
> Wagging their tails behind them

Little Rachel she is weeping in every street
Ba-ba-ba
All have strayed from the shepherds care
All are wand'ring in a cruel nightmare
All have forgotten it's time to prepare

"Thus saith the LORD; A voice was heard in Ramah, lamentation, and bitter weeping; Rachel weeping for her children refused to be comforted for her children, because they were not."

Jeremiah 31:15

Who was Rachel?

The younger of the daughters of Laban, the dearly loved wife of Jacob, and mother of Joseph and Benjamin (Gen. 29 - 31; Gen. 33: 1-2, 7; Gen. 35: 16, 24-25; Gen. 46: 19, 22, 25); her grave (Gen. 35: 19-20; Gen. 48: 7; 1 Sam. 10: 2). Jeremiah, in a very beautiful passage, pictures Rachel as weeping in Ramah for her children, the descendants of Benjamin, Ramah being the place at which the exiles were assembled before their departure for Babylon (Jer. 31: 15). Matthew quotes the passage in his description of the mourning at Bethlehem (where Rachel's grave was) after the murder of the children (Matt. 2: 18).

Bible Dictionary

Yes she was the wife of JACOB or JACK. Obviously LITTLE BO PEEP refers to Rachel who was the mother to Israel's sons Joseph and Benjamin, and Grandmother to Ephraim and Manasseh. They are the 'Lost Sheep' who have strayed from the Shepherd's care. Jeremiah looked into the future and saw the weeping and mourning of Rachael for 'lost' Israel. Sheep and Shepherds in olden days were symbols which the people could understand. But in all these fairy tales and nursery rhymes few understand their meaning. Only those who are spiritually minded and are acquainted with biblical history and stories will 'see' their deeper meaning, because most of our Anglo-Saxon people have strayed from the Shepherds care, and in consequence all are wandering in a spiritual nightmare of spiritual darkness.

LOST to the knowledge of their Israelitish identity (Romans 11:25)!

AND ALL HAVE FORGOTTEN IT'S TIME TO PREPARE!

Prepare for what? – To be sure, the return of the Master Shepherd: The Lord Jesus Christ.

Israel's Spiritual Decline

Our people are mostly like the unwise virgins – having no oil in their lamps – and having no 'LIGHT' to show the way or guide them back to the fold or accept their true identity. They will not be prepared for the marriage feast. They will not be ready for the Bridegroom when he comes.

Revelation 19:7-8   Marriage supper of the lamb
Matthew 25:1-13   Parable of the Virgins

It is not the author's intention to explain the symbolism of all the popular fairy tales or nursery rhymes, but one or two are selected to show examples of how imagery and symbolism are used to convey a message. That our forefathers and mothers were obviously aware of their hidden meanings. That the use of imagery and symbolism is not exclusive to the Bible – to Daniel, John the Revelator, or Ezekiel and others. Folklore and fairy tale symbols were used by our early forefathers to protect their lives from the 'Image of the Beast'. The purpose of introducing the symbolism of fairy tales and nursery rhymes is to acquaint the readers in the interpretation of symbols. To prepare your spiritual eyes for the task of interpreting the imagery and symbolism contained in the book of Revelation and Daniel.

Jack and Jill

> Jack and Jill went up the hill
> To fetch a pail of water
> Jack fell down and lost his crown
> And Jill came tumbling after

Who would suspect that in this innocent little rhyme there is a very outstanding piece of biblical history!

Jack is Jacob or Israel represented by the tribe of Joseph through his son Ephraim who received the birthright. Jill representing the House of Judah received the crown or monarchy over all the tribes of Israel.

> *"Now the sons of Reuben the firstborn of Israel, (for he was the firstborn; but, forasmuch as he defiled his father's bed, his birthright was given unto the sons of Joseph the sons of Israel: and the genealogy is not to the reckoned after the birthright.*
>
> *For Judah prevailed above his brethren, and of him came the chief ruler; but the birthright was Joseph's)."*
> 1 Chronicles 5:1-2

These tribes of Jacob did in fact 'go up the hill' Mt Sinai, there to receive the life giving water of the Law of the Gospel – the 'ordinances' of which would have, HAD THEY BEEN OBEDIENT, ensured their eternal salvation and exaltation.

This was echoed by Jeremiah

> *"O Lord, the hope of Israel, all that forsake thee shall be ashamed, and they that depart from me shall be written in the earth, because they have forsaken the Lord, **the fountain of living waters**."*
> Jeremiah 17:13
> Emphasis added

The Throne of David

Eventually the Lord installed the line of DAVID and SOLOMON – who were of the House of Judah through his son Pharez – as custodians of His (the Lords) throne.

> *"Then Solomon sat on the throne of the LORD as king instead of David his father, and prospered; and all Israel obeyed him."*
>
> 1 Chronicles 29:23

> *"And I was with thee whithersoever thou wentest, and have cut off all thine enemies out of thy sight, and have made thee a great name, like unto the name of the great men that are in the earth.*
>
> *Moreover I will appoint a place for my people Israel, and will plant them, that they may dwell in a place of their own, and move no more; neither shall the children of wickedness afflict them any more, as beforetime,*
>
> *And as since the time that I commanded judges to be over my people Israel, and have caused thee to rest from all thine enemies. Also the LORD telleth thee that he will make thee an house.*
>
> *And when thy days be fulfilled, and thou shalt sleep with thy fathers, I will set up thy seed after thee, which shall proceed out of thy bowels, and I will establish his kingdom.*
>
> *He shall build an house for my name, and I will stablish the throne of his kingdom for ever.*
>
> *I will be his father, and he shall be my son. If he commit iniquity, I will chasten him with the rod of men, and with the stripes of the children of men:*
>
> *But my mercy shall not depart away from him, as I took it from Saul, whom I put away before thee.*

And thine house and thy kingdom shall be established for ever before thee: thy throne shall be established for ever.

According to all these words, and according to all this vision, so did Nathan speak unto David."

2 Samuel 7:9-17

"I have found David my servant; with my holy oil have I anointed him:

With whom my hand shall be established: mine arm also shall strengthen him.

The enemy shall not exact upon him; nor the son of wickedness afflict him.

And I will beat down his foes before his face, and plague them that hate him.

But my faithfulness and my mercy shall be with him: and in my name shall his horn be exalted.

I will set his hand also in the sea, and his right hand in the rivers.

He shall cry unto me, Thou art my father, my God, and the rock of my salvation.

Also I will make him my firstborn, higher than the kings of the earth.

My mercy will I keep for him for evermore, and my covenant shall stand fast with him.

His seed also will I make to endure for ever, and his throne as the days of heaven.

If his children forsake my law, and walk not in my judgments;

If they break my statutes, and keep not my commandments;

Then will I visit their transgression with the rod, and their iniquity with stripes.

Nevertheless my loving kindness will I not utterly take from him, nor suffer my faithfulness to fail.

My covenant will I not break, nor alter the thing that is gone out of my lips.

Once have I sworn by my holiness that I will not lie unto David."

Psalm 89:20-35

In the land of Canaan they continued to live as a UNITED KINGDOM for nearly 500 years, and during the reign of David and Solomon they reached the zenith of power.

The Ancient Dispute

However in the year 975 BC when Solomon's son Rehoboam became king, ten of the tribes represented by Ephraim rebelled against the House of Judah, due to Rehoboam introducing a Poll Tax (shades of our modern days)! These ten tribes formed a separate nation calling themselves the House of Israel or Ephraim. Thus the UNITED KINGDOM of twelve tribes had become a DISUNITED KINGDOM of two separate nations. BUT THE MONARCHY AND THRONE OF DAVID REMAINED WITH THE SOUTHERN KINGDOM OF JUDAH with its capital at Jerusalem.

The northern kingdom of Israel (Ten Tribes) with its capital in Samaria, 'elected' a line of kings from the tribe of Ephraim to rule over them. BUT THEY DID IN FACT 'LOSE THE CROWN'.

Figure 1. Israel and Judah

The Disunited Kingdom

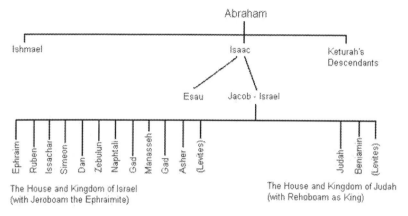

Figure 2. The Disunited Kingdom

And after this division, their histories, prophecies, and destinies all became completely different.

Benjamin: The Light Bearer

Only ten tribes of the kingdom were taken from Rehoboam – one of the eleven tribes was given to the king 'as a light' (1. Kings 11:36). This light bearing tribe was quite evidently BENJAMIN (1. Kings 12:21) which remained with the House of David and formed the Kingdom of Judah with the addition of some Levites and a remnant of others.

The tribe of Benjamin disproved the decision to be included with the Southern Kingdom, and eventually settled near Galilee after the Ten Tribes had been deported to Assyria. They became known as Galileans, and it is interesting to note that all the original Twelve Apostles were Galileans of the tribe of Benjamin (except for one – Judas Iscariot who was of the tribe of Judah)!

An echo of the ancient dispute between the House of Judah and the House of Israel is heard in a bit of old folklore.

> The lion and the unicorn
> Were fighting for the crown
> The lion beat the unicorn
> And chased him out of town

As most students of biblical history are aware, each of the twelve tribes had a tribal emblem. The emblem of Judah was a Lion. The emblem of Ephraim was a Unicorn or Bull Calf.

Judah and Ephraim did fight over the crown. And Ephraim was literally 'chased out of town' or out of the capital Jerusalem.

The Captivity of the House of Israel (10 Tribes)

The ten-tribed House of Israel was decadent from its very earliest days, practising wicked idolatry through the instigation of its first king JEROBOAM the son of Nebat,

> *"Who made two calves of gold, and said unto them "*
> *(unto the ten-tribed Israel) "it is too much for you to go up*
> *to Jerusalem" (to worship and sacrifice)": behold thy gods,*
> *O Israel, which brought thee up out of the land of Egypt"*
> 1 Kings 12:28
> Emphasis added

Thus from the very inception of the Northern Kingdom, their departure from God, His Commandments, Statues, and Judgement, led them to the depths of wickedness.

To learn the whole sad story of the sinfulness of these Ten Tribes, we need only to read a comparatively short section of the scriptures, from Jeroboam's sin (1 Kings 12:25) to the fall of Samaria (2 Kings 18). Their history is represented concisely by the following passage:

> *"For so it was that the children of Israel had sinned*
> *against the Lord their God... and walked in the statutes*
> *of the heathen ... they set them up images (images of the*
> *'Queen of Heaven' for example) and groves, (or shrines)*
> *in every high hill and under every green tree (painfully*
> *evident today in some Roman Catholic countries) ... and*

they built them high places in all their cities... and there they burnt incense in all the high places, as did the heathen ... to provoke the Lord to anger ... yet the Lord testified against Israel, and against Judah, by all the prophets and by all the seers, saying, turn ye from your evil ways, and keep my commandments and my statutes ... notwithstanding they would not hear, but hardened their necks... therefore the Lord was very angry with Israel."

2 Kings 17:7-18
Emphasis added

Unquestionably, one of the greatest lapses was king Omri's substitution of the 'Statutes of Omri' for the Commandments, Statutes and Judgements of God (Micah 6:16, 1 Kings 16:25-26). This struck at the very root of Israel's heritage and glory; namely the possession of Divine Law, of which man-made legislation was forbidden (Deuteronomy 4:2).

Ejection into Assyria

Since they would not hearken to the Lord, it was inevitable they should pay the full price of punishment about which they had been forewarned so often. The first to fall was the ten-tribed Kingdom of Israel. Living in the northern part of Palestine, the ten tribes blocked the expansion of the Assyrian Empire as it moved to gain control of the Mediterranean seaports. Consequently Israel was attacked and, after a long and bitter struggle, was conquered by the Assyrians who deported all of the survivors northward to the lands bordering the western shore of the Caspian Sea.

Racially, the Assyrians (ASSHUR-IANS) were close blood relatives of the children of Israel, being also descended from Shem, but through Shem's son 'ASSHUR' (Genesis 10:21-22). These Assyrians were also an idolatrous people, worshipping as their leader or god, the "Sacred Presence" of Asshur himself, calling him their 'Feroher' (Führer), a word familiar to everyone!

History reveals that God used no less than four Assyrian monarchs in succession to subdue the Ten-Tribed Israel, and carry them away captive. The first was TIGLATH-PILESSER II followed by SHALMANESER

IV; and his son SARGON II who captured Israel's capital city, Samaria, in the year 721 BC. The fourth and last was SENNACHERIB, who completed the work which the others had begun.

The complete removal of the northern Kingdom into Assyria embraced a period of 60 years, the invasions began in 745 BC. The second and greatest came in 721 BC with the fall of Samaria, and 'mopping up' operations continued for another 35 years, until 685 BC.

THE BABYLONIAN EMPIRE

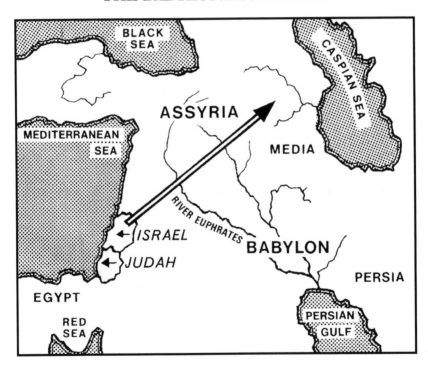

Figure 3. Captivity of the House of Israel into Assyria

Captivity of Judah

In the year 605 BC about 120 years after the fall of Israel, the Assyrian Empire fell to the Babylonians after a deciding battle at Carchemish.

From 604 BC through 587 BC they continued the expansion of their empire. In clearing a way for their conquest of Egypt, attacked and conquered the Kingdom of Judah, taking the 'Jews' captives into Babylon, crushing the monarchy of David and putting to death all the male lineage to the throne.

So ended an era ... and Jill (Judah) did in fact "come tumbling after" suffering the same fate as the House of Israel!

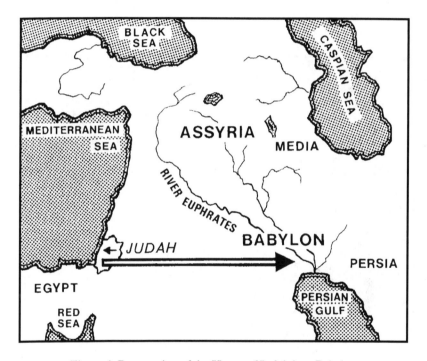

Figure 4. Deportation of the House of Judah into Babylon

THE PERSIAN EMPIRE

The Jews Return

About seventy years after the people of Judah were taken as slaves to Babylon. The Babylonian Empire itself fell to the Medes and Persians under the leadership of the great general Cyrus in the year 534 BC.

A small number of 'Jews' in Babylon were allowed to return to resettle in Palestine, under the leadership of Ezra and Nehemiah in the years 453/5 BC, but Judah was never again to rise as a complete and independent nation.

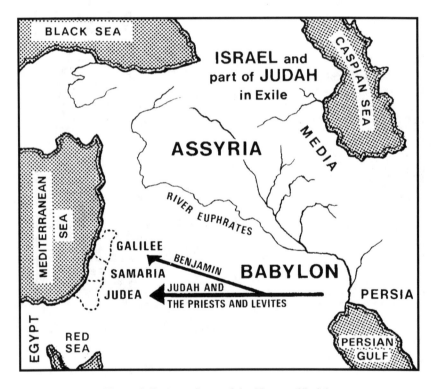

Figure 5. Return of part of the House of Judah

HEBREWS – ISRAELITES – JEWS

We must pause here to point out the difference between the titles HEBREW – ISRAELITE – JEW.

All the descendants of EBER or HEBER the tenth patriarch from Adam were EBER-EWS or HEBREWS. Abraham, Isaac and Jacob were all HEBREWS (see Gen 14:13). Jacob was re-named ISRAEL and so was the first Israelite, and all his descendants were Israelites <u>and</u> Hebrews, with his son Isaac receiving the birthright. They were all Semitic being descended from Shem. They were all Hebrews – but not Jews. Only the remnants of Judah's son Pharez returning from Babylon with a few proselytes and 'remnants' of other tribes were given the name 'Jew'.

> *"At that time Rezin king of Syria recovered Elath ot Syria, and drave the Jews from Elath: and the Syrians came to Elath, and dwelt there unto this day."*
>
> 2 Kings 16:6

This is the only reference to the word 'Jew' in the old testament!

To say that all Hebrews are Jews is like saying all Americans are Californians or all Englishmen are Yorkshire men. The 'Jews' were descended from <u>JU</u>-DAH. The title Jew is derived from the first syllablesof JU-DAH. JUDAH was only one of the twelve tribes of Israel. None of the other tribes were ever referred to as Jews.

(See fig 6 overleaf).

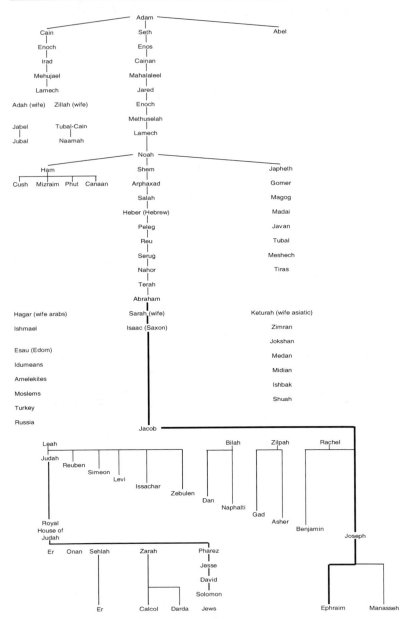

Figure 6. The Birthright

Humpty Dumpty

> Humpty Dumpty sat on a wall
> Humpty Dumpty had a great fall
> All the kings' horses and all the kings' men
> Couldn't put Humpty together again

> (From Lewis Carroll's: Alice in the looking glass)

Another simple rhyme with a profound biblical meaning.

Humpty Dumpty is the Kingdom of Judah, more especially referring to the remnants that returned to Judea from Babylon.

The Broken Kingdom

But the 'Jews' were never again from that time ever to become a restored kingdom. With the rise of the Roman Empire and the occupation of the Holy Land they were ever to be a 'broken' kingdom.

Then with the Jews uprising in 70 AD and eventual defeat by the Roman armies led by VESPASIAN and his son TITUS the Jews were forcibly expelled from the land as a punishment for their rebellion – only a few scattered remnants remained; from that day the 'Jews' have been 'wanderers' among the nations, without a homeland, until after 1917 when the British forces liberated Jerusalem and afterward a new homeland for the Jews being established.

The Parables of the Marred Vessel and Broken Bottle

In addition to Fairy Tales and Nursery Rhymes are the Parables.

The events surrounding the House of Israel and House of Judah were revealed to Jeremiah in the form of two parables.

Jeremiah 18:1-4   The marred vessel
Jeremiah 19   The broken bottle

The marred vessel represents the House of Israel. The potter was making a vessel or vase, when he made a mistake and the clay became distorted, so he took the same piece of clay – formed another lump on the wheel and made it again another vessel. The word of the Lord came to Jeremiah saying:

> *"O house of Israel, cannot I do with you as this potter?*
> *Saith the Lord: Behold as the clay is in the potters hand,*
> *so are ye in my hand, O house of Israel."*
>
> Jeremiah 18:6

The Broken Bottle (Judah: Humpty Dumpty)

In contrast to the illustration of the House of Israel the condition of the House of Judah was depicted in the command to Jeremiah to get a potters earthen vessel (fired pottery) with which he was to demonstrate the judgement upon Judah. Jeremiah was told to take with him some of the leaders among the people and the Priests and go to the valley opposite the pottery gate where he as to proclaim a message of judgement upon them for their evil ways. He was then to break the bottle in the sight of those who were with him and say to them:

> *"...thus saith the Lord of hosts; even so will I break this*
> *people and this city (Jerusalem), as one breaketh a potter's*
> *vessel,* **that cannot be made whole again...** *"*
>
> Jeremiah 19:11
> Emphasis added

The House of Israel was the vessel of clay damaged in the making but still workable clay capable of being re-shaped into a new nation.

But the House of Judah was the Broken Bottle.

In the rhyme Judah is named as Humpty Dumpty and depicted in the shape of an egg which symbolises the Broken Bottle of the parable, which none of the kings men in line of the Davidic monarchy could ever restore.

In the rhyme Humpty is heard to boast "With me nothing is impossible" and, in a rather scornful tone he added "When 'I' use the word, it means just what I choose it to mean, neither more nor less".

But of course once he had fallen off the wall and broken into pieces it was <u>impossible</u> for him to put himself together again!

The Reshaped Vessel (House of Israel)

Jeremiahs prophecy of the re-shaped vessel throws a great deal of light upon the words of Paul (Romans 9:20-28) when he quotes from Hosea, who referred to the House of Israel – firstly as 'Lo-Ruhama' meaning NOT HAVING OBTAINED MERCY and 'Lo-Ammi' meaning NOT MY PEOPLE (Hosea 1:6-9).

However, in chapter 2 Hosea records their redeemed condition. Firstly as 'Ammi' meaning MY PEOPLE and 'Ruhamah' meaning HAVING OBTAINED MERCY (Hosea 2:1-2).

In that redeemed condition the Lord declares

> *"Yet the number of the children of Israel shall be as the sand of the sea, which cannot be measured nor numbered; and it shall come to pass, that in the place where it was said unto them, Ye are not my people, there it shall be said unto them, Ye are the sons of the living God."*
>
> Hosea 1:10

> *"And I will sow her unto me in the earth; and I will have mercy upon her that had not obtained mercy; and I will say to them which were not my people, Thou are my people; and they shall say, Thou art my God."*
>
> Hosea 2:23

MODERN ISRAEL

The 'marred' House of Israel in the hands of the Lord, like clay in the hand of the potter, has today re-appeared as the Anglo-Saxon-Celtic people, fashioned again by the Divine potter now performing a special task in His service.

Judah, however, having deserted God, lost the Kingdom causing the Saviour to declare unto them:

> *"Therefore say I unto you, The kingdom of God shall be taken from you, and given to **A nation** bringing forth the fruits thereof."*
>
> Matthew 21:43
> Emphasis added

'A' nation: the article 'a' signifies a singular modern day nation. This could only mean modern Israel.

Only the nation of America (and its historical counterpart Great Britain) fill the requirements of this prophecy.

For we are told:

> *"And whosoever shall fall on **this** stone (nation) shall be broken: but on whomsoever **it** shall fall, **it** will grind him to powder."*
>
> Matthew 21:44
> Emphasis added

The 'stone' referred to in verse 42 which the builders (the Jews) rejected was the Saviour. But the pronoun 'it' mentioned in verse 44 can only refer to something inanimate not a living being, as opposed to the pronoun 'he'.

So '**this stone**' does not refer to Jesus Christ but to the 'Stone nation' mentioned in verse 43. The ecclesiastical Kingdom of God was given to the Anglo-Celtic nation of America in 1820 AD and through the administration of the Priesthood has brought forth the fruits thereof.

2
THE KEY CHAPTER
An Introduction

I wandered lonely as a cloud
That floats on high o'er vale and hills,
When all at once I saw a crowd
A host, of golden daffodils ...
William Wordsworth

For many years I have wandered lonely in my search for the everlasting light to the truths contained in the Book of Revelation. There was always the elusive factor to give me greater understanding. I searched and studied but all to no avail; the missing piece to form a clear picture always evaded me. Then one day as in the beautiful poem above by William Wordsworth – the truth burst upon me like a shaft of light, just as the vision of golden daffodils appeared to the poet. Wordsworth was so taken aback by what he saw that he sat down and wrote the poem there and then, it was an inspiration that just rolled off his pen. This book was conceived in exactly the same way. One day whilst in my daily studies, without effort on my part, I had a revelatory experience in which I found the missing link, the lost chord as it were!

The realisation that came to me was that the Book of Revelation WAS NOT A CONTINUOUS VISION chapter after chapter as in the links of a chain, with one chapter following the other in chronological order, BUT TWO SEPARATE DIVISIONS – RUNNING IN PARALLEL COVERING THE SAME TIME PERIOD as in the tracks of a railway. That John received and recorded **two visions**.

First Vision	chapters 1 to 11	The book with Seven Seals
Chapter 12		Israel's eternal destiny
Second Vision	chapters 13 to 22	The rise and fall of Babylon the Great

With chapter 12 forming the central corridor between the two divisions.

THE KEY CHAPTER
Revelation 12

Chapter 12 is the key chapter and vital link – not as a link in a chain, but a totally separate history from the other two visions. But welding them together like the 'sleepers' in a rail track.

To understand the true meaning of this chapter, which relates to Israel's destiny, is the vital key that makes the related history in the other two visions so clear.

THE LARGE CHART
THE SEVEN SEALS OF REVELATION

From the experience mentioned earlier the chart THE SEVEN SEALS OF REVELATION supplied with this book was conceived almost at once.

On the chart, Israel the 'woman' is portrayed as BRITANNIA with a circle of twelve stars over her head, symbolic of the twelve tribes – the Kingdom of Israel.

This shows Israel's journey through the 'corridor of time' commencing in the pre-existence and on through to the seventh millennium.

The choice of Britannia to portray the Kingdom of Israel was deliberate, as we shall see when we examine SECTION 2 – ISRAEL'S ETERNAL DESTINY and including Revelation chapter 12. The information contained in Section 2 is essential in the understanding of the content of chapter 12, and indeed, to the rest of the chapters of John's revelation.

Chapter 12 is in itself a literary masterpiece! In seventeen verses only, John explains Israel's history beginning in the pre-existence – with a war in Heaven and the struggle between the forces of Satan and those of Christ to establish the Plan of Salvation. He sees the birth of Christ, the attempt upon his life shortly after his birth, and his resurrection and ascension into Heaven. Also in two 'time' prophecies he portrays Israel's eternal destiny through seven thousand years! Finally arriving into a new island home – 'prepared of God' where she is to fulfil that destiny. Absolutely brilliant!

It must be born in mind that the books of the Holy Bible commencing with Genesis chapter 12 are just different versions of the same story and history of one family. Commencing with Abraham through Isaac – Jacob (Israel), his twelve sons and two grandsons Ephraim and Manasseh and the Book of Revelation is no exception. Other nations or empires are mentioned as and when they come into contact with that history.

3
JOHN'S FIRST VISION - A GUIDED TOUR

First vision   Chapters 1 to 11   Has two parts.
Part I   Chapters 1 to 3   The message to the Seven Churches.

Part II   Chapters 5 to 11   The Book with Seven Seals.
With chapter 4 forming the link between the two parts.

Chapters 1 to 3
These record the events of John's day and is addressed to the 'Branches' of the church in the Seven cities of Asia Minor.

Note Revelation 1:3: 'The time is at hand'; these three chapters show clearly that the 'Branches' of the Church of Jesus Christ in that day were rapidly going into apostasy (34 to 100 AD).

This book is concerned with events commencing with chapter 4, therefore we will proceed to that chapter immediately.

THE CAUSE OF CONFUSION

Revelation 4
This chapter records a visionary experience and commences with: "and I will show thee things which must be hereafter".

This statement has caused all the confusion. It has mislead all Bible students of Revelation to believe that the division between past and future events of John's revelation commences here – that all the chapters from this point through to the final chapter 22 are all linked together historically and chronologically as in the links of a chain.

And I have to admit that I also was influenced by this statement, which caused me years of confusion and frustration until, I discovered that which I have explained to you in 'The Key Chapter'.

We know that the 'hereafter' applied only to John's First Vision, concludes with chapter eleven.

The Four Beasts (Revelation 4:7)
Is it a coincidence, I wonder, that the imagery of the four beasts were exactly the four Brigade Emblems of the Twelve Tribes of Israel?

Israel's Tribal and Brigade Emblems
Each of the twelve tribes adopted an emblem or standard taken from the patriarchal blessing given by Jacob to each of his sons whilst in Egypt. This patriarchal blessing is to the twelve tribes by Moses in Deuteronomy 33 and Numbers 24:8.

And Jacob gave a special blessing to his two grandsons Ephraim and Manasseh in Genesis 48.

From these blessings the tribes choose a Primary Emblem which they carried upon a standard.

The Emblems of the tribes were as follows:

	Tribe	Primary Emblem	Secondary Emblems	Reference
1	Reuben	Face of a man	Water	Gen 49:3-4
2	Simeon	A sword	A castle gate/turreted gate	Gen. 49:5-7
3	Judah	Lion (couchant)	three lions rampant/a sceptre	Gen 49:11
4	Zebulon	Ship	A white horse, serpent or snake	Gen 49:13
5	Issachar	Laden ass		Gen 49:14
6	Dan	Eagle		Gen 49:17
7	Gad	Trooper on horse		Gen 49:19

8	Asher	Covered goblet		Gen 49:20
9	Naphtali	Leaping hind		Gen 49:21
10	Manasseh	Olive branch	A bunch of 13 arrows	Gen 49:20-24 Hosea 14:5-7
11	Ephraim	An ox or bull	A unicorn / a horn	Deut 33:17 Num 24:5-8 Rom 11:17-25
12	Benjamin	A wolf		Gen 49:27

These emblems or standards were in regular use during their forty years of wandering. This IS definitely stated in Numbers 2:2. These standards were their means of identification and rallying point. When on the march the tribes formed themselves into four columns of three tribes. Each three tribes were a 'Brigade'. Each brigade had a leading tribe; these were chosen to be JUDAH, REUBEN, EPHRAIM and DAN.

The first Brigade   Issachar **Judah** Zebulon
The second Brigade   Simeon **Ruben** Gad
The third Brigade   Benjamin **Ephraim** Manasseh
The fourth Brigade   Asher **Dan** Naphtali
The 'Brigade' emblem of JUDAH was a LION
The 'Brigade' emblem of REUBEN was a FACE OF A MAN
The 'Brigade' emblem of EPHRAIM was a BULL CALF
The 'Brigade' emblem of DAN was an EAGLE

This formation was adopted when the Israelites marched out of Egypt, for we are informed that:

> *"The children of Israel went up* **harnessed** *(in ranks) out of the land of Egypt"*
>
> *Exodus 13:18*

Figure 7. Israel's National Emblem

The three tribes forming the Brigade of Judah went first, followed in order by the Brigades of Reuben, Ephraim and Dan, with the tabernacle protected in the central position in the column escorted by the tribe of Levi.

As we read in the second chapter of Numbers we see that when not on the march, the Twelve Tribes encamped in a definite order around an open space at the centre of which was the tent like enclosure for national worship called the Tabernacle. It is assumed that the Twelve Tribes encamped around this open space in the form of a square,

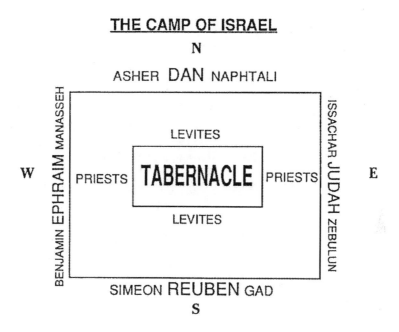

Figure 8. The camp of Israel

with three tribes in each of the four directions – East, South, West and North – facing inwards, with the Levites and Priests surrounding the Tabernacle in the centre.

The Order of Heaven

When one examines these tribal emblems closely it is observed that both the emblems and the formation of the camp are closely associated with the Zodiac and its signs. The formation of Heaven!

Ezekiel's Experience

Ezekiel had a similar experience to John (see Ezekiel 1:5-10). Both prophets are given a vision of the Throne of God and the Glory of Heaven.

Around the base of this glory they see the likeness of four living creatures. In these two visions we have an almost exact picture of the camp of Israel.

It is evident that this 'Glory' was a visible manifestation of God's presence at the centre of His own Kingdom (nation). Thus during their wanderings the Ark of the Covenant and the Tabernacle represented His earthly Throne, and hovering over this was the mysterious light called the 'Shekinah' or glory of the Lords presence in the midst of Israel.

A number of these tribal emblems are to be found in the British Coat of Arms – also Town and County arms.

Also in the Great Seal of the United States of America.

THE SEVEN SEALS
Chapter 5

If it were not for modern revelation we would, like many others be confused as to the real meaning of the Book Sealed with Seven Seals (Revelation chapter 5).

Section 77 of the Doctrine and Covenants provides the answer:

> *Q. What are we to understand by the book which John saw, which was sealed on the back with seven seals?*
>
> *A. We are to understand that it contains the revealed will, mysteries, and works of God; the hidden things of his economy concerning this earth during the seven thousand years of its continuance, or its temporal existence.*

Q. What are we to understand by the seven seals by which it was sealed?

A. We are to understand that the first seal contains the things of the first thousand years, and the second also of the second thousand years, and so until the seventh.

D&C 77:6-7

Each of the seven seals then, represents one thousand years of the Earths history beginning its 'temporal' existence, that is, from the Fall of Adam.

At this moment of time, 2006 AD, we are entering the period of the seventh seal or seventh millennium.

OVERVIEW
Revelation 6 to 11

These chapters form a **prophetical and panoramic overview**, a guided tour if you like, of events through the ages leading up to **and including** the events through the Seventh Seal (2001 – 3000 AD).

These chapters deal mainly with the events of the last three seals, that is from the birth of Christ.

5th Seal	Birth of Christ to 1000 AD
6th Seal	1001 AD to 2000 AD
7th Seal	2001 AD to 3000 AD

You must bear this in mind as you read these chapters.

The events of the 5th Seal	commence	Rev 6:9-11
	concludes	verse 11
The events of the 6th Seal	commence	Rev 6:12-17
	concludes	Rev 7:17
The events of the 7th Seal	commence	Rev chapter 8
	concludes	Rev chapter 11

Therefore the events of the **5th Seal**, that is the 1000 years from the birth of Christ – occupy only **three verses** of scripture!

The events of the **6**th **Seal**, that is the 1000 years from 1001 AD to 2000 AD occupy **twenty three verses** of scripture!

The events of the **7**th **Seal**, the 1000 years of what we call the millennium, 2001 AD to 3000 AD **sixty four verses**!

A total of 90 verses covering a prophetical overview of 3000 years.

However, we must remember that the second vision provides us with a *further historical overview* covering the same period.

THE FOUR HORSEMEN OF THE APOCALYPSE
Revelation 6

John does not record the events of the first four seals, that is, the first 4000 years of the Earth's temporal or prophetical history.

The first four seals are depicted as four coloured horses with their riders – known to bible students as 'The four horsemen of the Apocalypse'.

'Apocalypse': A Greek word meaning revealed or uncovered. But John did not reveal the contents of these years. His revelation was concerning the events of his own day and future.

I believe that John was showing us, in the imagery of these four coloured horses, the general events which occur in history in any given generation since Adam

Deception	War	Famine	Pestilence
White Horse	Red Horse	Black Horse	Pale Horse

The White Horse of Deception
The reason why I conclude that the White Horse in this revelation represents *deception* is because almost all bible students are deceived in thinking that the rider of this Horse is the Saviour.

You will notice that the rider of this White Horse is different to the one that the Saviour appears on in Revelation 19:11-16.

The Great Deceiver

The false Christ on the White Horse of chapter 6 carries a bow in his hand with which he goes to war, "and he went forth conquering and to conquer" and "receives a crown". A false crown as the Prince of this world.

The true Christ in Revelation 19 brandishes a 'Sword', but the sword is not in his hand, but comes out of his mouth, representing the word of God (the two edged sword), by which the deceiver Satan is overcome. The rider of the White Horse in Revelation chapter 6 is a *counterfeit* representing a false religion that would "fool the very elect".

> *"And then shall that Wicked be revealed, whom the Lord shall consume with the spirit of his mouth, and shall destroy with the brightness of his coming:*
>
> *Even him, whose coming is after the working of Satan with all power and signs and lying wonders,"*
> *2 Thessalonians 2:8-9*
>
> *"For such are false apostles, deceitful workers, transforming themselves into the apostles of Christ.*
>
> *And no marvel; for Satan himself is transformed into an angel of light.*
>
> *Therefore it is no great thing if his ministers also be transformed as the ministers of righteousness; whose end shall be according to their works."*
> *2 Corinthians 11:13-15*
>
> *"In whom the god of this world hath blinded the minds of them which believe not, lest the light of the glorious gospel of Christ, who is the image of God, should shine unto them."*
> *2 Corinthians 4:4*

When you read these verses you will be inclined to accept the interpretation that the rider of the White Horse in Revelation 6:2 is the great deceiver Satan, who is also the great counterfeiter, mixing truth with error and misleading the innocent.

THE EVENTS OF THE FIFTH SEAL
The First Great Tribulation of the Saints

50 Million Martyrs

> *And when he had opened the fifth seal, I saw under the altar the souls of them that were slain for the word of God, and for the testimony which they held:*
>
> *And they cried with a loud voice, saying, how long, O Lord, holy and true, dost thou not judge and avenge our blood on them that dwell on the earth?*
>
> *And white robes were given unto every one of them; and it was said unto them, that they should rest yet for a little season, until their fellow servants also and their brethren, that should be killed as they were, should be fulfilled.*
>
> *Revelation 6:9-11*

History tells us that in the middle ages more than 50 million people were killed, many for their faith and obedience to God and 'for the testimony which they held' refusing to submit to the authority of Rome.

This tribulation took place during the 5th Seal or 1000 years from the birth of Christ, even continuing into the period of the 6th Seal.

John is given a vision of these martyrs wearing 'white robes' exclaiming: "How long, O Lord, before thy judgement upon this system".

They were informed that the judgement would not come 'Until their fellow servants also their brethren should be killed as they were, should be fulfilled'.

Clearly indicating that there was to be a final Great Tribulation of the Saints before the second coming of the Saviour.

THE EVENTS OF THE SIXTH SEAL
The Sealing of the Saints (Revelation 7)

A Great Multitude

This 'sealing' process has been going on in Holy Temples of all generations in which the Holy Priesthood was upon the earth. In this generation multitudes have received the 'sealing' since the Endowment of the Priesthood was restored in 1836. It will be noticed that his sealing takes place in 'their foreheads' (verse 3). The forehead is the seat of intellect and learning.

Only in Holy Temples can one be instructed in the '**ordinances**' of Heaven, which are the ordinances of the Holy Priesthood (see JST Exodus 34:1).

This 'great sealed multitude' which no man could number, of all nations, kindred, and people, and tongues, stood before the throne, and before the Lamb, clothed in white robes', i.e. the robes of the Holy Priesthood.

John was asked: "What are these which are arrayed in white robes? And whence came they?" John replied that he didn't know, and was told by the Angel: "these are they which came out of the great tribulation, and have washed their robes and made them white in the blood of the lamb" (verse 9-17).

The washing in blood is symbolic of ones baptism and cleansing for the remission of sins through the atoning sacrifice of Jesus Christ.

The Overcomers

> "*These are they who have the name of the Lambs Father written in their foreheads*"
>
> *Revelation 14:1*
> Emphasis added

To have the Father's name written in the forehead means to know God the Father and His son Jesus Christ. These are they who have overcome the world (John 17:3).

> "**Him that overcometh** *will I make a pillar in the temple of my God, and he shall go no more out: and I will write upon him the name of my God, and the name of the city of my God, which is new Jerusalem, which cometh down out of heaven from my God: and I will write upon him my new name.*"
>
> Revelation 3:12
> Emphasis added

These are they,

> "*which have not defiled their* **garments**; *and they shall walk with me in white: for they are worthy.*
>
> **He that overcometh**, *the same shall be clothed in* **white raiment**; *and I will not blot out his name from the book of life, but I will confess his name before my Father, and before the angels.*"
>
> Revelation 3:4-5
> Emphasis added

> "*...* **To him that overcometh** *will I give to eat of the tree of life, which is in the midst of the paradise of God.*
>
> Revelation 2:7
> Emphasis added

> "*...* **He that overcometh** *shall not be hurt of the second death.*"
>
> Revelation 2:11
> Emphasis added

> "*...***To him that overcometh** *will I give to eat of the* **hidden manna**, *and will give him a white stone,*

and in the stone a **new name** *written, which no man knoweth saving he that receiveth it."*

Revelation 2:17
Emphasis added
See also D&C 130:6-11

"To him that overcometh *will I grant to sit with me in my throne, even as I also overcame, and am set down with my Father in his throne."*

Revelation 3:21
Emphasis added

"And hast made us unto our God kings and priests: and we shall reign on the earth."

Revelation 5:10

"And it was commanded them that they should not hurt the grass of the earth, neither any green thing, neither any tree; but only those men which **have not** *the seal of God in their foreheads."*

Revelation 9:4
Emphasis added

"Behold, I come as a thief. Blessed is he that watcheth, and **keepeth his garments**, *lest he walk naked, and they see his shame."*

Revelation 16:15

"Let us be glad and rejoice, and give honour to him: for the marriage of the Lamb is come, and **his wife** *hath made herself ready.*

And **to her was** *granted that she should be arrayed* **in fine linen, clean and white**: *for the fine linen is the righteousness of* **saints**."

Revelation 19:7-8
Emphasis added

"And the armies which were in heaven followed him upon white horses, clothed in fine linen, white and clean."

Revelation 19:14

"Blessed and holy is he that hath part in the first resurrection: on such the second death hath no power, but they shall be **priests** *of God and of Christ, and shall reign with him a thousand years."*

Revelation 20:6

"He that overcometh *shall inherit all things; and I will be his God, and he shall be my son."*

Revelation 21:7

Emphasis added

"And they shall see his face; and his name shall be in their foreheads."

Revelation 22:4

Does not this sound familiar?

The Lords people are called 'Saints' and 'Overcomers'.
They will eat of the 'hidden manna'.
They will be wearing 'garments'.
They will be dressed in 'white linen robes'.
They will be 'pillars' in God's Temple.
They will be 'sealed'.
They will be 'priests' of God and of Christ.
They will receive a 'new name'.
Also they will receive a 'white stone' which we are to understand is a Urim and Thummim.

"… to each individual who receives one, whereby things pertaining to a higher order of Kingdoms will be made known."

D&C 130:10

The Calling of the 144,000

> *"And I looked, and lo, a lamb stood on Mount Sion,*
> *and with Him am hundred and forty and four thousand,*
> *having His father's name written in their foreheads".*
> *Revelation 14:1*

> *"These are they which were not defiled with women; for*
> *they are virgins. These are they which follow the Lamb*
> *whithersoever he goeth. These were redeemed from among*
> *men, being the firstfruits unto God and to the Lamb."*
> *Revelation 14:4*

This last scripture alludes to the special calling of the 144,000 High Priests *"For they are virgins – not defiled with women"*. The meaning being that they have not committed fornication or adultery and have kept their garments unspotted – have lived worthily in accordance to their Priesthood covenants and callings.

It is not usual to describe a man as a 'virgin'. Therefore the meaning is obvious; it means a man who is spotless and <u>un</u>defiled, morally clean.

> *"And in their mouth was found no guile: for they are*
> *without fault before the throne of God."*
> *Revelation 14:5*

The scriptures and Church teach the sanctity of marriage, in fact it is essential for exaltation; therefore a man is not 'defiled' <u>in</u> marriage, only by immoral acts before or whilst married.

The scripture mentioned will have great significance to those who have received the endowment of the Holy Priesthood.

REVELATION 7

The Calling of the 144,000

In this chapter John names the tribes of Israel from whom the 144,000 are to be called and 'sealed'.

> Judah, Reuben, Gad, Asher, Naphtali, Manasseh, Simeon, Levi, Issachar, Zebulon, Joseph and Benjamin.

You will notice that John does not record them in the order of their birth, which is:

> Reuben, Simeon, Levi, Judah, Zebulon, Issachar, Dan, Gad, Asher, Naphtali, Joseph, Benjamin.

You will also notice that the tribes of Dan and Ephraim are missing from his list!

Whether this was intentional, or for what reason they were not included were are not told. Alternatively it could have been a translating error.

However, Ephraim and Manasseh were not sons of Jacob but grandsons, although they were 'adopted' as sons or tribes (Genesis 48:16).

So if we remove Manasseh from the list and include Dan it would be complete.

The question of Ephraim and Manasseh's 'share' could be obtained through that allocated to Joseph, their father.

Of course this is just speculation but it is a possible answer to the question as to why Dan and Ephraim are missing in John's list.

During the Sixth Seal

I also draw your attention to the fact that the Sixth Seal is opened in chapter 6 verse 12 and the Seventh Seal or beginning of the Seventh Millennium is opened commencing chapter 8.

That places the events of chapter 7 in those of the Sixth Seal. The millennium ending the year 2000 AD. This is confirmed by the chapter introduction and further by D&C 77:10-11.

> *"Q. What time are the things spoken of in this chapter to be accomplished?*
> *A. They are to be accomplished in the sixth thousand years, or the opening of the sixth seal.*
> *Q. What are we to understand by sealing the one hundred and forty-four thousand, out of all the tribes of Israel — twelve thousand out of every tribe?*
> *A. We are to understand that those who are sealed are high priests, ordained unto the holy order of God, to administer the everlasting gospel; for they are they who are ordained out of every nation, kindred, tongue, and people, by the angels to whom is given power over the nations of the earth, to bring as many as will come to the church of the Firstborn."*
>
> *D&C 77:10-11*

According to this, then the selection and 'sealing' of the hundred and forty-four thousand (144,000) High Priests should have by now been accomplished!

John also records the calling and selection of the hundred and forty-four thousand in chapter 14 which, if the chapters of the Book of Revelation are in chronological order would place this event as the taking place in the seventh seal, or this millennium we are now in!

Because this would place all events after Revelation chapter 8 as taking place in this the Seventh Millennium commencing 2001 AD.

This would also place the coming of Moroni in this millennium. But John is not recording two separate callings of the 144,000. If this were so there would of necessity be 288,000.

There can be only one answer: Yes! That chapter 14 records the same event as chapter 7 in a totally new vision covering the same period of time. That the first vision ends with chapter eleven, and contains the prophetical overview of the events of the seven seals through to and including the millennium we are now in.

That chapter 13 commences a new vision beginning with the 5th Seal or events of the early century after Christ through to the 6th Seal and even including the events of this 7th millennium.

Chronologically then this would place the events of Revelation chapter 12 in the period of the 5th and 6th Seals, except for those verses portraying the events 'in heaven' or the pre-existence.

The chronological order of the chapters 13 to 22 is seen as containing the historical events of the 5th, 6th and 7th seals in a completely new version of the same story. So the coming of Moroni was recorded by John in its correct chronological setting. The correct order of theses chapters should be:

13	Through fifth and sixth seals
14 to verse 7	Through fifth and sixth seals
17	Through fifth/sixth **but mainly the seventh seal**
18	Through seventh seal
14 verse 8 to 13	Through seventh seal
15	Through seventh seal
16	Through seventh seal
14 verse 14 to 20	Through seventh seal
19	Through seventh seal
20	Through seventh seal
21	Through seventh seal
22	Through seventh seal

EVENTS OF THE SEVENTH SEAL
Revelation 8 to 11

Commencing 8: verse 1

The '½ hour silence' represents the interlude of time between the sealing of the Saints and calling of the 144,000 High Priests, and the beginning of the Plagues.

The ½ hour is figurative. If it is to be calculated on the principal of 1 DAY FOR 1000 YEARS, then this ½ hour would represent 20 years 10 months.

If it is calculated on 1 DAY FOR 1 YEAR principle then the ½ hour would represent 7 ½ years.

This calculation being based on prophetical time of 360 degrees. Each degree representing 1 year of time. 15 degrees being one hour or 15 years of time. ½ hour would therefore represent 7 ½ degrees or 7 ½ years. In a literal year of 360 days, it would represent 7 ½ days.

Angels with the Seven Trumpet Plagues

Rev 8:2 through Rev 11:15.

These trumpet blasts represent various disasters which will befall the Earth <u>AFTER</u> the commencement of the Seventh Seal, that is, after the year 2001 AD, then on through part of that <u>millennium</u> (D&C 77:12).

THE FIRST FIVE TRUMPET PLAGUES
Revelation 8:2-13

Pollution.

During this period the Earth will experience the loss of one third of trees and grass. This process is already commencing with acid rain and human pollution. A great mountain (asteroid) hits the earth.

One third part of the sea becomes blood and one third of sea creatures die. With new and ever increasing viruses affecting marine life, human pollution and dumping of nuclear waste at sea, this is the outcome.

At the sounding of the 3rd Angel – A 'Great Star' falls upon the rivers and fountains of waters. The name of the Star is called *Wormwood*, causing the third part of waters to become wormwood – *"Because they are bitter"*.

Is it a coincidence I wonder that the Ukrainian word for 'Wormwood' is 'polyn' or 'chernobyl'? And is it a further coincidence that the nuclear disaster in Russia was at the power plant at Chernobyl?

Since 'gall' is often associated with wormwood, I observed that this word in Youngs Concordance is the Hebrew word for 'Rosh'. This word also being associated with Russia and Ukraine: Chief Prince of Rosh – Meshech (Moscow) and Tubal-Cans (Ezekiel 38:1-2)!

THE SIXTH TRUMPET PLAGUE
Revelation 9:15

World War

This trumpet plague records a war of complete destruction of universal conflict which will last for 13 months (World War III)! A nuclear conflict.

This war will devastate the nations of Europe and most of other nations and one third of humanity will be slain.

The events of the 6th trumpet plague are closely associated with the 5th plague where John sees an army of 200 million who he describes as symbolic of locusts devouring all before them which had the power of scorpions; which had power in their mouth <u>and in their tails</u>. He also describes this army sitting on horses, which he described as having heads of lions, and out of their mouths issued fire, smoke and brimstone.

I think John did a great job, because these descriptions are identical of modern tanks, artillery and jet aircraft!

This 13 month war will result in the total collapse of practically all governments in Europe and elsewhere. There will be no organised governments, armies, police or security forces to maintain law and order. Looting and unlawfulness will be rampant.

THE TWO INTERIM EVENTS

(Between the sounding of the sixth and seventh Trumpets)

The First Interim Event (Revelation 10)

A Mission to the Apostle John
This is a personal vision to John himself. Through modern revelation we are informed that the 'Little Book' represents a mission for John to prepare the Ten Tribes for their return shortly after the war just mentioned. Due to the devastation and death resulting from this war the Tribes will experience no opposition in their return (D&C 77:13-14).

John's experience in eating the 'Little Book' was that it made his belly bitter, but in his mouth it was as sweet as honey (verses 9-10).

How can one better describe the work of the Lord? The work is not easy, but it is also a means of great satisfaction, with bitter and sweet experiences.

Serving Christ a Bitter-Sweet Experience
Trying to bring souls to the Saviour's true gospel is a bitter-sweet experience. All the door knocking, the setbacks, the opposition, the trials and temptations, are all forgotten when one soul responds to the message: What joy there is to baptise a repentant soul in the waters of salvation. That's the honey!

John's mission will be hard and trying yet at the end with great satisfaction.

THE SECOND INTERIM EVENT
Revelation 11

The Battle at Armageddon

It seems that coinciding with <u>or as the result of</u> the World War mentioned, there will be an attack on the Holy Land. This war is recorded in Ezekiel 38 and 39 and in the books of Joel and Zechariah, and is known as the Battle of Armageddon.

The Two Witnesses

These are two prophets sent as special witnesses of Christ, who will prophecy for 3 ½ years prior to and during the battle. They will be killed by the opposing forces and their bodies left in the streets, but will be resurrected after 3 ½ days. At this time Christ will appear to redeem and save the Jews and Jerusalem, and appear on the Mount of Olives.

With divine assistance the opposing armies will be defeated, and the 'Jews' will recognise the Lord Jesus Christ as their Messiah.

The Angel with the Seventh Trumpet

When this period of conflict and tribulation are ended the Seventh and last Angel sounds his trumpet, declaring the political Kingdom of God is established on Earth, and Christ will rule.

The Angels with the Vials

The reader should compare these seven trumpet plagues with the plagues mentioned in Revelation chapter 16.

Consulting the chart: <u>The Seven Seals of Revelation</u> it will be evident to everyone that the plagues poured out by the Angels with the seven vials are almost identical with the plagues of the Angels with the seven trumpets.

Confirming yet once again that John received two distinct visions. This will be made more evident when the second vision is under discussion.

The Angel with the Everlasting Gospel

<u>Furthermore in Revelation 14:6</u> John records an Angel visiting the earth bringing "the everlasting gospel" which we believe to be the "the everlasting covenant" mentioned in D&C 22, and was fulfilled with the Angel Moroni when he appeared to Joseph Smith the prophet (D&C 27:5, 128:20, see also Joseph Smith – History 1:27-54)

This being so, if we believe or teach that all the chapters of the Book of Revelation run in chronological order from chapter 4 through 22, where in time would that place the events of chapter 14? Yes, it would have to be during the events of the Seventh Seal or Seventh <u>Millennium</u> commencing 2001 AD.

The events of the Seventh Seal commenced with Chapter 8, therefore it would be logical and chronological to assume that all chapters from 8 to 22 ARE YET TO BE FULFILLED!

Consequently chapter 12 and 13 would also be yet future and the vision of Revelation 14:6 would yet to be fulfilled! BUT WE NOW KNOW DIFFERENT.

THE GREAT MISCONCEPTION

Most professors of theology and students have been led in this misconception, that is why they find it hard to give an explanation to chapter 12, which gives a vision of the pre-existence and Israel's earthly destiny.

But we know the event recorded in Revelation 14:6 took place in the late 1820's. In the events of the sixth seal! Therefore it is logical that there must be two visions containing two separate and distinct histories, covering the same time periods of the first vision – WITH THE DIVISION ENDING WITH CHAPTER ELEVEN AND COMMENCING AGAIN AT CHAPTER TWELVE

The first vision, chapters 4 to 11 containing the <u>PROPHETICAL</u> EVENTS of the earths seven thousand years of temporal existence. The second vision, chapters 13 to 18, containing the <u>HISTORICAL</u>

EVENTS of the same period. With chapter 12 forming the link. And chapters 19 to 22 recording the final events of Christ's coming in glory – Jesus Christ triumphant.

SECTION 2: ISRAEL'S ETERNAL DESTINY

4

BRITISH AND AMERICAN ROOTS IN BIBLICAL HISTORY

Inherited Blessings

By relating the blessings given by God to <u>ABRAHAM</u> – <u>ISAAC</u> – <u>JACOB</u> – and by Jacob to his two grandsons <u>EPHRAIM</u> and <u>MANASSEH</u> to the facts of history, we can readily see that the nations of Great Britain and the Commonwealth, and America and Canada are a fulfilment of those blessings.

To Abraham the Lord said:

> *"And I will make of thee a* **great** *nation, and I will bless thee, and* **make thy name great***; and thou shalt be a blessing:*
> *And I will bless them that bless thee, and curse him that curseth thee: and in thee shall all families of the earth be blessed."*
>
> *Genesis 12:2-3, Abraham 2:9-11*
> Emphasis added

Surely this prophecy has literally been fulfilled for the only nation on earth to have the pre-fix **Great** to its name is Great Britain, with its Empire, now a Commonwealth representing the fantastic geographical blessings, making it literally a 'Great' Nation. "And in these all the families of the earth will be blessed".

In this prophecy we see that spiritual blessings which the world would receive through the colonizing efforts of Israel, mingling the blood of Abraham within all nations, and in a more important way being the instruments in proclaiming the Gospel of Salvation to all peoples through the restoration of the true Church and Priesthood.

In blessing Jacob the Lord said:

> *"And God said unto him, Thy name is Jacob: thy name*
> *shall not be called any more Jacob, but Israel shall be thy*
> *name: and he called his name Israel.*
>
> *And God said unto him, I am God Almighty: be fruitful*
> *and multiply;* **a nation and a company of nations**
> *shall be of thee, and kings shall come out of thy loins;"*
> *Genesis 35:10-11*
> Emphasis added

So from Jacob was to come:

1. A singular Great Nation
2. A company (Commonwealth) of Nations (see Ephesians 2:12)
A prophecy fulfilled in the two Israelite nations of Great Britain and her Commonwealth, and the United States of America.

In the forty-eighth chapter of Genesis is recorded Jacob's blessings upon his grandsons Ephraim and Manasseh. When Jacob blessed the sons of Joseph he was under the necessity of crossing his arms in order that he might place his right hand from which the blessings of the birthright would come, upon the head of Ephraim, the one whom the spirit had designated as the birthright inheritor, and his left hand upon the head of Manasseh. Ephraim was the younger of the two boys. Joseph tried to correct Jacob in this action reminding him that <u>Manasseh</u> was the firstborn.

> *"And his father refused, and said. I know it my son, I*
> *know it: He (Manasseh) shall also become a GREAT*
> *PEOPLE (singular great nation), and he also shall be*
> *GREAT: But truly his brother (Ephraim) shall be*
> *GRE<u>ATER</u> THAN HE (Manasseh) and his*
> *(Ephraim's) seed shall become a multitude*
> *(Commonwealth) of nations."*
> *Genesis 48:19*
> Emphasis added

And so we see that what in fact took place in this action was that Jacob had transferred his own blessing given him by Almighty God – upon the heads of his grandsons Ephraim and Manasseh and their descendants.

And in the crossing of his hands, Jacob necessarily made the sign of the Celtic cross (✖). This is the Celtic pre-Christian cross of which relics are found wherever Israel travelled. This 'sign' is found in what is known as the 'Union Jack' – the British national flag, and the same sign is found in the ensign of the British Royal Navy vessels. The sign is also buried in the very name SAXON. Which is a shortened version of the name ISAAC or ISAAC-SONS = SAXONS, a blessing given to Isaac by God even before his birth.

"For in Isaac shall thy seed be called" (Genesis 21:12). Also to be found in the 'Union Jack' is the Christian cross (✚) of Christ. Let us not spiritualise away national things, nor nationalise spiritual things. Let us understand the sacred word of God as it is.

The title or name BRITISH is composed of two Hebrew words 'BRITH' meaning COVENANT and 'ISH', MAN or PEOPLE. The whole meaning 'MY COVENANT PEOPLE'!

Again the word ANGLE or nGA-EL-ISH (English) means Sons of God in Hebrew. The name of the tribe, which migrated into Britain is also the Hebrew word for Bull or Bull Calf, which was as we have discovered the emblem of EPHRAIM! Ever since that day the English have been referred to as 'JOHN BULL'. Another national emblem and characteristic being the 'BULL DOG' or Bull Dog Breed.

Figure 9 Anglo-Saxon destiny - Jacob's prophetic blessing

Further Evidence

Ephraim and Manasseh's Monoliths

We are informed in scripture that JACOB/ISRAEL and his family entered Egypt in 1702 BC.

DURING THE REIGN OF THOTMES III OF THE 18TH DYNASTY.

It was during this reign that the famine occurred and at which time Joseph became Prime Minister to Pharaoh.

Joseph married Asenath the daughter of Potpherah. A priest of the Temple of ON in ancient Memphis (capital of Egypt).

It was there that Joseph's twin sons Ephraim and Manasseh were born.

Joseph had two Obelisks' erected to commemorate their birth. These were placed in the public square at Memphis.

Where are they today?

It may surprise you to know that one is 'Cleopatra's Needle' standing on the Embankment, London.

The other stands in Central Park New York City.

'Cleopatra's Needle' was given to the British people in 1819 by Mohammed Ali. Its 200 ton bulk did not reach London until 1878. Due to the craft built to ship it to London breaking away from its towing vessel.

The 'Obelisk' was presented to the American people by Ishmael, Khedive of Egypt in 1877. Mr H.C Vanderbuilt brought it to New York in 1880.

The inscriptions on the two monoliths shows they were erected during the reign of Thotmes III. At this time Joseph would have been about 30 years of age.

The 'Needle' represents Joseph's son Ephraim.
The Obelisk represents Joseph's son Manasseh.
They were standing in Memphis when the aged patriarch Jacob gave God's blessings and promises of their future to these two grandsons.

Cleopatra's name is associated with the London monolith, because it was removed to Alexandria (her Royal City) and erected there 12 BC.

How many people passing along the Embankment, London or in Central Park, New York are aware of their history?

If these stone monuments could speak what a tale they would tell!

TWO MONOLITHS ERECTED IN EGYPT AT THE TIME OF THE BIRTH OF MANASSEH AND EPHRAIM

Figure 10. Two monoliths erected in Egypt at the time of the birth of Manasseh and Ephraim

Cleopatra's Needle and Thutmose III
Biblical Chronology (KJV)

Jacob born	1836 BC	
Joseph born	1745 BC	
Thutmose III reigned	1717 BC	
Joseph made Prime Minister of Egypt in his 30th year	1715 BC	Genesis 41:40
Followed by seven years of plenty Joseph marries Asenath	1715 to 1708 BC	Genesis 41:45
Ephraim and Manasseh born	1708 BC	Genesis 41:50
Seven years of famine commences	1708 BC	
Jacob and his family arrive in Egypt at age 130 years	1706 BC	Genesis 45:13 Acts 7:15-16
Famine ends	1701 BC	
Jacob blesses Ephraim and Manasseh (age 18/19)	1689 BC	Genesis 48
Jacob dies, age 147	1689 BC	

Notes:
The years in which THUTMOSE III reigned is an enigma.

The Internet gives the reign as -	1458 to 1427 BC
The British museum gives -	1504 to 1450 BC
(Room 4 – Egyptian Sculpture)	
Other scholars give the reign as -	1710 to 1661 BC
And still others give the years as -	1744 to 1690 BC

But we can dismiss all these dates because they do not fit in with Biblical chronology, and Biblical chronology must be the yardstick by which we work.

Biblical chronology informs us that Joseph was 30 years of age when he became Prime Minister of Egypt in 1715 BC, so any dates that do not fit in with that event must be dismissed.

I am of the opinion that THUTMOSE III began his reign 2 years before Joseph's 30th birthday in 1715 BC. My reasoning for this is the evidence given in Genesis 41:1, where it states:

> *And it came to pass at the end of two full years the*
> *Pharaoh dreamed…*

Then followed the dreams of the kine and corn: verse 2-7.

Why would the scribe state that the event was at the end of two full years – what two full years? I believe it indicates that two full years of his reign had elapsed. It was his father THUTMOSE II who had restored the butler and hanged the baker.

There is evidence in the British Museum that THUTMOSE II died in his very late twenties. However, the butler, the baker, and Joseph were all in the dungeon together when Joseph interpreted their dreams as we can read in Genesis 40. But the butler forgot Joseph's kindness until he was in the service of THUTMOSE III when he informed the Pharaoh of Joseph's ability to interpret dreams.

THUTMOSE III had had the two dreams of the kine and the corn that all the magicians of Egypt could not interpret – Genesis 41: 8.

The butler told the Pharaoh how Joseph had interpreted both his dream and that of the baker. He states:

And it came to pass, as he interpreted to us, so it was, me
'He' *restored unto mine office, and* **'him'** *(the baker)*
'He' *hanged.*

Genesis 41:13-14

(Brackets added)

The **'He'** in question was THUTMOSE II, the previous Pharaoh.

If the butler had been referring to the present Pharaoh THUTMOSE III, he would have said 'you':

> ... *when* **'you'** *restored me to my office...*
> And
> ...*when* **'you'** *hanged the baker...*

So it is clear that the events of **Genesis 40** were during the reign of THUTMOSE II. And the events of **Genesis 41** were during the reign of THUTMOSE III. And THUTMOSE III had reigned for two years when he had the dreams of the kine and corn.

At the butler's recommendation, Joseph was sent for from the dungeons. This was at the beginning of Joseph's 30th year in 1715 BC.

The inscription on the two monoliths show that THUTMOSE III erected them, and give the period of their origin with accuracy.

The two monoliths must have been set up at the time of the birth of Joseph's twin sons, Ephraim and Manasseh, and were therefore standing in MEMPHIS when the aged patriarch Jacob/Israel gave God's blessing and birthright promise to these young teenage lads a few months before he died in 1689 BC at the age of 147 years. By that time the twins would have been 18 or 19 years of age confirming the chronology.

The city of ON was the ancient capital of Egypt, and was known to the Egyptians as MEMPHIS, to Greeks as HELIOPOLIS, and to the Jews as BETH-SHEMISH. From this city these ancient monoliths originated,

All of this leads to the conclusion that the two monoliths were erected in MEMPHIS by THUTMOSE III in commemoration of the birth of Joseph's twin sons – Ephraim and Manasseh – due to the Pharaoh's great respect for Joseph.

RAMESES II used them to inscribe his military victories (a sort of ancient vandalism) at a later date, thereby giving scholars the impression that they were erected during his reign – 1559 to 1491 BC.

The People of the United States of America

Another interesting fact which arises from the blessing given to Manasseh was that Jacob (Israel) stated that (He) Manasseh would become a great 'PEOPLE' and shall be 'GREAT'.

Jacob did not use the word 'nation' in respect to Manasseh, and this was very prophetic indeed for, America is never referred to as a NATION but always the 'People' of the United States of America. OF THE PEOPLE, BY THE PEOPLE, FOR THE PEOPLE! – A GREAT PEOPLE!

Am-eri-ca

Another interesting fact is in the name of the nation; many suggestions have been offered as to the origin of AMERICA. Some historians have suggested it was derived from AMERIGO VESPUCCI (1451 – 1512 AD). A Florentine merchant and explorer, who claimed, on dubious authority to have been the first to sight and charter the mainland of South America in 1497. The name of AMERICA is said to have been derived from his own first name.

But the name of America was more divinely inspired, 'America' is formed in three syllables: AM-ERI-CA.

It will be remembered that Hosea was instructed by the Lord to give his children certain names (see Hosea chapter 1). To the firstborn son the name JEZREEL which means 'God may scatter' or 'God may sow'. To the second, a daughter, the name LO-RUHAMA which means 'Not having obtained mercy'. And the third, a son, the name LO-AMMI meaning 'Not my people'.

Of course the names of Hosea's children depicted the sorry state of Israel would find herself in due to her adultery with false gods and disobedience to Gods laws. They would be scattered, and in the scattering the sowing; not having God's mercy. And being issued a bill of divorcement.

Then in chapter 2 Hosea records the redeemed condition of Israel through the 'Door of Hope' of the Lords sacrifice and atonement for her transgressions. This redeemed condition is symbolised in the changed names of Hosea's children. The prefix 'LO' being dropped.

> *"Say unto your brethren ammi: and to your sisters Ruhamah"*
>
> *Hosea 2:1*

Ammi: Meaning now 'My People'
Ruhamah: Having obtained mercy.

You will notice that the expressions are NOT MY PEOPLE and MY PEOPLE not as one would expect 'MY NATION' or 'MY KINGDOM'. The shortened version of the word AMMI is AM, which forms the first syllable of AM-ERI-CA.

The central syllable 'ERI' is pure Hebrew and means 'MY WATCHERS'. Another form of ERI is URI another Hebrew word meaning 'ENLIGHTENED' (references from Youngs Analytical Concordance to the Bible). The whole meaning: MY ENLIGHTENED PEOPLE or WATCHERS HAVING OBTAINED MERCY. The meaning of the word WATCHER being WATCHMEN, GUARDIANS or CUSTODIANS.

This reference is used extensively throughout the scriptures for those entrusted with a Divine calling on behalf of the Almighty God of Israel (refer to Topical Guide under Watchman, Watchmen).

It is interesting to note that the original name was not AM-ERI-CA but AM-ERI. This is clearly evidenced by reference to MERCATORS WORLD MAP of 1538. this map is displayed in a book MAPS OF THE ANCIENT SEA KINGS by Charles Hapgood (Turnstone Books, 37 Upper Addison Gardens, London, W14).

This <u>CA</u> in AM-ERI-<u>CA</u> is purely a suffix added at a later date.

Israel's New Names

So we find that in the name of AM-ERI and BRIT-ISH are hidden the new names which were to be given to Israel (Isaiah 45:4, 62:2 and 65:15-16). MY COVENANT PEOPLE, ENLIGHTENED, WATCHERS, HAVING OBTAINED MERCY – SONS OF ISAAC.

Isaiah's Testimony

Isaiah records the creation of America with a similar symbolism to John in Revelation 12:1-2.

He likens this to a woman ready to give birth:

> *"Before 'she' travailed, she brought forth: before her pain came she was delivered of a 'man child'.*
> *Who hath heard such a thing? Who hath seen such things?*
>
> *Shall the earth be made to bring forth in one day? Or shall 'a nation; be born at once? ..."*
>
> Isaiah 66:7-8
> Emphasis added

This is not natural: Who has heard of such a thing – a woman giving birth before her travail or before her pain came, and in one day! The prophet is speaking of the birth of a nation in one day – practically overnight.

A 'man child' from the 'mother nation'.

America being the first nation that Britain gave birth to. Born on the 4th July, 1776.

And 'her pain' came after her birth in the Civil War, between brothers!

This act of God is similar to the making of the two nations of the House of Israel and the House of Judah.

> *"...for this thing is of me..."*
> *1 Kings 12:24*

And the 'man child' was named 'SAM'. This name is short for SAM-SON or SAM-U-E-L. The word is from the Hebrew SEMES, or SUN-ONE (SEMES-SON). The modern form being SYMONSON, SIMSON etc. SAM-SON was the supreme champion in Israel his parents gave him the name in anticipation of his heroic sun like strength and miraculous energy.

The Lord God is both Sun and Shield towards His people who in their covenant power and glory reflect His great light to be as the sun among other nations and people, literally

> *"... a light unto the Gentiles ..."*
> *Isaiah 42:6*
> Emphasis added

Jacob had also received a further blessing:

> *"And thy seed shall be as the dust of the earth, and thou shalt spread abroad to the WEST (America), and to the EAST (India), and to the NORTH (Canada), and to the SOUTH (Australia/New Zealand)."*
> *Genesis 28:14*
> Emphasis added

Is not this a marvellous revelation?

> *"Thus saith the Lord, in an acceptable time, have I heard thee, and in a day of salvation have I helped thee.*
> *And I will preserve thee, and give thee for a covenant of the people, TO ESTABLISH THE EARTH, TO CAUSE TO INHERIT THE DESOLATE HERITAGES".*
> *Isaiah 49:8*
> Emphasis added

The acceptable time for Great Britain's growth as an Empire Nation began in the fifteenth century. Through the previous centuries this Island Nation had been preserved, and is still preserved from the aspirations of those who attempted invasion and subjugation of its people, except those who were part of God's overall plan for His Israel people, in the Isles of the Sea.

The Day of Salvation, referred to the ending of Israel's period of chastisement, the Seven Time Punishment period i.e. 2,500 years (see Leviticus 26), which extended from the time of Israel's captivity into Assyria 721 BC to 1800AD.

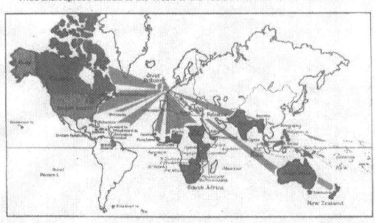

Figure 11. The Old British Empire

The nation was preserved for the purpose of colonising the 'desolate places' of the earth. Britain's colonising activities followed the exact way in which God had said. Firstly to the *West* – America being the first colonising effort in the sixteen hundreds. Then to the *East* – India. *North* – to Canada, and finally *South* to Australia and New Zealand.

In this new Island Home, the 'House of Israel' was to be called by a new name, they were no longer to be called 'Israel'.

> *"And the Gentiles shall see thy righteousness, and all*
> *kings thy glory: and thou shalt be called by a new name,*
> *which the mouth of the Lord shall name."*
>
> *Isaiah 62:2*

These two nations, descendants of Ephraim and Manasseh were to inherit all of the Sea Gates of the Earth, promised to their Great Progenitor – Abraham.

> *"… and thy see shall possess the gate of his enemies…"*
> *Genesis 22:16-17*

This prophecy was also fulfilled, for, between them Great Britain and the United States of America have at one time or another held all the 'sea gates' of this earth e.g. Gibraltar, Malta, Suez, Aden, Singapore, Hong Kong, Cape of Good Hope, The Falklands, Panama, Hawaii, The Philippines. And in keeping with the prophecy these have been mostly, if not all in, or near, Territories and Nations who have not been friendly in fact, quite the opposite.

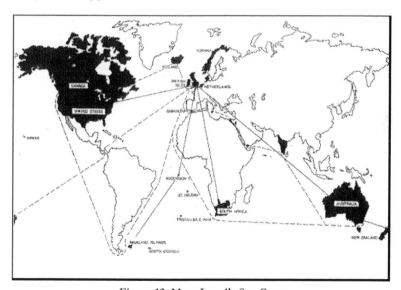

Figure 12. Map: Israel's Sea Gates

After the Tribes of Israel had settled in their new Island Home, and had eventually repulsed Roman and other invaders, their numbers began to increase and they began to say, 'this place is too small, such a small island cannot support us all". So between 1500 AD and 1800 AD they began to colonise. The prophet Isaiah foresaw these events 1000 years (millennia) previously. He states:

> *"For thy waste and thy desolate places, and the land of thy destruction (exile), shall even now be too narrow by reason of the inhabitants, and they that swallowed thee up shall be far away."*
>
> *Isaiah 49:19*

It was Assyria who had 'swallowed up' the nation of Israel. But here in the land of their 'exile' (the British Islands) the Assyrians would be 'far away'. However, the islands were too small to support a growing population, and so the work of colonising began, if it had not commenced this island would now be attempting to support all of the populations of British origin in the White Commonwealth, and those of the United States and Canada!

The story is depicted in the nursery rhyme – 'There was an old woman who lived in a shoe' – or rather an 18th century woman's bootee which resembles the outline of England/Britain. The old woman representing Israel in her new Island Home.

Then Isaiah continues:

> *"The children which thou shalt have, after thou hast lost the other (colony), shall* **say again** *in thine ears, The place is too strait for me: give place to me that I may dwell."*
>
> *Isaiah 49:20*
> Emphasis added

The first major colony which the British acquired was the American colonies, which they eventually lost in the American War of Independence 1776 AD. Therefore 'Again' it became necessary for the Island Israel People to seek new colonies, which they did, firstly to the

East in India, then to the North in Canada, and finally to the South: Africa, Australia and New Zealand.

Isaiah also informs the 'Children of Israel' in the Islands:

> *"... is my hand shortened... that it cannot redeem...*
> *Isaiah 50:2*
> *"Look unto the rock whence ye are hewn, and to the hole of the pit whence ye are digged... the isles shall wait upon me, and on my arm shall they trust."*
> *Isaiah 51:1-5*

Then in chapters fifty three and fifty four, God expressed Divine love for his people Israel:

> *"For the mountains shall depart, and the hills be removed; but my kindness shall not depart from thee, neither shall the covenant of my peace be removed, saith the Lord that hath mercy on thee."*
> *Isaiah 54:10*

The covenant which God made with Abraham, Isaac and Jacob was unconditional, and God would not, could not, ever annul it. However, they could be punished, which they were, but when the period of chastisement came to and end in 1800AD the Lord began to emancipate his people.

> *"In righteousness shalt thou be established: thou shalt be far from oppression; for thou shalt not fear: and from terror; for it shall not come near thee.*
> *Behold, they shall surely gather together, but not by me: whosoever shall gather together against thee shall fall for thy sake.*
> *No weapon that is formed against thee shall prosper; and every tongue that shall rise against thee in judgement thou shalt condemn. This is the heritage of the servants of the Lord, and their righteousness is of me, saith the Lord."*
> *Isaiah 54:14-15, 17*

This is about as clear as it could be. The Lord is not speaking of a church here, he is speaking to His new born nations of Israel, Britain and America, and it is significant that since 1800 AD, no nation has been successful in their attempts to subjugate our nations. Isaiah gives us an insight to the growth of this Island Nation and the 'Lost Colony' of America.

> *"A little one shall become a thousand, and a small one a strong nation: I the Lord will hasten it in his time."*
> *Isaiah 60:22*

The 'little one' that grew into 'a thousand' or Empire and Commonwealth, were the British.

The 'small one' (colony) which was lost and became a strong singular 'Great' nation is the United States of America.

> *"Thy sun shall no more go down; neither shall thy moon withdraw itself: for the Lord shall be thine everlasting light. And the days of thy mourning shall be ended."*
> *Isaiah 60:20*

Was there not a saying that 'The sun never sets on the British Empire', and after 1800 AD her 'days of mourning' (2,520 years) were surely ended.

> *"For ye are my witnesses, saith the Lord, and my servant whom I have chosen ... this people **(Israel)**, have I formed for myself; they shall shew forth my praise."*
> *Isaiah 43:10, 21*
> Emphasis added

These witnesses are nothing to do with a church, **any church**, but purely a message to God's Covenant Nation, informing them of their great commission.

After the period of chastisement was ended in 1800 AD , the redemption took effect, and the Lord restored the everlasting Gospel to the Earth, and the true authority to administer the ordinances represented by the

Melchezedeck Priesthood, which would once again be manifest in Israel.

> *"But ye shall be named priests of the Lord, men shall call you the ministers of our God: Ye shall eat the riches of the Gentiles …*
> *…and I will direct their work in truth, and I will make* **an everlasting covenant** *with them.*
> *And their seed shall be known among the Gentiles, and their offspring among the people: all that see them shall acknowledge them, that they are the seed which the LORD hath blessed.*
> *I will greatly rejoice in the LORD, my soul shall be joyful in my God; for he hath clothed me with the garments of salvation, he hath covered me with the robe of righteousness, as a bridegroom decketh himself with ornaments, and as a bride adorneth herself with her jewels."*
>
> Isaiah 61:6-10
> Emphasis added

This is just about one of the most sublime statements in the whole of the 'Book of Israel'.

What a revelation these verses portray.

The priests of the Lord, those who hold the true priesthood will be recognised by **all** people. I think this is true of Mormon missionaries, even though they dress like others, somehow people, 'just know' who they are.

"I will direct their work in truth", can only refer to the true restored gospel.

I will make "an everlasting covenant" with them, this also has been fulfilled, and he has in that "everlasting covenant" clothed his servants with *"garments of salvation"* and a *"robe of righteousness"*.

In this brief exposition on Isaiah, are not our eyes now to be opened? That this is the Lord's message to our peoples of Great Britain and

America, surely this must be so with so much weight of evidence. In one bold sweep across the centuries both Hosea and Isaiah tell the story of the rejection, the punishment, redemption, and ultimate restoration of the 'House of Israel'.

Hosea's whole message is central to this theme. Isaiah introduces his message in chapter twenty four, then from chapter forty through to chapter sixty six his whole message is to the Hebrew-Israel people, descendants of SHEM-EBER-ABRAAHM-ISAAC AND JACOB, "In the Isles of the Sea", and their descendants throughout the world.

Finally the Lord says:

> *"Who is blind, but my servant? or deaf, as my messenger*
> *that I sent? who is blind as he that is perfect, and blind as*
> *the Lord's servant?"*
>
> *Isaiah 42: 19*

It is not the servants of God who hold the true Priesthood which are blind, it is not the true church which is blind.

It is our nations of Britain and America, and the other Anglo-Saxon Celtic nations in the Earth, they are blind, **blind to their identity.**

Paul said:

> *"For I would not, brethren, that ye should be ignorant of*
> *this mystery, lest ye should be wise in your own conceits;*
> *that blindness in part is happened to Israel, until the*
> *fulness of the Gentiles be come in."*
>
> *Romans 11: 25*

The fullness of the Gentiles has now come in, and Israel's blindness is being removed.

5
THE SEVEN TIMES PUNISHMENT

At this point we again pick up our story of Israel the marred vessel, the lump of clay in the hand of the potter, being reshaped and moulded into a new nation.

With reference to the chart THE SEVEN SEALS OF REVELATON we see Israel's journey through the 'corridor of time'.

In this and the following chapters we see the 'woman' Israel in her road of destiny through history, beginning in the pre-existence; of her selection as Jehovah's national earthly helpmate, where she is depicted in the scriptures (metaphorically speaking) as the 'wife' and He the 'husband', and on to her ultimate destiny and glory.

In the next few chapters we shall discuss:

- Israel's pre-mortal selection and foreordination.
- Her national birth.
- Her training and preparation. A period of correction in a 'wilderness' experience. A 'nourishing' period and a time of 'revival'
- And ultimately to a complete restoration as a new nation with a new identity.

And how this history applies to the contents of John's second vision (Revelation chapters 13 to 18).

The 'IF' and 'BUT' Covenant

In Leviticus chapter 26 and in the 28, 29 and 30th chapters of Deuteronomy are contained the specific conditions under which the Israelite nation could retain possession of the promised land and also sets forth the terms of the marriage contract between Jehovah the husband and the Israelite 'wife' nation.

This is known as the 'IF' and 'BUT' covenant (Leviticus 26).

The 'If' Covenant

The 'IF' covenant was:

> *"YE shall make you no idols nor graven image, neither rear you up a standing image, neither shall ye set up any image of stone in your land, to bow down unto it: for I am the LORD your God* **(condition 1).***
> Ye shall keep my Sabbaths* **(condition 2)***, and reverence my sanctuary* **(condition 3)***: I am the LORD.*
> *If ye walk in my statutes* **(condition 4)***, and keep my commandments* **(condition 5)***, and do them;"*
>
> *Leviticus 26:1-3*
> Emphasis added

'If' the nation as the wife would be faithful to him through obedience to these simple conditions then blessings of surpassing magnitude would be showered upon her (Leviticus 26:1-13). These conditions seemed reasonable considering the blessings they were to receive in return.

But both the House of Israel (Ephraim) and the House of Judah broke every one of them, not once, but many times. Occasionally there would be a period of repentance, but they soon slipped back into their old ways, until Jehovah her husband became wearisome of the ritual.

The 'but' Covenant

Commencing verse 14 through to verse 46 is contained the 'BUT' conditions of the contract or covenant.

> *"But if ye will not hearken unto me and will not do all these commandments..."*
>
> *Leviticus 26:14*

Then the punishment clauses of the covenant would become operative, she would be divorced from her husband, his land, and home, and would even lose his name.

This punishment or period of correction was for a definite period of time

I will punish you seven times for your sins

I will bring seven times more plagues upon you

I will punish you seven times

I will chastise you seven times

These punishments are not to be taken as seven individual punishments, but rather an era of time, during which Israel would be sent into captivity and punishment, for correction, training, and eventual redemption, and at the end of this period would be cleansed, purified and brought back to God, ready and willing to administer the laws of God, contained in the Commandments, Statutes and Judgements as the national laws of the land, the people at last being a faithful wife acknowledging Jehovah as her king (Jeremiah 31:31, Hebrews 8:8).

> *"For I will take you from among the heathen, and gather you out of all countries, and will bring you into your own land.*
> *Then will I sprinkle clean water upon you, and ye shall be clean: from all your filthiness, and from all your idols, will I cleanse you.*
> *A new heart also will I give you, and a new spirit will I put within you: and I will take away the stony heart out of your flesh, and I will give you an heart of flesh.*
> *And I will put my spirit within you, and cause you to walk in my statutes, and ye shall keep my judgments, and do them."*
>
> *Ezekiel 36:24-27*

Both the House of Israel and the House of Judah were rebellious and unworthy of Gods love, having apostatised and committed adultery, worshipping false gods, neglecting the Sabbaths and failing to keep His Statutes and Judgements. For this she was given a Bill of Divorce.

To Jeremiah the Lord said:

> *"The LORD said also unto me in the days of Josiah the king, Hast thou seen that which backsliding Israel hath done? she is gone up upon every high mountain and under every green tree, and there hath played the harlot.*
>
> *And I said after she had done all these things, Turn thou unto me. But she returned not. And her treacherous sister Judah saw it.*
>
> *And I saw, when for all the causes whereby backsliding Israel committed adultery I had put her away, and given her a bill of divorce; yet her treacherous sister Judah feared not, but went and played the harlot also.*
>
> *And it came to pass through the lightness of her whoredom, that she defiled the land, and committed adultery with stones and with stocks.*
>
> *And yet for all this her treacherous sister Judah hath not turned unto me with her whole heart, but feignedly, saith the LORD.*
>
> *And the LORD said unto me, The backsliding Israel hath justified herself more than treacherous Judah.*
>
> *Go and proclaim these words toward the north, and say, Return, thou backsliding Israel, saith the LORD; and I will not cause mine anger to fall upon you: for I am merciful, saith the LORD, and I will not keep anger for ever.*
>
> *Only acknowledge thine iniquity, that thou hast transgressed against the LORD thy God, and hast scattered thy ways to the strangers under every green tree, and ye have not obeyed my voice, saith the LORD.*
>
> *Turn, O backsliding children, saith the LORD; for I am married unto you: and I will take you one of a city, and two of a family, and I will bring you to Zion:*
>
> *And I will give you pastors according to mine heart, which shall feed you with knowledge and understanding."*
>
> *Jeremiah 3:6-15*
> Emphasis added

If only the House of Israel had repented and "acknowledged their iniquity" they would have been forgiven their transgressions then and there and the Lord promised that then he would give them "pastors according to his own heart which shall feed you with knowledge and understanding". However, repentance never came and therefore Israel had to learn the hard way for 2520 years before she was given the blessings of these promised pastors.

And in the following verses even greater blessings were pronounced upon the condition of their repentance.

This appeal was repeated through the prophets Hosea, Isaiah, Ezekiel and others (Isaiah 54:1-8, Ezekiel 36:16-38)

But they failed to respond causing the Lord to declare:

> "...*their way was before me as the uncleanness of a removed woman.*"
>
> *Ezekiel 36:17*

> "*Surely as a wife treacherously departeth from her husband, so have ye dealt treacherously with me, O house of Israel, saith the LORD.*"
>
> *Jeremiah 3:20*

It was for this treachery that the Lord pronounced a punishment of Seven Times upon His people.

TIME MEASURES REVIEW

A Time

In biblical terms 'a time' has the value of 360 given in either degrees, days or years. There were no man made clocks in those days. Time was calculated on the degrees of a circle (360 degrees). On the daily count 15 degrees would represent one hour of time and 15 years as 'one hour' of prophetical time.

15 x 24 = 360

In all 'Time' prophecies 'days' should be interpreted as 'years'. Therefore 'Seven Times' is translated as 7 x 360 = 2520 and in prophetical terms this would mean 2520 years.

3 ½ Times is rendered as:

A time, times, and half of time
or
A time, times and dividing of time

A Time	360	
And Times (360 x 2)	720	
Half of Times	180	
	1,260	years

One Day as a Thousand Years

Sometimes certain prophets used the 'day for a thousand years' principle.

One Day = 1,000 years
Two Days = 2,000 years
Three Days = 3,000 years

The only prophet to use this principal was the prophet Hosea (Hosea 6:1-3).

The Millenniums

Time measures can have a further application.

1.	On the reckoning of a Lunar Calendar	354.367 Days
2.	On the reckoning of a Biblical Calendar	360 Days
3.	On the reckoning of a Solar Calendar	365.242 Days

According to the science of Chronology we are sure that from the fall of Adam to the birth of the Savour was 4,000 years. It is now 2,000 years since the first advent of the Saviour – total of 6,000 years.

The Solar millennium or Seventh thousandth year commenced in the year 2001 AD.

However Lunar Time is 30 years per thousand shorter than Solar Time: Over a period of 6,000 years Lunar time would be 180 years (half of 360) less than Solar Time. Therefore the lunar millennium would have commenced in the year 1820/1 AD! Biblical Time is 15 years per thousand shorter than Solar Time. Therefore over a 6,000 year period would be 90 years less than Solar Time, making the Biblical time millennium commence in 1911 AD!

The years in which the first two of these millenniums commenced hold great significance in both secular and religious history, particularly to Latter-day Saints.

The Millenniums
Lunar   1820 AD
Biblical   1911 AD
Solar   2001 AD

A Biblical Year

One year consisted of 360 Days
Each moth had 30 days
30 x 12 = 360

A Biblical Day

Symbolically it could mean 1000 Years. The day was counted from sunset to sunset.
One day consisted of 360 Degrees.
The night period had a value of 180 Degrees.
The day period had a value of 180 Degrees.
One hour consisted of 15° of the cycle 24 x 15 = 360

A Day For a Year Principle

360 degrees would represent 360 years.
Each 15 degrees of the cycle would represent 15 years (one hour).

A Biblical Time

The 360 day year is referred to as 'a time' in the Bible. 3 ½ years is rendered: 'a time, times and half of time'.
'Times' meaning 360 x 2 (or twice 'time') = 720 days

Sometimes it is rendered 'a time, times and dividing of time'

'Time'	= 1 year	or 360 days
'Times'	= 2 years	or 720 days
'Half of time'	= 6 months	or 180 days

Total 1260 Days (3 ½ years or 42 months)

Seven years is rendered as 'seven times' 7 x 360 = 2520 days.
Applying the day for a year principle, these 'days' become years and they are then known as 'Prophetic Days'.

Figure 13. Time Measures Review

We know from chronology as it relates to biblical history that the House of Israel (10 tribes) were taken into captivity to Assyria in 721 BC. Therefore, the seven times punishment period would end in 1800 AD (Solar Time).

721 BC------------------------2520 years----------------------------1800 AD

Applying this same principal to the dispersion of the House of Judah who were taken into captivity in Babylon in 604 BC we arrive at a terminal date of 1917 AD.

604 BC------------------------2520years----------------------------1917 AD

1800 and 1917?

What is significant about these two terminal dates? We shall look at this question from various view points and we shall show that these terminal dates apply to the House of Israel and Judah.

(1) Nationality, (2) Historically and (3) Ecclesiastically

Ecclesiastically

It will not be difficult for members of the Church of Jesus Christ of Latter-day Saints to see the significance of the terminal date of 1800 AD, for we know that the Gospel was restored shortly afterwards for, in the spring of 1820, Joseph Smith received the first vision.

Why 1820?

This in itself answers the question. Why did the Lord wait until 1820 before restoring the Gospel and true Church?

It was because the House of Israel was serving its Seven Times period of correction, *and blessings of such nature were withheld.*

Some people may think the God of Israel to be harsh. But the Lord is wiser than man, and, in actual fact this seven times period of punishment and correction was a blessing in disguise for both Israel and the whole world.

> *"For my thoughts are not your thoughts, neither are your ways my ways, saith the LORD.*

*For as the heavens are higher than the earth, so are my
ways higher than your ways, and my thoughts than your
thoughts."*

Isaiah 55:8-9
See also verses 10 and 11

The Lunar Millennium 1820

The year 1820 marked the end of 6,000 Lunar years from Adam, with
this date, the world entered upon an epoch of 180 years (half of a Time!).
A transitory period, to which the prophet Daniel gave the designation,
'the *time* of the end' (Daniel 12:4). Another term may be 'the fullness of
time'. Daniel informs us that during these 180 years there would be an
increase in knowledge through the inventive genius of man, in new
powers which would be developed and in travel.

Up to the beginning of the 19th century there had been no practical
change in man's condition, except for the possibility of the invention of
the printing press; for millenniums he had been labouring by the sweat of
his brow to provide for his material needs. During those years the fastest
mode of travel upon land was by horse, and upon the sea, in sailing
vessels.

Explosion of Knowledge

Then suddenly there was an explosion of knowledge. In 1818 the first
steam boat to cross the Atlantic was the Rising Sun. In 1831 Michael
Faraday discovered the principal of electromagnetic induction, and many
more inventions were forthcoming. We call it the age of industrial
revolution.

A Restitution of All Things

Thus in 1820/1 AD the terminal date of 6,000 Lunar years inaugurated a
period of invention that enabled man to harness the forces of nature. In
all ways the ground work was laid for the development of modern
civilisation which became highly industrialised as a result of the
application of steam and electric power.

And so it was an appropriate time for the *restitution of all things spoken by God through the mouth of the holy prophets since the world began* (Acts 3:19-21).

Is it any wonder then why the Gospel was restored at this time! However, the restoration of the Gospel in 1820 was only seen as in the 'moonlight' period of time –

not clear – not distinct, but, nevertheless, outlined by the light of the moon, giving only a general idea of its shape and form, and so the world in general did not appreciate the wonderful event which had taken place.

1911 – The Biblical Millennium
The End of Isolation
Applying biblical time measure to the given event of the Lunar millennium 1820 we arrive at 1911 the central date of the 'Time of the End' (or the 180 year period from the Lunar Millennium to the Solar Millennium).

After the persecutions which the Mormon people experienced in Kirtland Ohio in 1836/7 and Jackson County Missouri, they moved into the state of Illinois and built a city which they called 'NAUVOO', an American Indian name meaning 'The beautiful place'. However, by 1846, due to the continuing persecutions and the foul murder of Joseph Smith and his brother Hyrum at Carthage, the Saints were once again forced to evacuate that place. Many books have been written about the Mormon pioneers who migrated over 1,000 miles to the West, some pushing hand carts and eventually arriving at the Great Salt Lake Basin in the year 1847. This was a land that no one desired – it was a desert wilderness. However, it became a sanctuary of safety for God's people, a place that gave them respite from persecution.

After the death of Joseph Smith, almighty God raised up another great Leader, Brigham Young. The isolation which Brigham Young obtained for his people in the sanctuary of the Rocky Mountains gave the Church of Jesus Christ of Latter-day Saints the opportunity of becoming a permanent institution. The roots of the church became firmly planted. Its organisation and beliefs became fixed and crystallised. The isolation which the people endured for 60 years from 1847 to 1911 preserved the church from destruction. It was not preserved, however, without great cost. Despite the interest of the church in schools and education, the circumstances were such that a whole generation developed with little formal education. But for the continual influx of immigrants and the contact of missionaries with the outside world, the Mormons would have witnessed a period of stagnation and learning. As it was, the development of men of letters, scientists, artist, doctors, surgeons and many other professions, suffered greatly. Furthermore, isolated as the people were, deep seated convictions crystallised into doctrines in the minds of many, and religious forms into unchangeable laws.

This isolation, however, did not continue. Nor was it the desire of Brigham Young or of the church that it should continue. Once the Saints were established in the west, the church exerted its full influence to open new channels of communication with the world – to invite industry to Utah – and welcome contacts in every way with the rest of the nation.

The first event to break into this isolation was the great gold rush to California which made of Utah a national highway to the gold fields. This brought numerous non-Mormons into Utah and resulted in a number of non-Mormon merchants establishing themselves in Salt Lake City.

The organisation of a territorial form of government and the coming of federal appointees encouraged other non-Mormons to enter the territory for political or economic purposes.

The next development was the opening of the mining industry in Utah during, and immediately following the Civil War. Foreign capital and labourers were attracted to the state and the non-Mormon population rapidly increased in the cities and mining centres.

In **1861**, the overland telegraph connecting Salt Lake City with the rest of the nation was installed.

In **1869**, an event occurred which, more than any other, removed barriers created by time and distance and revolutionised the economic conditions of the Territory. In that year the first transcontinental railroad was completed – the Union Pacific from the west and the Central Pacific from the east. The two lines were connected at Promontory, Utah and engines from east and west rubbed noses. The period of Utah's isolation was coming to an end. Once again, the Divine Clock was on time.

By **1911** the modern system of house to house communication had become a reality as a result of Alexander Graham Bell's invention of the telephone and mass production had been perfected without which it would have been impossible. It is most significant that 120 years (the same period of warning as given to Noah concerning the Deluge – Gen 6:3) after 1820 we reached the third and final phase in the progress of scientific achievement when, in the year 1941, the secret of unlocking the power contained in the atom became known. Four years later the first use made of the new power was to destroy the two Japanese cities of Hiroshima and Nagasaki in World War II with a tragic toll of death amongst the inhabitants.

Without exception, all the prophets, Jesus Christ and his apostles, prophesied that as the present age came to a close, the accompanying events would bring despair upon all men for fear of the possible annihilation of all mankind. After speaking words of warning concerning this time of tribulation Jesus climaxed his remarks with a pronouncement of marked significance:

> *"And except those days should be shortened, there should no flesh be saved: but for the elect's sake those days shall be shortened."*
>
> *Matthew 24:22*

Men are therefore living in dread of what might happen and consequently the words of Jesus Christ are being literally fulfilled in our generation:

> *"Men's hearts failing them for fear, and for looking after those things which are coming on the earth…"*
>
> *Luke 21:26*

Following this statement of universal fear Jesus gives the reason why men will be afraid: "For the powers of heaven shall be shaken". The reference here is the unlocking of the secrets of the atom. The destructive use for which this knowledge is utilised has put the world in fear.

However, looking at the period of time since 1820 and the Restoration of the Gospel, especially since 1911 great strides have been made in bringing a period of enlightenment and truth to mankind as the church began to embark on a world wide program of growth through missionary work and temple building, which will continue up to and through the *Solar Millennium commencing 2001 AD.*

6
MIGRATIONS AND WAYMARKS

The Captivity Period

Here we should note another significant fact regarding this deportation of the Israel people. The Assyrian name for their Israel captives was KHUMRI. The Persians called them SAKI (SAKAE), the Babylonians – GHIMRI, and the Greeks named them SCYTHIANS (SCYTH pronounced SKYTHS) = SCOTS today. The name KHUMRI is derived from OMRI. The title KHUMRI is continued in the CYMRY of Wales. The name is good Hebrew and significant of Israel, for it means 'Priests' – CUMRI pronounced KUMRI. These names should never be pronounced as if 'C' was 'S', just as Celtic should always be pronounced KELTIC. We find the tribal names CIMMERIANS, CIMBRAINS, and CRIMEA all pronounced with a hard 'C'. It was pronounced KIMMEROI in Greek.

In the great inscription of king Darius on the rocks of BEHISTUN, in what was Persia, a list of tribal names given in each of the three languages in which the records are there inscribed. The people named SAKA in one version are called GIMRI in the second; obviously 'SAKA' and 'GIMRI' are two names for the same race. Strange that we should have 'SAXONS' and 'CYMRY' side by side in these islands associated in the building up of modern Britain. BETH KHUMRI is another form in which the name "House of OMRI" occurs in some Assyrian inscriptions as a designation for the people of Israel. As also BETH SAK is the Phoenician name for the "House of Isaac".

Israel Kumri	Original name Assyrian name	Israel names well known to archaeologist
Ghimri Sakae	Babylonian name Persian name	Names linked to the "Behistun Rock"
Sakae Scythians	Persian name Greek name	Names linked by "Herodutus"
Sake	Persian name	Names linked by "Ptolemy"

Saxones	Modern name	
Saxons or	Anglo-Saxon name	Immigrants to Britain
Saac-Sons	Sons of Isaac	approximately 500 AD
Angels	Anglo-Saxon name	

Escape from Assyria

As early as the ninth century BC the growing Assyrian power began to harass the people of Syria and Israel and struck terror into the inhabitants of the whole land of Phoenicia. It was then that a great immigration of Israelites took place to the Ionic States on the coasts of Asia Minor, the Aegean Islands and Macedonia where they were safe from Assyria.

However, of those that remained, it is estimated that up to 2 million were taken in all to Assyria. Living there semi-independently for the next hundred years, those SAKS or SAKI, as they appear on various eastern inscriptions, like the BEHISTUN ROCK, became the predominant element in Media. They, in fact, were the leaders in the Medic wars of rebellion, first against Assyria and later against Babylon. It was they, who under CYAXARES, joined with the Babylonians under NABOPOLASSAR, and marched against NINEVEH in 606 BC, and destroyed it after a two year siege, when the last 'CZAR' of Assyria, ASHURETILILIANI perished in the flames of the capital. *It was there that the people of Israel began to fulfil their Divine Destiny of God's Battle Axe as we read in Jeremiah:*

> *"Thou art my battle axe and weapons of war: for with thee will I break in pieces the nations, and with thee will I destroy kingdoms;*
> *And with thee will I break in pieces the horse and his rider; and with thee will break in pieces the chariot and his rider;"*
>
> *Jeremiah 51:20-21*

The power of Assyria had been the chosen medium to take Israel into captivity – to commence her Seven Times Punishment, but only a century later that power was destroyed by the sons of the prisoners they took into captivity.

After the fall of ASSHUR (Assyria) the SAKS or SAKI became the dominant power in that region and, let it be noted at the very time that the Kingdom of Judah ended in Palestine and were being deported to Babylonian captivity. About that time a large host of SAKS moved northward across the Araxes River and through the Caucasus Mountains into what today is southern Russia, where they became known as the SCYTHIANS, pronounced "SKYTS", and in more modern language: SCOTS. By that time of course they were speaking a different language to Hebrew, which we know today as Gaelic – in fact the word Wales is only a derivation of GAEL'S!

In Isaiah we read:

> *"For with stammering lips and another tongue will he speak to this people."*
>
> *Isaiah 28:11*

Strong's Concordance gives the Hebrew word for stammering as 'GAEL' while Young's Analytical Concordance gives stammering as 'LEAG'. It is most striking therefore that one of the old names for the Irish Scots should be 'LEAGAEL', or in Hebrew, a stammering people, the double word representing the left-to-right Phoenician and the right-to-left Hebrew!

Since 720 BC and more particularly since 600 BC these wanderings of Israel into Europe had been in progress. After the fall of NINEVAH in 606 BC the parent stock of the SAKS and CYMRI left their homes in Assyria and departed for a region north-west of the Black Sea named ARSARETH, taking the plunder of NINEVAH with them.

The Apocrypha's Witness

The prophet EZDRAS, who was none other than the prophet EZRA (as shown by Josephus Antiquities 11 chapter 5, paragraph 1. And also Ezra 7:13-26) is also described in 2 Esdras 12:11 as the brother of the prophet Daniel! His prophecies, like Daniel's, were given during Judah's captivity in Babylon approximately 150 years after the captivity of the Ten Tribes. Regarding the migration of the Ten Tribes from Assyria he states:

"Those are the ten tribes, which were carried away
prisoners out of their own land in the time of Osea the
king, whom Salmanasar the king of Assyria led away
captive, and he carried them over the waters (Euphrates),
and so come they into another land.

But they took this counsel among themselves, that they
would leave the multitude of the heathen, and go forth into
a further country, where never mankind dwelt,

That they might there keep their statutes, which they never
kept in their own land.

And they entered into Euphrates by the narrow passages
of the river.

For the most High then shewed signs for them, and held
still the flood, till they were passed over.

For through that country there was a great way to go,
namely, of a year and a half: and the same region is called
Arsareth."

2 Esdras 13:40-45
Apocrypha
Emphasis added

Our map Migrations of Israel shows the region named by Ezra. Starting from Assyria, they crossed the Araxes river and through a pass in the Caucasus mountains, named the Dariel Pass, into the steppes of Southern Russia, moving westward along the shores of the Black Sea as far as the Carpathian mountains. From these mountains flows a river named Sereth mentioned by Ezra, 'AR' meaning river or hill. The Sereth is a tributary of the Danube and as can be seen, the Danube crosses Europe in a North Westerly direction, linking up with the river Rhine in Germany, and into the North Sea – a natural line of migration for the wandering Israelites in their course for the island of the sea.

This is in harmony with the statement by the prophet Micah

"I will surely assemble, O Jacob, all of thee; I will surely
gather the remnant of Israel; I will put them together as
the sheep of Bozrah, as the flock in the midst of their fold:
they shall make great noise by reason of the multitude of
men.

The breaker is come up before them: they have broken up, **and have passed through the gate, and are gone out by it:** *and their king shall pass before them, and the LORD on the head of them."*

> *Micah 2:12-13*
> Emphasis added

The clause 'They... have passed through the gate', and the one by Ezra, 'They have entered into the narrow passages' are parallels and refer to the same circumstances and place. It is at this time that Hosea wrote:

> *"...the children of Israel (10 Tribes) shall abide many days without a king, and without a prince, and without a sacrifice, and without an image..." or as the marginal reading gives it: "without a standing pillar"*
>
> *Hosea 3:4*
> Emphasis added

Young's exhaustive Concordance gives, among other definitions of the original Hebrew word, both 'Memorial Stone' and 'Pillar'. Other authorities give us 'pillar rock' and 'pillar stone' as the correct rendering: which justifies the conclusion that the 'Pillar Stone' in question was the Bethel Pillar Stone – Jacob's Stone – which had been retained by the royal family which ruled over the remnant of Judah until the overthrow of Zedekiah.

To understand Hosea's statement it must be borne in mind that the last king of the Ten Tribed Israel was Hoshea 730 – 721 BC, **however the royal throne of David continued to exist in the nation of Judah until the deportation of that nation to Babylon in 604 BC.**

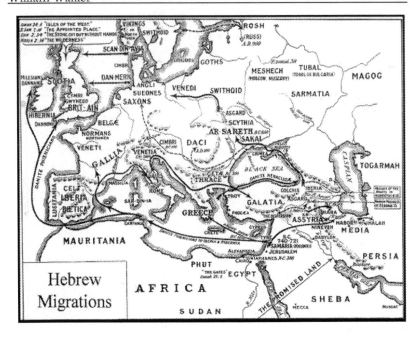

Figure 14. Hebrew Migrations

7
THE WILDERNESS YEARS
(10 Tribes)

The prophet Hosea informs us that the House of Israel would be "Wanderers among the nations" (Hosea 9:17).

Also that Ephraim "followed after the east wind", and everyone knows that an east wind blows west (Hosea 12:1)!

> *"Therefore, behold, I will allure her, and bring her into the wilderness, and speak comfortably unto her."*
> *Hosea 2:14*

The 'wilderness' being an expression for Israel's divorce, captivity and period of wandering in exile among the nations. It is this same 'wilderness' to which reference is made by Ezekiel, where God declared that he would plead with his people following the period when his fury would be poured out upon them for their sins:

> *"And I will bring you into the wilderness of the people, and there will I plead with you face to face.*
> *Like as I pleaded with your fathers in the wilderness of the land of Egypt, so will I plead with you, saith the Lord GOD."*
> *Ezekiel 20:35-36*

In a footnote in the Companion Bible, the following statement is made about this wilderness:

> *"The wilderness of the people!, Probably another country which would be to them another wilderness in which they were to be tested as to whether they would hear*
> *Israel is 'swallowed up': now shall they be among the gentiles as a vessel wherein is no pleasure*
> *Hosea 8:8*
> *For Lo, I will command and I will sift the House of*

Israel among all nations, like as corn is sifted in a sieve,
yet shall not the least grain fall upon the earth."
Amos 9:9
See also *Romans 11:1-11*

Josephus the Great Jewish Historian Bears Testimony

Concerning the whereabouts of the Ten Tribes at the time of Christ and after, Josephus says, in an account written probably forty years after the crucifixion:

> *"Wherefore there are but two tribes in Asia and Europe subject to the Romans, while the ten tribes are <u>beyond Euphrates till now</u> (70 AD) and are an immense multitude, and not to be estimated in numbers."*
> *Book 11, chapter 5, Paragraph 2*
> Emphasis added

The previous statement given by the greatest Jewish historian of his day, clearly refutes all the misguided arguments of those who have endeavoured to destroy the truth by stating erroneously that the 'Jews' were composed of all twelve tribes. Josephus makes it abundantly clear, even after our Lord's day, that the Ten Tribes were distinct from the 'Jews', and were an immense multitude of people who had not re-crossed the river Euphrates to return to their old home in the Holy Land. They had on the contrary, wandered out of Assyria, moving further north and west.

Herodotus the Ancient Greek Historian Bears Witness

The Scythains told Herodotus that their nation had been in existence for a thousand years previous to the invasion of Darius. If we date, therefore, a thousand years backward from the Time of Darius, 515 BC, we arrive at 1485/6 BC, the date of the Exodus when Israel was founded. This referred to what Herodotus called the Royal Scythians, who considered the other tribes in the light of slaves. These lived on the river Gerrhus, a tributary of the present Dniester. Herodotus includes among the Scythian tribes the Massagetai or Getae, which is the Median form of Gutti and means "wanderers" or "adventurers". Massagetai, means "great wanderers", they lived on the shores of the Danube, i.e. the Arsareth mentioned by Esdras. (Regarding this subject we shall include the testimony and evidence of other respected historians in the forthcoming chapters.)

This "wilderness period" was for Israel's good and salvation for the Gentiles. It became a period of training, preparation, submission, repentance, and eventual emancipation for the great commission they had been selected to fulfil (Romans 11:25). Micah informs us 'In that day', that is, the day in which their wandering in the wilderness would end, the Lord would restore his blessings to them in fulfilment of the promises made to Abraham, Isaac, and Jacob.

> *"In that day, saith the LORD, will I assemble her that halteth, and I will gather her that is driven out, and her that I have afflicted* **(ten Tribed Israel);**
> *And I will make her that halted* **(Judah)** *a remnant, and her that was cast far off* **(Israel)** *a strong nation* **(a singular great nation)***: and the LORD shall reign over them in mount Zion from henceforth, even for ever.*
> *Micah 4:6-7*
> Emphasis added

The location for this re-gathering and place of refuge and safety had been selected by an all-wise God long before Israel's captivity, for the Lord had revealed that there was an "<u>Appointed place" prepared for his people</u> – this revelation was given to the prophet Nathan during the days of King David about 1000 years BC.

> *"Moreover I will appoint a place for my people Israel, and will plant them, that they may dwell in a place of their own, and move no more; neither shall the children of wickedness afflict them any more, as beforetime,"*
> *2 Samuel 7:10*

Was it only a mere coincidence I wonder that Cotton Mather took up his Bible just before the Mayflower left England, and, after reading this passage of scripture, he then said, "we are now going to that land"!

Israel's Waymarks and High Heaps

Speaking to Ephraim, the Eternal says in Jeremiah

> *"Set thee up* **waymarks**, *make thee* **high heaps**: *set thine heart toward the highway,* **even the way which thou wentest...**"
>
> *Jeremiah 31:21*
> Emphasis added

From this instruction we should expect some kind of signs or 'waymarks' to have been left along the trail by which the ancient Hebrews and House of Israel journeyed.

Dan the Serpent's Trail

In Genesis 49:17 Jacob foretelling what should befall each of the tribes, says: "Dan shall be a serpent by the way", or "Dan shall be a serpents trail". It is a significant fact that the tribe of Dan, named every place they settled after their father Dan. A few points in the history of the children of Dan will show us how they became a serpent's trail.

The tribe of Dan originally occupied a strip of coast country on the Mediterranean, west of Jerusalem. But this division of the land soon became too small for the tribe, as we are told the following:

> *"And the coast of the children of Dan went out too little for them: therefore the children of Dan went up to fight against Leshem, and took it, ... and called Leshem, Dan, after the name of Dan their father."*
>
> *Joshua 19:47*

Also in Judges 18:11-12 it is recorded that Danites took Kirjathjearim, and 'called the place Mahaneh – Dan unto this day'.

A little later the same company of 600 armed Danites cam to Laish, captured it, and 'they called the name of the city Dan, after the name of Dan their father' (see verse 29).

So we notice how these Danites left their 'serpents trail' by the way – set up waymarks by which they may be traced today.

In the original Hebrew language vowels (a, e, i, o, u) were very rarely given in the spelling. The sound of the vowels had to be supplied in speaking. Thus, the word 'Dan' in its English equivalent could be spelled, simply, 'DN'. It may therefore have been pronounced as "DAN, "DEN", "DIN", "DON" or "DUN" and still could be the original Hebrew name.

The tribe of Dan occupied two different portions of the Promised Land before the Assyrian captivity. One colony lived on the seacoast. They were principally seamen, and it is recorded Dan abode in ships (see Judges 5:17). When Assyria captured Israel, these seacoast Danites struck out in their ships and sailed west through the Mediterranean and north to Ireland. Just before his death, Moses prophesied of Dan: "Dan is a lion's whelp: He shall leap from Bashan" (Deuteronomy 33:22). Along the shores of the Mediterranean they left their trail in names, 'Den', 'Don', 'Din', 'Dar-Dan-ells', and just before passing out through the straight into the Atlantic they left their mark in Iberia on the peninsula of Spain, i.e. ME-DIN-A, SI-DON-IA, SAR-DIN-IA, etc.

Irish annals and history show that the new settlers of Ireland, at just this time, were the 'TUATHA DE DANAANS', which means, translated, 'Tribe of Dan'. Sometimes the same appears simply 'TUATHE-DE', meaning the 'People of God'. And in Ireland we find these 'waymarks': DANS LAUGH, DAN-SOWER, DUN-DALK, DUN-DRUM, DON-EGAL bay, DUN-EGAL CITY, DUN-GLOW, LON-DON-DERRY. There is also the name DIN-GLE, DUN-GARVEN AND DUNS-MORE (which means "more Dans"). Moreover the name Dunn in the Erse-the ancient Irish language means the same as DAN in the Hebrew: judge. DAN-I-EL which means the Judge of God.

Dan's Overland Migration

But the northern colony of the Danites were taken to Assyria in the captivity, and thence in the escape with the rest of the tribes of Israel they travelled from Assyria by the overland route. After leaving Assyrian captivity, they inhabited for some time the land just west of the Black Sea, the region of Arsereth. There we find the rivers DNIEPER, DNIESTER, and the DANUBE, the DAN-INN, the DAN-ASTER, the DAN-DARI, the DAN-EZ, the DON, the DAN, and the U-DON, the ERI-DON, down to the DANES. Denmark means 'DANS-MARK', meaning 'DANS last resting place'. As also we find the identity in the word SCAN-DIN-AVIANS.

The Scandinavian Connection

The 'Danoi' settled in Thrace and Macedonia. They formed part of the Grecian Empire ruled over by Alexander the Great 300 BC.

After the sudden death of Alexander and the dissolution of his Empire 323 BC these Danoi of Macedonia trekked northwards into central Europe – Russia – Germany – Sweden about the year 250 BC under the leadership of Odin.

He had five sons whom he established as ruling monarchs in all the areas which the conquered; including Greece, Russia, Germany, Hungary, Sweden, Denmark, Norway. All the ruling monarchs of Europe trace their lines back to <u>Odin,</u> including the Royal House of Britain!

<u>Macedonia:</u> MASS-E-DON-IA meaning the multitudes (Mass) of (E) the tribe of Dan. (IA) is only a suffix to round the name off.

This gave rise to the great legends of Odin and the 'ASA'-men. 'Asa' could mean Asia. But the real meaning is that it was the shortened version of ASHER, another of the tribes of Israel. Asher as we have discovered was one of the tribes assigned to Dan's brigade; the other being the tribe of Naphtali. The three emblems being an Eagle or White Horse, Covered Goblet and a Leaping Hind. All of these emblems are predominant in the heraldry of the Scandinavian countries, and the hillside white horses of England are well known.

Odin's headquarters was a fortress at Asgard in Asaheim where his castle the Valhalla was located. Asgard can be located on the river Dnieper. This tribe eventually moved northwards, following the course of the rivers Dnester, Dnieper and then by the rivers Elbe, Oder, Vistula, crossing the Baltic Sea into Finland, Sweden, Norway and also Denmark by land route.

The name Odin has DANish connections. The 'O' in Odin should be written as a prefix thus O-Din. The 'O' indicating the ancestral line 'O' (of the family of) Dan!

The practise of using the prefix 'O' before a name was, and is still, continued in Ireland as in the names of O'Connor, O'Leary, O'Sullivan, etc. Another indication that Ireland was one of Dan's many settlements. Another Israelistish identity was the Viking helmet of 'Bulls Horns'!

Vowels were very rarely used in the Hebrew or Phoenician written language.

ISAAC would be written as 'SC' or 'SK'
DAN would be written 'DN'
SCANDINAVIA would be written SC-N-DN

The SC pronounced with a hard 'C', SK in Gaelic. The whole title being a monogram or patronymic of ISAAC and DAN. SC (Isaac)-n-DN (Dan) or the tribes of Isaac-n-Dan-ians. The 'AVIA' of Scandin-avia is once again only a suffix to complete the name.

Donske

This is the ancient name of the one section of Swedish settlers, it is still used today. It is made up of the monogram DN-SK in other words descendants of Isaac and Dan (DON-SKE).

The monogram of Isaac can be found in many countries, cities and towns, such as <u>SAC</u>RAMENTO, <u>SASK</u>-ATCHEWEN, NAGA-<u>SAKI</u>, O'<u>SAKA</u>.

When they came to the British Isles as Vikings and earlier settlers they set up the 'waymarks' names of DUN-DEE, DUN-RAVEN, E-DIN-BURGH etc. in Scotland and in England DON-CASTER, LON-DON.
We are told in the days of Solomon, "Every three years came the ships of Tarshish". Eight hundred and sixty years before Christ we are told that Jonah went to Joppa, a seaport within the borders of DAN, and found a ship going to Tarshish – the ancient name of the Britannic Isles! This will surprise most people. However Jonah was going away as far as possible from the responsibilities which the Lord had given him. Just how long the ships of Palestinian seaport had been replenishing, or colonising, the isles, even before the Assyrian captivity of the Ten Tribes is not known, but historians place the time as early as 900 BC. However, there is evidence to prove it was as early as 1900 BC.

ELDUD, an eminent Jewish writer said: "The Danaans were a people of great learning and wealth; they left Greece after a battle with the Assyrians and went to Ireland and also to Danmark, and called it, 'Danmares', 'Dans country'".

In the 'Annals of Ireland' we find: "The Danaans were a highly civilised people, well skilled in architecture and other arts from their long residence in Greece." Their first appearance in Ireland was 1200 BC.

It is also a well authenticated fact of history that the Milesains, or Scots, inhabited the north of Ireland as well as the tribe of Dan, that they were the same race of people and the word SCOTS means wanderers, i.e. 'dwellers in booths', or tents, of which the Israelites were well noted (see Lev 23:42). The 'CLANS' of Scotland gives note of a tribal beginning, as does the plaid of the multi coloured kilt identify this nation with the coat of many colours of Joseph the son of Jacob.

Many other such identities of Israel's 'waymarks' could be offered.

Israel's High Heaps

The shores of the Mediterranean and Atlantic seaboard are dotted with megalithic stone shrines. As the people who set them up moved further on, their ideas evidently expanded and so we have the great stone circles of Stonehenge and Avebury in England and Callernish in the Hebrides. The period of the erection of these circles is given as 1800 BC, under the leadership of Hu-Gadarn, known as Hu the Mighty.

A traditional custom that indelibly bound the Kelts, Celts and Gaels (the meaning of the word in each case is 'stranger') indicating, they were strangers or wanderers to the land which they rested on their trek to the isles. Today their passage across the world can be clearly traced by the relics of the altars they raised in stone, enduring memorials to their great pilgrimage.

This tradition lingers today, and, as then, only among the Keltic-Saxon people. In our times the custom of erecting these memorials to some great historic event is chiefly practiced by the Scots and Canadians. They comprise pyramids of stones piled to a peak and are known as 'CAIRNS'. This is the Keltic name for the word used in the Bible, as 'heaps', 'stones of witness', and were normally erected to a height of 4 to 6 feet.

The first stone altar in the biblical record was erected by Jacob, after his significant dream of the ascending ladder between heaven and earth, known as Jacob's ladder.

He built it as a witness to his contract and covenant with God on that occasion (see Genesis 28 and 31:45-46).

Stone Circles

Scripture also informs us that the Israelites erected stone circles; generally, these consisted of twelve standing stones formed in a circle of 360°, with a central stone in the horizontal position representing the tabernacle.

The first stone circle we read of is the one erected by Moses at the foot of Sinai 1486 BC (Exodus 24:4). Firstly Moses erected the altar upon which the blood sacrifice was to be made and around this 'altar' a circle of standing 'pillars' (as we see at Stonehenge, England), one for each of the tribes of Israel.

This practice continued wherever Israel migrated, for we find in the fourth chapter of Joshua, that the Lord commanded him to erect a circle of twelve stones at Gilgal, which means 'circle' (Joshua. 4:19-21). Also we read of Elijah erecting a similar circle in his contest with the prophets of Baal (1 Kgs. 18:31-32).

Even after the erection of such altars (cairns) or stone circles became a religious custom of the wandering Hebrews and Keltoi, as they passed through strange lands; a declaration and a witness to their belief and faith in the covenant with the one and only Eternal God.

In contrast to the pyramid type stone heaps or 'cairns' were the 'High Mounds' formed from natural or artificial grass covered mounds up to 500 feet in height. Upon the summit were erected 12 standing stones with a larger one in the centre, the MAENLLOG or LLOGAN stone, which was symbolic of the Tabernacle or the Rock of Christ.

The Cymric word 'Pro GORSETH' means 'high seats' which term was applied to the seat of the monarchs or 'place of Assembly', where the king or chieftain, the clergy and the freemen assembled and enacted law and justice. Those early Keltic 'Gorsedds' were the first parliaments of a free people. Keltic tradition has it that it was within the circles of Avebury that the Gorsedds were instituted, a national institution not known outside of Britain.

In the national *Gorsedds* and *Eisteddfods* of Wales the traditions of the Druidic Assemblies on the Wiltshire downs survive to this day.

The Cymric words 'TON, 'TOT', 'TOR', signify a sacred mount. The word 'circle' in the ancient British tongue was 'COR' and in those 'cors' they gathered. The word has come down to us in our 'court' and in another sense in the word 'choir'.

The approach to the 'COR' or summit of the High Place was reached by 'serpent like' avenues in the form of a footpath or avenue of stones. The avenues at Avebury are several miles long.

The words 'TON', 'TOT', 'TOR', survive unto this day. The Tower of London with which is connected so much of the romance of the British history, was erected on the site of the ancient Celtic White Mount, the 'BRYN GWYN' in the Welsh language (BRYN – 'hill', GWIN – 'white') – White Hill.

> "Some miles north of the Tower was the Llandin from the Welsh Llan, 'sacred and din, 'eminence', meaning a high place of worship. Llandin is also the original derivation of London.
>
> Two miles west of the Tower, near where Westminster Abbey now stands was another 'high place', with a circle and a druidic college named TOTHILL. The hill was levelled after the reign of Elizabeth I, but the name still survives in TOTHILL STREET and TOTHILL FIELDS."
>
> Ref: Prehistoric London. E.O Gordon P.

These London mounds referred to, were from one hundred to three hundred feet in height and must have been with their stone circles, striking monuments in pre-historic London, towering like great cathedrals, above the flat landscape of the Thames marshes. On the high ground where St. Paul's now stands, might have been silhouetted against the sky the mighty unhewn monoliths of the Druidic circle – however no trace of the circle remains today.

Other mounds or Gorsedds are to be found all over Britain. At Avebury (Silbury Hill). The word Avebury is derived form 'ABRI' being the ancient form of the word Hebrews. Then twenty miles south of Avebury is Stonehenge. Its original Celtic name is COR-GAWR, or 'the great circle of the Ambresbiri' (The Holy Anointed Ones). And another at Glastonbury in Somerset named the 'Glastonbury Tor' which is five hundred feet in height and is associated with Joseph of Arimathea, and still further at Winton (Winchester) and at Windsor, London, known as the Round Table mound upon which King Arthur (871 AD) reorganised the old Druidic order on Christian principles. Later on, Edward III (1328 AD) built his Round Tower on Round Table Mound, and for many centuries the assemblies of the orders of St. George and the Garter, Britain's highest orders have been held there.

The Windsor Gorsedd, the Win-de-sieur, the White or Holy Mount of the Sieur or Lord (according to the Welsh derivation of the name) is the only Gorsedd which is unbroken. Historical continuity has literally fulfilled its Keltic title as the great seat of the throne of the Monarch from the sixth century to the present day.

8
THE SCOTTISH DECLARATION OF INDEPENDENCE

Fig 15. The Scottish Declaration of Independence Document

6th April 1320 AD

This document is sometimes referred to as the 'Declaration of Abroath'!

This document is of supreme interest, but which is seen by few, and further still, it is unknown to many, owing to their ignorance of its existence, lying in the Register House at Edinburgh, Scotland.

This document is a parchment to which are attached some twenty red and green seals (being the seals of subscribing Scottish nobles).

It was drawn up by Bernard-de-Linton, 'Abbot of Aberbrothock' and 'Chancellor of Scotland' in the year 1320, and was sent to Pope Jon XXII by the Scottish Estates in Parliament assembled in the 'Abby of Aberbrothock' under the presidency of King Robert the Bruce, 6th April 1320. Officials of the Register House have described it as, "probably our most precious possession", and it may be seen in a shallow glass case in the Register House at Edinburgh.

King Edward I of England had failed in his attempt to subjugate Scotland, having met a crushing defeat at the 'Battle of Bannockburn' in 1317 AD. He enlisted the support of the Pope (John XXII) to whom he sent lavish gifts of jewels, as a result of which the Pope refused to acknowledge the Bruce as King of Scotland, and indeed sent emissaries to him with a view to securing his submission to the English King. These papal messengers, Cardinal Gaucelin, and Cardinal Luke, were not received by the Scottish King, who would not even read their letters. Instead he summoned the Scottish Parliament, and the document proclaiming 'The independence of the Scottish People' was drawn up and despatched.

The point of particular interest to us is the remarkable testimony which the document contains concerning the origin and previous migrations of the Scottish people, a declaration which, it must be remembered, is attested by the seals of not only King Robert the Bruce, but of all the Scottish Nobles of the day. It is not, therefore, a statement by a single (possibly fallible) historian, but, the official declaration of a king and his Estates in Parliament assembled and consequently being of overwhelming authority.

"We know, most Holy Father and Lord, and from the chronicles and books of the ancients gather, that amount other illustrious nations, ours, to wit the nations of the Scots, has been distinguished by many honours; **which passing from the greater Scythia through the Mediterranean Sea and Pillars of Hercules**, and sojourning in Spain among the most savage tribes through a long course of time, could nowhere be subjugated by any people however barbarous; **and coming thence one thousand two hundred years after the outgoing of the people of Israel**, they, by many victories and infinite toil, acquired for themselves the possessions in the West which they now hold... In their Kingdom one hundred and thirteen kings of their own royal stock, no stranger intervening, have reigned."

It is surely deeply interesting to have this statement, so unimpeachably attested, that the ancestors of the Scottish people come from Greater Scythia, sojourned a while in Spain and settled in Scotland 1,200 years after the going out of the people of Israel.

720 BC----------------------1200 years-------------------------480 AD

As we shall discover this terminal date is in keeping with John's Revelation prophecy of Israel's Wilderness period of 1,260 years. A difference of only forty years!

The Scottish nobles who placed their seals to this document, had no knowledge of John's 'Time Prophecies' in chapter 12 of the Book of Revelation; so it is a completely independent witness to the migration of the House of Israel and the fulfilment of John's prophecy; of Israel's wilderness years and nourishing period.

The 6th of April 1320 AD will be of great significance to members of the Church; this date is exactly 500 years to the day, previous to the date in which the Church was organised by revelation: 6th April 1830 AD.

Of course there are these so called 'historians' who surmise that the 'Declaration' was based on the long procedure of a Master Baldred Bisset of 1301AD; and that Baldred's account of the origin of the Scots (from Greater Scythia to Spain, Ireland and Scotland) was altered to make more palatable, the claim of Robert the Bruce to the legitimate heir to the throne of a sovereign Scotland, and to...

> "make the conversation of the Scots to Christianity by the Apostle Andrew, brother of Peter, sound more plausible. For one of the very few reasonably early statements recorded about Saint Andrew was that he had preached to the Scythians. There was a stubborn tradition that the Picts had come from Scythia, and the letter of 1320 seems to be an early example of the confusion of Pictish and Scottish origins."
>
> *G.W.S. Barrow: 'Robert the Bruce' p. 426*

Now we ask you, would Robert the Bruce and the Scottish Nobles mentioned in the 'Declaration' knowingly put their 'Seals' to a statement or document that they knew to be false? Would these Earls, Barons, Freeholders and 'The whole community of the Realm of Scotland', subscribe to a fraud enacted in the Scottish Parliament? Of course not. These were men of honour and dignity; they would not have placed their 'Seals' to a falsehood, and to imply so commits a terrible injustice to their character and nobility.

The King and his Noblemen declared their independence from any other nation, declaring that... "They journeyed from Greater Scythia by way of Tyrrhenian Sea (Mediterranean) and the Pillars of Hercules (Gibraltar) and dwelt for a long course of time in Spain among the most savage of tribes, but no where could they be subdued by any race, however barbarous. Thence they came (by way of Ireland)... to their home in the West, where they still live today... In their Kingdom there have reigned one hundred and thirteen Kings of their own Royal Stock, THE LINE UNBROKEN BY A SINGLE FOREIGNER."

In their Declaration these Scottish leaders claim to have been the first to accept Christianity, saying: "That the King of Kings and Lord of Lords, our Lord Jesus Christ, after his Passion and Resurrection, called them, even though settled in the uttermost part of the earth, almost the first to His Most Holy Faith. Nor would he have them confirmed in that faith by merely anyone, but by the first of His Apostles by calling – though second or third in rank – the most gentle St. Andrew, the Blessed Peter's brother, and desired him to keep them under his protection as their patron forever."

Many of those one hundred and thirteen Kings mentioned in the Declaration were Kings of the Gael Sciot Iber in Spain, and many others in and unbroken line were Kings of Eri (Ireland) where they stayed for over a thousand years before migrating to Scotland.

Further information can be obtained from Volume I of the Acts of the Parliament of Scotland, or part II of the National Manuscripts of Scotland, or from the 'Scot's Magazine' issue April 1934, from which the illustration is produced.

9
THE KEY CHAPTER
Revelation Chapter 12

¹ AND there appeared a great wonder in heaven; a woman clothed with the sun, and the moon under her feet, and upon her head a crown of twelve stars:

² And she being with child cried, travailing in birth, and pained to be delivered.

³ And there appeared another wonder in heaven; and behold a great red dragon, having seven heads and ten horns, and seven crowns upon his heads.

⁴ And his tail drew the third part of the stars of heaven, and did cast them to the earth: and the dragon stood before the woman which was ready to be delivered, for to devour her child as soon as it was born.

⁵ And she brought forth a man child, who was to rule all nations with a rod of iron: and her child was caught up unto God, and to his throne.

⁶ And the woman fled into the wilderness, where she hath a place prepared of God, that they should feed her there a thousand two hundred and threescore days.

⁷ And there was war in heaven: Michael and his angels fought against the dragon; and the dragon fought and his angels,

⁸ And prevailed not; neither was their place found any more in heaven.

⁹ And the great dragon was cast out, that old serpent, called the Devil, and Satan, which deceiveth the whole world: he was cast out into the earth, and his angels were cast out with him.

¹⁰ And I heard a loud voice saying in heaven, Now is come salvation, and strength, and the kingdom of our God, and the power of his Christ: for the accuser of our brethren is cast down, which accused them before our God day and night.

¹¹ And they overcame him by the blood of the Lamb, and by the word of their testimony; and they loved not their lives unto the death.

¹² Therefore rejoice, ye heavens, and ye that dwell in them. Woe to the inhabiters of the earth and of the sea! for the devil is come down unto you, having great wrath, because he knoweth that he hath but a short time.

¹² Therefore rejoice, ye heavens, and ye that dwell in them. Woe to the inhabiters of the earth and of the sea! for the devil is come down unto you, having great wrath, because he knoweth that he hath but a short time.

¹³ And when the dragon saw that he was cast unto the earth, he persecuted the woman which brought forth the man child.

¹⁴ And to the woman were given two wings of a great eagle, that she might fly into the wilderness, into her place, where she is nourished for a time, and times, and half a time, from the face of the serpent.

¹⁵ And the serpent cast out of his mouth water as a flood after the woman, that he might cause her to be carried away of the flood.

¹⁶ And the earth helped the woman, and the earth opened her mouth, and swallowed up the flood which the dragon cast out of his mouth.

¹⁷ And the dragon was wroth with the woman, and went to make war with the remnant of her seed, which keep the commandments of God, and have the testimony of Jesus Christ.

Revelation 12

Let us briefly analyse these verses – the place, the setting and the actors.

It is obvious that John saw some of the action of the vision taking place in HEAVEN and some of it upon the EARTH.

Firstly, who represents the 'woman' in this vision? There should be no doubt now with our readers as to who the 'woman' is in this scripture, but National Israel represented firstly by the Twelve Tribes – The Kingdom of Israel and later by the Ten Tribes – The House of Israel.

The woman with a crown (or circle) of twelve stars over her head is clearly a symbol of Israel. Comparing a similar revelation given to Joseph, the son of Jacob (Gen 37:5-10) it is clearly shown that Jacob and his wife Rachel were represented by the sun and moon, and the other eleven sons by the eleven stars – Joseph himself being the twelfth star.

> *"And Joseph dreamed a dream, and he told it his brethren: and they hated him yet the more.*
>
> *And he said unto them, Hear, I pray you, this dream which I have dreamed:*
>
> *For, behold, we were binding sheaves in the field, and, lo, my sheaf arose, and also stood upright; and, behold, your sheaves stood round about, and made obeisance to my sheaf.*
>
> *And his brethren said to him, Shalt thou indeed reign over us? or shalt thou indeed have dominion over us? And they hated him yet the more for his dreams, and for his words.*
>
> *And he dreamed yet another dream, and told it his brethren, and said, Behold, I have dreamed a dream more; and, behold, the sun and the moon and the eleven stars made obeisance to me.*
>
> *And he told it to his father, and to his brethren: and his father rebuked him, and said unto him, What is this*

> *dream that thou hast dreamed? Shall I and thy mother and thy brethren indeed come to bow down ourselves to thee to the earth?"*
>
> *Genesis 37:5-10*

And of course eventually they did!

In this chapter John gives us a brief 'overview' of Israel's pre-existent commission and future destiny among the nations of the earth.

Israel – the worthy sons and daughters of God, those who had fought valiantly for the cause of Christ and the Plan of Salvation in the pre-existence, where "pained to be delivered" meaning to come to earth to fulfil that plan.

There is no doubt that there was a pre-mortal grading of spirits and many were foreordained for special duties upon the earth.

A woman knows by her birth pains when she is ready to be delivered, and so did Israel in the pre-existence.

> *"And the dragon stood before the woman which was ready to be delivered, for to devour her child as soon as it were born."*
>
> *A.V. Rev 12:4*

> *"... the dragon stood before the woman which was delivered, ready to devour her child after it was born."*
>
> *J.S.T. Inspired Version*

Here we are informed of Satan's attempt to kill the newborn Saviour of mankind and Israel's redeemer. These verses clearly indicate that the woman brought forth the 'Man Child' – Jesus Christ, born though the loins of Jacob's son, Judah.

Israel's Emblem

A Circle of Twelve Stars on a Blue Background

This is clearly a symbol of Israel. The Star of David was the emblem of the House of David only. This is the emblem used by the Jewish State of Israel today. But the circle of twelve stars on a blue background (representing the Heavens) was the symbol of the Kingdom of Israel – The Kingdom of Heaven.

We find that this emblem has been appropriated by Satan's apostate Kingdom in the flag of the European Federation. And it is also used in Roman Catholic Churches all over the world depicting Mary in the same way.

Figure 16. Phoenician Goddess

In Fig 16, Astarte the Phoenician goddess of fertility was associated with the crescent moon. The Egyptian goddess of fertility Isis was represented as standing on the crescent mood with twelve stars surrounding her head. In Roman Catholic churches all over Europe may be seen pictures of Mary exactly the same way. The accompanying illustration above pictures Mary with twelve stars circling her head and the crescent moon under her feet. The crescent moon is the symbol of unknown influences.

(Mysteries).

It must be remembered that during the period of events portrayed to us by John in the first eleven chapters of the Book of Revelation, that is, from the time of the Saviour's first advent, and even before that day until now – the woman – the House of Israel was writing its own history as portrayed to us in Revelation chapter 12.

In this chapter we have another symbolic and historical representation of the seven times prophecy only it is given in two parts each of 1260 years.

The first period is found in Revelation 12 verse 6.

The Wilderness Period

The First Period of 1,260 Years

> *"And the woman fled into the wilderness, where she hath a place prepared of God, that they should feed her there a thousand two hundred and threescore days (years)."*
> *Revelation 12:6*
> Emphasis added

The 'woman' (the Ten Tribes) was likened to a **marred vessel** by Jeremiah (see Jer 18:1-6) that was to be moulded into a new vessel with a new home, a new identity, a new name, and a new language.

That new home was to be in the isles of the sea (the British Isles). There they were to be given a new name (British) and speaking English not Hebrew.

This new home was foreseen by the prophet Nathan

> *"Moreover I will **appoint a place** for my people Israel, and will plant (transplant) them, that they may dwell in a place of their own, and move no more; neither shall the children of wickedness afflict them any more, as beforetime,"*
>
> 2 Samuel 7:10
> Emphasis added

This island home was seen by many other prophets including Balaam – Isaiah – Ezekiel – Jeremiah.

Balaam prophesied:

> *"For from the top of the rocks I see him, and from the hills I behold him: lo, the people shall dwell alone, and shall not be reckoned among the nations."*
>
> Numbers 23:9

The only geographical location in which Israel could dwell alone, and not be reckoned among the nations (that is have boundaries with other nations) IS AN ISLAND HOME.

Isaiah in chapters 40 to 66 directs his message to Israel – both Great Britain and America.

> *"KEEP silence before me, O islands; and let the people (Israel) renew their strength:..."*
>
> Isaiah 41:1
> Emphasis added

And again

> *"Listen, O isles, unto me; and hearken, ye people, from far..."*
>
> Isaiah 49:1

Yes! Israel in their new island home were from 'afar', that is, in captivity in Assyria. Here in the islands they were to "<u>renew their strength</u>", that is, to experience a nourishing and a revival period.

> *"...and they that swallowed thee up shall be far away."*
> *Isaiah 49:19*

Yes! '<u>They</u>', the Assyrians, would be far away and long forgotten, and the "<u>children of wickedness</u>" would no longer afflict them anymore "<u>as before time</u>".

As we have clearly shown in the previous chapter the Wilderness period was the amount of years it took Israel to cross Europe to her new island Home – the place prepared of God. We are also informed that this journey took a period of a "thousand two hundred and three score days" meaning 1260 years.

The main captivity of the Ten Tribed House of Israel into Assyria began in 720 BC.

	1260	Years
Less	720	BC
Terminal Date	540	AD

720 BC------------------------1260 years----------------------------540 AD

The Providence of God

It was the providence of God which brought about the collapse of the Western Roman Empire in the late 4th century. This resulted in the withdrawal of Roman forces from the British islands to help protect Rome from invasion. The withdrawal of Roman forces began about 450 AD and was completed by 476 AD making way for Israel in the form of Angles, Saxons, Vikings, Norsemen to occupy the islands by 540 AD, and later the Norman conquest of 1066 AD.

The Roman occupation of Britain beginning with the Claudian campaign in 42 AD had also been the providence of God because it had protected the islands from Barbarian invasion for almost 450 years, "until the purposes of God were fulfilled"

The Nourishing Period

The Second Period of 1,260 Years

> *"And to the woman were given two wings of a great eagle,*
> *that she might fly into the wilderness,*
> *into her place, where she is nourished for a time,*
> *and times, and half a time, from the face of the serpent."*
> *Revelation 12:14*

The expression of the 'woman' Israel being given 'two wings of a Great Eagle' reminds us of Jehovah's statement to Israel when he brought them out of Egyptian captivity:

> *"Ye have seen what I did unto the Egyptians, and how I*
> *bare you on eagles' wings, and brought you unto myself."*
> *Exodus 19:4*

It was the providence of God which brought Israel out of Egypt. It was also the providence of God which brought Israel out of Assyrian captivity. In this second period of 1260 years we find Israel "*in her place*" (after 540 AD) where it says she is "*nourished*" for a further period of 1260 years. If we add this second period of 1260 years on to the first period it results this.

	540	AD
Add	1260	years
Terminal Date	1800	AD

540 BC------------------------1260 years------------------------1800 AD

We find that the woman Israel experienced four periods after her escape from Assyrian captivity:

1. The Wilderness and Affliction Period

2. The Nourishing Period

3. The Revival Period

4. The Restoration Period

The Nourishing Period (540 AD to 1300 AD)

After arriving *"into her place"* in the British isles under the protection of Almighty God, *"there"* she is to be *"nourished"* for a period of 1260 years.

During this period commencing 1300 AD she was also to experience a period of revival.

The Nourishing Period was the period of time for Israel in her new island home to begin re-moulding herself into a new nation, with a new name and a new language.

This period can be likened to a person recovering in hospital from a serious illness. The Nourishing Period begins, being fed with strength giving foods.

We are told in the concluding verses of Revelation 12 that Satan was wroth with the Woman, and cast out of his mouth water as a flood after the woman. But the earth helped the woman, and the earth opened up her mouth and swallowed up the flood which the Dragon cast out of his mouth:

> *"And the dragon was wroth with the woman, and went to*
> *make war with the remnant of her seed..."*
> *Revelation 12:17*

The 'flood' which Satan cast out of his mouth were the Assyrian and Mongolian hordes who pursued after them. But the 'earth' – the Roman armies then occupying Europe – swallowed up the flood in the protection of their empire. These were turbulent years in the history of theses island people, however, the nation survived and this led up to the next stage of her development. The Revival Period.

The Revival Period (1301 AD to 1800 AD)

Of the ancient House of Israel the Lord declared:

> *"I will go and return to my place, till they acknowledge their offence, and seek my face:* **in their affliction** *they will seek me early."*
>
> Hosea 5:15
> Emphasis added

Yes! Isn't that true of us all? Men soon turn to God when the hard times come, and we are no different to the Children of Israel in our response.

> *"Come, and let us return unto the LORD: for he hath torn, and he will heal us; he hath smitten, and he will bind us up.*
>
> *After two days will* **he revive us***: in the third day he will* **raise us up***, and we shall live in his sight.*
>
> *Then shall we know, if we follow on to know the LORD: his going forth is prepared as the morning; and he shall come unto us as the rain, as the latter and former rain unto the earth."*
>
> Hosea 6:1-3
> Emphasis added

In the first two verses of chapter 6, Hosea records the day when Israel would acknowledge her offences, and the effects of her repentance and reconciliation with her husband.

The years of Affliction	First Period
After two days He will revive us	Second Period
In the third day He will raise us up	Third Period
And we shall live in His sight	Fourth Period

The "*Years of Affliction*" were their years in Assyrian captivity beginning 721 BC.

These days are obviously 'days' of 1000 years.

'After' two days He will revive us (the Revival year)

721 BC-------------------------2000 years-------------------------1280 AD

(1300)

In the third day He will raise us up (makes us great)

1300 AD-----------------------500 years-------------------------1800 AD
(half of the 3rd 1000 years)

And we shall live in His sight

1800 AD-----------------------500 years-------------------------2300 AD
(final part of the 3rd 1000 years)

Therefore according to this prophecy Israel's *national* and *spiritual* revival would commence about 1300 AD.

The term 'raise us up' means a restoration to greatness (make us great again). This greatness would commence in the Revival year and reach its fullness after 1800 AD and eventually to be reconciled to her true God and live in His sight.

The Kingdom of Israel became a 'Disunited Kingdom' after the death of Solomon in 975 BC. Here we see the vision of a new 'United Kingdom' and in respect it is interesting to see the fulfilment of this prophecy.
Was it a co-incidence then that we see the beginning of a United Kingdom starting in 1280 AD?

In **1283** AD England and Wales were united

In **1707** AD England, Wales and Scotland were united

In **1801** AD England, Wales, Scotland and Ireland were united, forming a new United Kingdom of Israel!

The ultimate restoration of this Kingdom will come to pass when the Anglo-Saxon-Celtic peoples (British and American) awaken to a recognition of their origin and identity as the House of Israel in the world to-day.

The Revival period saw the nation experience the pains of re-birth, nationally, politically and religiously. Nationally in the welding together of the Celts-Angels-Saxons-Normans into a union of a new United Kingdom.

Further the English Civil War (1642 – 1644 AD) gave the nation political stability and the Parliamentary system. Followed by the brave reformers commencing with John Wycliffe, William Tyndale and later with Coverdale, Huss, Luther, Calvin, Knox, John and Charles Wesley, etc. who challenged the power of Rome, and gave the people a new spiritual liberty. All of the events of these turbulent years were the preparation for the greater spiritual light of truth which was to come in the year 1820 AD.

This was the period of Israel's National and Spiritual Revival portrayed by Ezekiel in his description of the valley of dry bones (see Ezekiel 37:1-14).

No one will deny that the British people need to be revived to-day – morally, materially and, above all, spiritually.

The Restoration Period (1800 AD)
This period witnessed the miraculous growth of the British Empire.

The 'Disunited Kingdom' of Israel commenced after the death of King Solomon in 975 BC.

975 BC-------------------------2520 years--------------------------1545 AD

The terminal year of 1545 AD witnessed the beginning of a Restoration into a new United Kingdom – and was secured when Elizabeth I confirmed England a Protestant nation in 1558 AD.

We also witnessed the birth of the United States of America. The captivity of ancient Israel commenced in 745 BC.

745 BC------------------------2520 years--------------------------1776 AD

The main captivity took place in 721 BC

721 BC------------------------2520 years--------------------------1800 AD

The 'mopping up' operation continued until 685 BC

685 BC------------------------2520 years--------------------------1836 AD

The final terminal date has great significance for members of the Church for on the 3rd April 1836 the Lord restored all the 'Keys' of the Holy Priesthood. The Lord warned ancient Israel that he would punish her Seven Times for her sins if she did not mend her ways. **And so He did.**

But after that this period she was to be restored to greatness. **And so she was.**

In the conclusion to Isaiah chapter 60 the Lord confirms the extent of this great emancipation:

> *"Thy sun shall no more go down; neither shall thy moon withdraw itself: for the LORD shall be thine everlasting light,* **and the days of thy mourning shall be ended.** *"*
>
> *Isaiah 60:20*

The 'days' of Israel's 'mourning' was her Wilderness and Affliction period in the **'graveyard'** of captivity (Hosea 13) until the period of Nourishing and Revival. Her 'mourning' ended in 1800 AD. From that time began the miraculous growth of the British Empire, until it was said, "the sun never sets on the British Empire".

Isaiah adds further:

> *"A little one shall become a thousand, and a small one a strong nation: I the LORD will hasten it in his time."*
>
> Isaiah 60:22

This little island nation did become a thousand or rather a Great Empire and Commonwealth. And America the small colony gained its independence in 1776 AD became a singular strong nation. Confirming the covenants and promises to Abraham, Isaac, Jacob, Joseph, Ephraim and Manasseh. And the Lord brought it about according to plan and **in His time.**

The Angel with the Everlasting Gospel

After John had received the vision given to us in chapter 12 of his revelation, he sees the rise of Papal Rome (chapter 13) which was followed by another vision:

> *"And I saw another angel fly in the midst of heaven, having the everlasting gospel to preach unto them that dwell on the earth, and to every nation, and kindred, and tongue, and people,"*
>
> *Revelation 14:6*

The scripture clearly alludes to the Angel Moroni who visited Joseph Smith to reveal the whereabouts of the Book of Mormon, which, of course, could only have occurred after 1800 AD according to the chronology and prophecies of the vision.

Regarding the visit of the Angel Moroni, Joseph Smith relates:

> *"He called me by name, and said unto me that he was a messenger sent from the presence of God to me, and that his name was Moroni; that God had a work for me to do; and that my name should be had for good and evil among all nations, kindreds, and tongues, or that it should be both good and evil spoken of among all people.*

> *He said there was a book deposited, written upon gold*
> *plates, giving an account of the former inhabitants of this*
> *continent (America), and the source from whence they*
> *sprang. He also said that the fullness of the everlasting*
> *Gospel was contained in it, as delivered by the Saviour to*
> *the ancient inhabitants;"*
>
>

JS-H 1:33-34
Emphasis added

And so John saw through the conduit of time the Angel Moroni restoring this ancient gospel to the earth again after emancipation of his people Israel in 1800 AD.

Chronology of 'Lost' Israel's Revival Period

AD	
540	Israel's arrival in the isles: the nourishing period commences
554	Imperial restoration of the holy Roman Empire with Pope as the head
1066	Norman invasion: last of the tribes to arrive in Britain
1283	England and Wales unite: the revival period commences
1320	John Wycliffe commences the reformation
1490	William Tyndale translates and prints the scriptures into English
1545	Britain's divorce from Roman Catholicism
1558	Elizabeth I declares Britain Protestant
1559	John Knox establishes a Protestant state in Scotland
1588	Spain attempts to subjugate Britain – the Armada defeated
1603	King James VI of Scotland becomes James I of England
1606	American colonies established
1611	The Protestant movement established – King James bible translated
1620	Pilgrim Fathers depart for America
1642	English Civil War. A parliamentary system established
1688	The 'Glorious' Revolution
1707	Union of England, Wales and Scotland

1776	American colonies gain independence: exactly 2,520 years from commencement of Israel's captivity (745 BC)
1800	Israel's Seven Times punishment ends
1801	England, Wales, Scotland and Ireland unite into a new United Kingdom. Britain adopts the Union flag and the title Great Britain
1805	French fleet defeated at Cape Trafalgar
1814	Holy Roman Empire brought to an end
1815	French army defeated at Waterloo
1820	Lunar millennium commences
1820	Joseph Smith's first vision. Visitation of the angel Moroni
1830	Church of Jesus Christ of Latter-day Saints organised (6th April)
1836	Restoration of the 'keys' of the priesthood
1841	Orson Hyde dedicates Palestine as a Jewish homeland
1844	Joseph and Hyrum Smith martyred
1847	The sanctuary is cleansed (Dan 8:13, 14)
1847	The decline of the Turkish Empire
1911	The 'biblical time' millennium commences
1917	Jerusalem liberated by British forces
1948	'Jewish' state of Israel established
1987	The fall of 'Babylon the Great' commences
2001	'Solar Time' millennium commences

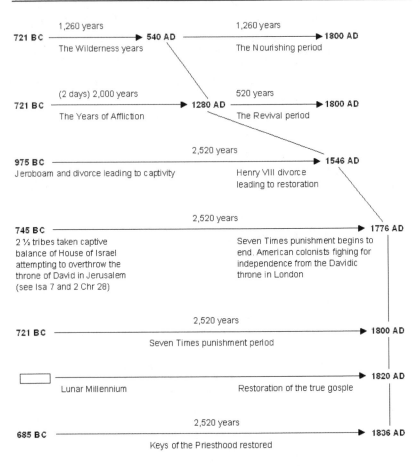

Fig 17. Israel's Divorce - Captivity and Restoration Era

The Eight Incorruptible Witnesses

How do we know that the great predictions to Israel will be fulfilled? To this same Israel and not to some other people? What proof have we of all this, and of their absolute certainty? Man, in a court of law, requires witnesses, and he takes the evidence of his fellow man. So in like manner, the Great and Faithful Promiser has not left himself without witnesses.

Is the word of Jehovah enough? Surely, it ought to be! And would be, to believing men! But, alas, God has to deal with men who are not that! Even in this our day, men do not believe God, and professedly Christian men, and even ministers too! Then what is God to do, with this faithless people, who, with His word in their hands, do not believe it?

Jehovah himself gave the law of witnesses (Deuteronomy 19:15) so he himself must live by that law. So what is God to do to convince His people of His unalterable love for them and of His unchangeable purpose to fulfil every jot and tittle of His promises respecting them? What can He do?

Is He to appoint mere man as His witnesses? Or any number of men? If he did, they would be disregarded, just as the prophets had been, and also they would die and the witness would end.

No! God would not entrust His great witness to mere man, frail, uncertain, faithless man! He must have a witness that would be impartial and could not be influenced or removed by mortals.

His witnesses are eight in number, and are all divinely appointed. They are not men, nor are they dependent on man's faulty understanding, nor His prejudiced and blind eyes!

His witnesses are eight, and they are right before the eyes of all men, 24 hours a day. They cannot be hidden. God himself names them and appoints them (Jeremiah 31-35-37). They are:

- The Sun
- The Moon
- The Stars

- The Heavens
- The Earth
- The Sea
- The Day
- The Night

> *"Thus saith the LORD, which giveth the sun for a light by day, and the ordinances of the moon and of the stars for a light by night, which divideth the sea when the waves thereof roar; The LORD of hosts is his name:*
>
> *If those ordinances depart from before me, saith the LORD, then the seed of Israel also shall cease from being* **a nation** *before me* **for ever.**
>
> *Thus saith the LORD; If heaven above can be measured, and the foundations of the earth searched out beneath, I will also cast off all the seed of Israel for all that they have done, saith the LORD."*
>
> Jeremiah 31:35-37
> Emphasis added

Thus does God the Eternal, the Immortal, Unchangeable, solemnly declare that nothing that Israel has done shall ever disinherit her, and thus does He pledge himself to bless and preserve Israel as <u>a nation before him forever.</u>

But, note, in the last quoted text God anticipates a controversy with some men who will say He has abandoned Israel. Looking down the centuries God could see a vilification of His Holy name in that infamous ascertation. So he challenges these men in the tremendous words just spoken.

Has any man ever measured the Heavens?

Has any man ever been able to reach the core of the Earth?

Can any man remove the Sun, Moon, Stars, Day, Night, and the Sea?

Then, if man says that Israel (10 Tribes) no longer exist as 'a nation' on this earth then he must do these impossible things.

When you wake up in the morning, there you have God's witness.
When the night comes there you have God's witness.
When the stars appear there you have the witness.
When you walk upon the land or listen to the sea there you have God's witness.

> *"That the seed of Israel will be a nation before Him forever".*

'A nation' means a singular great people existing on this earth today. Not some people living on another planet. Not some nomadic people living in a remote or secreted part of the earth. Not a church. Not a people scattered throughout all nations (although most nations do have an infusion of the blood of Israel). But **a nation** existing on earth today.

This language is not ambiguous. There is none clearer in the whole book. There are no more positive words, or more pronounced statements in any book, in any language.

Do you believe that? If so, we respectfully submit to you that you have either to find that nation or admit that the word of God is false and untrue.

You won't find that nation bearing the name Israel today (Isaiah 62:2-4). You won't find that nation speaking Hebrew today (Zephaniah 3:9-11) or consider themselves to be of Israel (Hosea 2:23). But would be considered as a Gentile nation (John 7:35).
They are the *Anglo-Saxon-Celtic* race and to them has been committed the ecclesiastical Kingdom of God on earth. The Church of Jesus Christ of Latter-day Saints, commonly known as the 'Mormon' Church.

To those who are not members of the 'Mormon' Church this may seem a bold statement indeed, but we intend to show in this work that the

Church was established by Divine revelation in fulfilment of prophecy and in accordance with the Divine Timetable.

Winston Churchill, addressing the United States Congress stated:

> "He must indeed have a blind soul who cannot see that some great purpose and design are being worked out here below, of which we have the honour to be faithful servants."

A few days later he told the people of Canada:

> "I believe the World's salvation lies in some organisation with the English speaking peoples at its core".

Prophetic words indeed!

Identity Marks of Israel

In the latter days the Bible shows that the people of Israel should respond to the following prophecies. Most of them as listed here are *unconditional* promises of God, but a few of them are *conditional* upon obedience. The reader should note carefully those which are conditional and those which are unconditional.

Identity Mark	Scriptural Reference
They must exist as a "nation"	Jer 31:35 Jer 33:20-26 Jer 30:11
They must be an island nation	Jer 31:10 Isa 41:1 Isa 42:12 Isa 11:11 Isa 24:14 Isa 49:1-3 Isa 49:12
Their islands must be north west from Palestine	Jer 3:12 Jer 28:8 Isa 49:12
Their number must be as the sand of the sea	Hosea 1:10 Gen 22:17 Gen 32:12

They must have found their island home too small	Isa 49:19
They must have found their island home too small more than once	Isa 49:20
They must be living under a monarchy and	1 Chr 22:10
Have a descendant of David as King (or Queen)	2 Chr 13:5 Jer 33:17-26 2 Sam 7:13-16 Ps 89:3, 4, 25-37
They must be a Company (or Commonwealth) of nations	Gen 35:11 Eph 2:12
They must have a great nation springing from them but independent of them	Gen 48:10 Isa 49:20
They must have immense colonies	Isa 49:8 Isa 49:20
They must push the aborigines into corners	Deut 33:17
They must be the "Chief of Nations"	Jer 31:7 Amos 6:1 Deut 28:1, 13
They must be an undefeated nation	Isa 54:17 Micah 5:8 Deut 28:7
They must conquer by a small army (conditional)	Lev 26:8 Deut 20:1
They must be a wealthy nation	Deut 8:18
They must lend to other nations (gentile) but not borrow from them (conditional)	Deut 15:6
They must abolish the slave trade	Isa 58:6
They must have the finest fruit and cattle (conditional)	Deut 28:4
Their national heraldry must be a lion and unicorn	Num 24:8, 9
They must be a great missionary people	Isa 27:6 Isa 43:21 Mark 16:15 Matt 7:20
They must be known by another name – British (NB Hebrew Brith = Covenant and Hebrew 'ish' = man giving a Hebrew etymology of British meaning 'Covenant man')	Isa 65:15 Isa 62:2
They must be named after Isaac, not Israel i.e. Saxon = Isaacson	Gen 21:12 Rom 9:7
The nation's name must be called Great	Gen 12:2
They must speak another language, not Hebrew	Isa 28:11
Noted for not sounding their H's	Judges 12:6
The Canaanites must trouble Israel	Num 33:55 Josh 23:13 Ch 9
Israel must be a Christian nation	Hos 1:10 Isa 9:2, 8

	Isa 45:17-19
	Isa 48:20
	Isa 49:3
Israel must possess the sea-gates of the earth (Gate of his enemies)	Gen 22:17, 18
They must observe the Sabbath, nationally	Ex 31:13, 16, 17
Israel must be a great sea power	Ps 89:25
	Num 24:7
Israel's benefactors will succeed and her enemies fall	Gen 12:3
They must eventually come into possession of all the land between the Nile and Euphrates	Gen 15:18
They must be tolerant of strangers	Lev 19:33, 34
They must be successful in war to be invincible in the "last days"	Isa 41:11, 12
	Isa 54:15-17
	Num 24:8
	Lev 26:7
	Deut 33:27, 28
	Deut 28:7
To be God's battle axe amongst nations	Jer 51:20
Their enemies to be found liars	Deut 33:29
Israel to be the Lord's portion – the lot of his inheritance	Deut 32:8, 9
They must not be subject to a foreign power	Deut 15:16
They will hold a most honourable place among the nations "if"	Deut 26:19
They must be in possession of an "appointed" haven, invincible from enemies, outside Palestine	1 Chr 17:9
	Num 23:9
	2 Sam 7:10
	Lev 26:6
To be envied and attacked	Gen 49:23, 24
Israel's preservation will be due to divine protection and intervention against her foes	Ps 124
	Deut 20:1-4
Israel will be joined by Judah and return representatively to Palestine	Jer 3:14, 18
	Ezek 37
Israel must exist as "a Nation" as long as the sun, moon and stars endure; and until heaven can be measured and the earth's foundations searched out.	Jer 31:33-37
	Jer 33:24-26
They must have a lineal descendant of David reigning over them forever	2 Sam 7:16
	Jer 33:17-21
They will be used as instruments in the hand of God in war to destroy the Gentile nations	Jer 51:20
	Dan 2:44
They were instructed to set up "waymarks" and high heaps	Jer 31:21
Israel to be under a new covenant	Jer 31:31
To spread abroad to the West, East, North and South, in that order	Gen 28:14
Israel to dwell alone	Num 23:24

	Num 24:9
Israel to lose a colony and then increase in the isles, then seek more room	Isa 49:20
Israel not to be found in circumcision	Gal 5
In multiplying, the Israel people were not to be crowded. They would expand and become a company of nations	Deut 32:8
The Israel people are the only people in the Bible to be called "sheep". At the time of the end "sheep nations" are to be separated from the "goat" nations	Matt 25:31-34
The Israel nations would feed the hungry, clothe the naked and liberate the captives	Matt 25:31-46
To enjoy spiritual blessings from above	Gen 49:25
To enjoy the blessings of the deep (sea power, oil)	Isa 60:5 Gen 49:25
To have blessings from the sand (oil, treasures)	Deut 33:19
To be addicted to drunkenness	Isa 28:1

These marks are so clear and pronounced that the identity of the nations literally jumps out of the pages.

They obviously refer to Great Britain and the Commonwealth and the United States of America. These facts being correct, then we have here a new method for proving that God lives and His word is true. Not proving it in a way that the Christian accepts it, but as a means by which it can be clearly proved true to the ordinary man and woman in the street. This surely is important then, not just to the congregations of all churches, Church of England, Roman Catholic, Mormon, Baptist, Methodist, Congregationalists and Jehovah's Witnesses, etc., but those of no church or persuasion at all.

If we can show that every warning and prediction in the Bible can be followed by the event, it should have the greatest effect upon all mankind, it will eliminate wild speculations, and will give the greatest impetus and backing to all schemes for the welfare and help of suffering humanity.

Can the Bible be proved true? It can! Indeed, it can!

Section 3:

John's Second Vision: The Rise and Fall of Babylon the Great

10
THE SEVEN HEADED BEASTS

Introduction

John's first vision contained in chapters 4 to 11 gave the 'overall events' up to and including the second advent of our Lord Jesus Christ, and the establishment of the political Kingdom of God on earth during the Seventh Millennium.

In chapter 12 John has a vision of the woman Israel in the pre-existence and her desire to come to earth to fulfil her destiny. John provides us with little historical information of Israel's sojourn on earth except, two very important 'time' prophecies, and some other clues to assist the seeker of knowledge in tracing the identity of 'lost' Israel.

These clues along with the abundant knowledge available to us in books of secular history, the author presented enough evidence in Section 2 to convince even the hardened critic that 'Lost Israel' has been located and identified. This evidence also gives us a clearer understanding of Isaiah's message to Israel in the 'Isles of the Sea'. From chapter 40 through to 66, his whole message was to 'lost' Israel, repeating the messages of Hosea and Amos who preceded him and, Micah who followed Isaiah adding his witness and evidence. We discovered that the reason for Israel's lost identity was the imposition of the 'Seven Times' punishment, which terminated in 1800 AD with Judah's punishment terminating in 1917 AD. And with the ending of this period the beginning of her emancipation and restoration of all things.

Revelation, chapters 13 to 18

These chapters form a completely distinct and separate vision from the other two **but marking the same period of historical events as that contained in the others**.

In this vision and these chapters John is shown the vision of various Beasts which, represent the Satanic influence exercised upon earthly

Kingdoms through **political power**. A false **economic system** and the influence of **counterfeit religion**.

These three phases of Babylon the Great are mentioned by John. He records the historical events leading to the rise and fall of this beast.

1. Counterfeit political system

2. Counterfeit economic system

3. Counterfeit religious system

In chapter 17 John is shown how Satan attempts to unite these three divisions of his power into a modern Political – Economical and Religious Order composed of Ten European Nations brought together in a Federal European Community in the Treaty of Rome.

Chapter 18 Babylon the Great has fallen

In this chapter John sees the final collapse of this 'Babylon the Great'.

Chapters 19 to 22 Jesus Christ triumphant

After the fall of Babylon the Great, John records the second advent – Christ's coming in glory, to enter into a new marriage covenant with his Bride the Church, the setting up of His political Kingdom upon the earth, and the reward of the faithful.

Chapters 13 and 17 are closely related in history therefore they will be used together.

Chapters 14, 15, 16, 18

The events of these chapters are closely interwoven with the prophecies and history contained in chapters 13 and 17.

Therefore for this presentation we shall rearrange the chapters as follows:

Chapter	
13	Through 5th and 6th seal
14 verses 1 to 7	Through 5th and 6th seal
17	Through 5th and 6th seal, **but mainly the 7th seal**
18	Through 7th seal
14 verses 8 to 13	Through 7th seal
15	Through 7th seal
16	Through 7th seal
14 verses 14 to 22	Through 7th seal
19	Through 7th seal
20	Through 7th seal
21	Through 7th seal
22	Through 7th seal

I shall provide enough evidence to prove that this is the correct chronological order of these chapters.

In our investigation into John's second vision, it must be borne in mind that the Apostle John had access to the writings and prophecies of all the Old Testament prophets.

Chapters 4 to 12 were closely linked with the writings of Hosea, Amos, Isaiah, Micah, Jeremiah and Ezekiel.

Chapters 13 though 18 are closely linked with the writings and prophecies of Daniel; so we shall be making reference to some of Daniel's prophecies as they relate to John's second vision.

The Seven Headed Beasts
Revelation chapters 12, 13 and 17 speak of various 'Beasts' having 'Heads', 'Crowns' and 'Horns'. It is the objective of this section to identify who or what these symbols represent.

It is appropriate for our readers firstly, to read the following scriptures:

Revelation 12:3

Revelation 13 – The whole chapter (noting verses 1, 2 and 11)

Revelation 17:1-3

All Symbols

These Beasts – Heads – Horns and Crowns are all symbols. All we have to do is to determine what or who they represent; this will assist our readers in the interpretation.

What we need then is a yardstick or standard of comparison to work with.

Interpretation of Symbols in the Books of Daniel and Revelation

Symbol	Interpretation
Days	Literal days of 24 hours or 'years' in prophetic terms
A Time	360 days or 360 years
Times	360 * 2 days or 720 years
Half of Time	180 days or 180 years
Time – Times and Dividing of Time	360 + 720 + 180 = 1,260 days or years
Seven Times	360 * 7 = 2,520 days or years
In that day In the last days Time of the end The end time	After 1800 AD
Beast – dragon / animals	Represents empires or kingdoms
Wings on a beast or animal	Denotes speed, rapid growth or conquest
Singular head on beast	An empire or kingdom
Multiple heads on one beast	Division of an empire or kingdom
Heads	Divisions of an empire
Heads with crowns	Division of an empire with imperial status
Horns	Divisions of an empire (politician rulers)
Horns with crowns	Division of an empire with imperial status
Dual of horns on the head one animal or beast	Two outstanding emperors or military leaders of an allied empire
Ten horns on one head	(1) Divisions of an empire or a group of ten nations forming an empire ruling one after the other in continuity Or (2) A group of nations forming a federation and a ruling together under one leader.
Ten toes	A group of nations forming a federation in the last days.
Notable or great horn	A great emperor or military leader
Notable ones	Military commanders, field marshals, generals (generally serving in one empire)
Little horn of Daniel 7	Apostate prominent religious leader
Little horn of Daniel 8	Another false religious leader
A two horned lamb / dragon	Apostate religious leader ruling over a divided kingdom or empire

Water	Mulitudes / nations
Flood	Israel's enemies/war like tribes
Sea (out of the sea)	Like unto previous empires or kingdom: An alliance of nations
Earth (out of the earth)	Ruling empire at that time
Mountain of the Lord	Zion, New Jerusalem or the true church
Mountain	A singular great nation
Mountains	Nations of high status
Top of the mountains	A singlular nation of supreme status
Hills	Nations of lower status
Trees (of the field)	Nations of lower status
Mad dogs	Nations envious of Britain and America

The last two 'Sea' and 'Earth' relate to the 'Beast' prophecies only. These rules are not hard and fast but are close enough. This 'yardstick' is not exclusive to John's vision but, applies to the prophecies of Daniel and others.

It will not go unnoticed that the 'Heads' and 'Horns' are almost interchangeable symbols, and will often be treated as such in this work.

With this yardstick before you our readers, when reading scriptural references related to prophecies you should attempt to analyse the meaning – you will amaze yourself with how close you are to the meanings; and with practice and a better understanding of Biblical and Secular history, the symbols and imagery will no longer be a mystery.

The Four Beasts

In chapter 12:3

The First Beast
John sees 'a great red dragon' "in heaven"

1. Having Seven Heads
2. with Ten Horns
3. and upon the Seven Heads Ten Crowns

Chapter 13:1-2

A second Beast coming up out of "the sea"
1. Having Seven Heads
2. Ten Horns
3. And upon the Horns Ten Crowns
4. And upon the Heads The name of Blasphemy

Chapter 13:11

A third Beast coming up out of "the earth"

This beast is described as having
1. Two Horns like a lamb
2. and who spake as a dragon

Chapter 17:1-3

A fourth Beast described as

1. A woman riding a scarlet coloured beast
2. the beast having Seven Heads and Ten Horns

But note: **No Crowns**

The woman is wearing robes of Purple and Scarlet decked with gold, precious stones and pearls. And in her hand a Golden Cup, which was full of abominations, filthiness and fornications.

It will not go unnoticed to our readers that these Beasts, except for the one in Revelation 13:1 are all similar having Seven Heads and Ten Horns some with crowns and others without crowns etc.

In the Likeness of Things on Earth

The first beast which John saw in Heaven – "was in likeness of things on earth" (JST Revelation 12:1). The beast representing the earthly forces through which Satan would use his power and influence to oppose the work of Christ and persecute the woman Israel.

The Seven Heads with crowns representing seven Imperial Empires or Kingdoms, the seven divisions of Satan's Beast. And we are aware through Biblical history how the Holy Roman Empire ruled over by the Popes were involved with Britain and Israel.

However we must remember that John was living in the era of the Roman Empire, so it is obvious that the visions or revelations he received were for that period of time and future.

Therefore the 'Beasts' seen by John in chapters 13 and 17 were related to the *Roman Head only*!

The Mark and Number of the Beast

> *"And the third angel followed them, saying with a loud voice, If any man worship the beast and his image, and receive his mark* **in his forehead,** *or in his hand,*
>
> *The same shall drink of the wine of the wrath of God, …*
> Revelation 14:9-10
> Emphasis added

> *"And I heard a great voice out of the temple saying to the seven angels, Go your ways, and pour out the vials of the wrath of God upon the earth.*
>
> *And the first went, and poured out his vial upon the earth; and there fell a noisome and grievous sore* **upon the men which had the mark of the beast,** *and upon them which worshipped his image."*
> Revelation 16:1-2
> Emphasis added

> *"And* **he** *causeth all, both small and great, rich and poor, free and bond, to receive a* **mark in their right hand, or in their foreheads:**

And that no man might buy or sell, save he that had the
mark, or the name of the beast, or the number of his
name.
Here is wisdom. Let him that hath understanding count
the number of the beast: for it is the number of a man;
and his number is Six hundred threescore and six."

Revelation 13:16-18
Emphasis added

Before we can determine the **mark** of the Beast, or his **number** we must first determine who or what the Beast is!

It is important to find out; for we are told it is those of this present generation who will be:

1. Worshipping the Beast and his image.
2. Who have received his 'mark in their foreheads'.
3. Or who have received his 'mark in their hands'.

And we are further informed that only these people will suffer the torture of the Seven Plagues.

Revelation 9:4
Revelation 15:1
And
Revelation 16:1-2

Therefore to discover the identity of this beast is of paramount importance to all.

John the Revelator was acutely aware how closely related his vision of these beasts were to those of Daniel and therefore must have 'compared notes' as it were. So we shall do exactly what John must have done. Because Daniel's vision offer the clues to the identity of John's Beasts in the 13th and 17th chapters of Revelation.

We therefore ask our reader to turn to Daniel chapter 7 and compare this visionary experience with those of Revelation 13:1-2.

Figure 18. Daniel's dream of four great beasts

"In the first year of Belshazzar king of Babylon Daniel had a dream and visions of his head upon his bed: then he wrote the dream, and told the sum of the matters.

Daniel spake and said, I saw in my vision by night, and, behold, the four winds of the heaven strove upon the great sea.

And four great beasts came up from the sea, diverse one from another.

*The first was **like** a lion, and had eagle's wings: I beheld till the wings thereof were plucked, and it was lifted up from the* earth, and made to stand upon the feet as a man, and a man's heart was given to it.

*And behold another beast, a second, **like** to a bear, and it raised up itself on one side, and it had three ribs in the mouth of it between the teeth of it: and they said thus unto it, Arise, devour much flesh.*

*After this I beheld, and lo another, **like** a leopard, which had upon the back of it four wings of a fowl; the beast had also four heads; and dominion was given to it.*

After this I saw in the night visions, and behold a fourth beast, dreadful and terrible, and strong exceedingly; and it had great iron teeth: it devoured and brake in pieces, and stamped the residue with the feet of it: and it was diverse from all the beasts that were before it; and it had ten horns.

*I considered the horns, and, behold, there came up among them another **little horn**, before whom there were three of the first horns plucked up by the roots: and, behold, in this horn were eyes like the eyes of man, and a mouth speaking great things.*

> *I beheld till the thrones were cast down, and the Ancient of days did sit, whose garment was white as snow, and the hair of his head like the pure wool: his throne was like the fiery flame, and his wheels as burning fire.*
>
> *A fiery stream issued and came forth from before him: thousand thousands ministered unto him, and ten thousand times ten thousand stood before him: the judgment was set, and the books were opened.*
>
> *I beheld then because of the voice of the great words which the horn spake: I beheld even till the beast was slain, and his body destroyed, and given to the burning flame.*
>
> *As concerning the rest of the beasts, they had their dominion taken away: yet their lives were prolonged for a season and time.*
>
> *I saw in the night visions, and, behold, one like the Son of man came with the clouds of heaven, and came to the Ancient of days, and they brought him near before him.*
>
> *And there was given him dominion, and glory, and a kingdom, that all people, nations, and languages, should serve him: his dominion is an everlasting dominion, which shall not pass away, and his kingdom that which shall not be destroyed."*
>
>

Daniel 7:1-14
Emphasis added

In this vision Daniel saw *four* beasts – come up out of the sea, just as John's beast.

On the other hand John saw only **one Beast**, John's beast was described as being *like unto* a leopard, with the feet *as* the feet of a Bear, and his mouth *as* the mouth of a Lion, and the Dragon gave this Beast his power, and his seat, and great authority (Revelation 13:2)

With Daniels vision however:

- The first Beast was like a Lion with One Head
- The second Beast was like a Bear with One Head
- The third Beast was like a Leopard with Four Heads
- The fourth Beast was terrible to describe with One Head, it was unlike any beast known to Daniel. This beast had only One Head and upon the Head Ten Horns.

Therefore there were in total Seven Heads and Ten Horns! The 10 horns being upon the head of the forth Beast only. And coming up among these horns came forth *another 'little' horn*. And by this little horn – three of the 10 horns "were plucked up by their roots". So, in actual fact when this little horn 'came up' only seven of the original horns of the Beast remained!

Daniel was puzzled by all this:

> *"I Daniel was grieved in my spirit in the midst of my body, and the visions of my head troubled me."*
> *Daniel 7:15*

He then asked one of the heavenly beings the truth of all this, "So he told me, and made me know the interpretation of the things." (verse 16)

Daniel was informed that the Beasts were four Kings or Kingdoms "which shall arise *out of the earth*" or, upon the earth.

The Four Great Empires

It is accepted by almost all students that these Beasts represent the four Empires associated with Biblical history.

The Lion	Babylonian Empire
The Bear	Persian Empire
The Leopard (with four heads)	Greek Empire
The Terrible Beast	Roman Empire

The Image of Daniel Chapter 2

These same four world ruling gentile kingdoms are described in the second chapter of Daniel. The imagery being different but with the same meaning.

King Nebuchadnezzar of the Chaldean/Babylonian Empire had a dream, the meaning of which God revealed to Daniel.

This dream is described in verses 31-35. The king saw a Great Image.

Its head was of	Gold
Its breast and arms of	Silver
Its belly and thighs of	Brass
Its two legs of	Iron
And its feet and toes	A mixture of Iron and Clay.

Finally, he saw a stone being cut out of a mountain but not by the hands of men which, smote the image upon its feet and toes, "that it brake in pieces the iron, the clay, the brass, the silver, and the gold", and the image was blown away like chaff. And the stone that smote the image became a great mountain and filled the whole earth.

The interpretation is given in verses 36-45.

The Head of Gold	Chaldean/Babylonian Empire 625 – 534 BC
Breast and Arms of Silver	Mede/Persian Empire 534 – 332 BC
Belly and Thighs of Brass	Greek/Macedonian Empire 331 – 160 BC
Legs of Iron with Feet and Toes of Iron and Clay	Roman Empire 160 BC – 476 AD

Plainly in Daniel 2 are described the same four universal world ruling gentile powers that are described by Daniels four beasts in chapter 7.

The Two Legs of Iron

Nebuchadnezzar's image, by the two legs of iron, describes the two divisions of the Roman Empire after 330 AD. West with its capital at Rome and East with its capital at Constantinople.

The Ten Toes

There is enough evidence to prove that these 10 toes represent 10 nations or governments; who will make up the final stages of the Great Image – **and are yet future.**

These 10 governments will be unified in a *political, economic* and *religious* treaty. But will be as iron and clay! Symbolising that just as iron and clay has no adhesion, these nations will not be completely unified.

Not a Continuing Succession of Governments

These 10 toes **do not** represent a continuing succession of governments one following the other – developing out of the Roman Empire after its collapse in 476 AD as most scholars believe.

This will be proven at a later stage in this section.

The Ten Horns – A Continuing Succession

However, the 10 horns of Daniel 7, which are in the head of the 4th beast **do** represent the ten stages of government continuing in succession – one after another out of the Roman Empire after its fall in 476 AD.

THESE ARE VITAL FACTORS AND SHOULD BE NOTED BY OUR READERS.

The Fifth Kingdom

The Stone Kingdom

This is the Stone Kingdom - the 5th Kingdom of the Great Image - a **future,** *world-ruling,* political Kingdom of God. The Kingdom of Jesus Christ formed by the True Church and nations of modern Israel

> *"And in the days of these kings shall the God of heaven*
> ***set up a kingdom,** which shall never be destroyed:*

and the kingdom shall not be left to other people, but it
shall break in pieces and consume all these kingdoms, and
it shall stand for ever."

Daniel 2:44
Emphasis added

This Stone Kingdom is to be "set up" – "in the days of these kings".

That is after and during the union of the 10 nations represented by the toes of the Great Image. We shall explain this further in the following chapters.

Kingdom	Image of Daniel 2	Beast of Daniel 7	Years
1. Babylon	Head of Gold	A Lion	625 – 534 BC
2. Medo/Persian	Breasts and Arms of Silver	A Bear	534 – 332 BC
3. Greek	Belly and Thighs of Brass	A Leopard with 4 wings and four heads	331 – 160 BC
4. Roman	Legs of Iron with feet and toes of Iron and Clay	A Terrible Beast with iron teeth and ten horns	160 BC – 476 AD
Rome Divided: The two legs of the Image			
Eastern Empire			395 – 1453 AD
Western Empire	Lapsed in 476 AD and was revived in 554 until the fall of Napoleon in 1814.		554 – 1814 AD
The 10 Toes	Represents the final stages of the Great Image. A future union of 10 nations: unified in a *political, economic* and *religious* treaty.		
5. The Stone Kingdom	The future *world-ruling* political Kingdom of God		

Figure 19. The Four Kingdoms Identified

DANIEL refers 'to the previous four' Empires as 'KINGDOMS'. And also to this 5th Empire as a **'KINGDOM'** And a KINGDOM must of necessity, have a King!!

Progressive Development

This 'KINGDOM' has developed in three progressive stages since 1801 AD when the **'UNITED' 'KINGDOM'** of modern Israel was formed. This was the **FIRST STAGE** of the (STONE KINGDOM). Over which the descendants of King David and Solomon have ruled continuously.

The Second Stage (The Stone Nation)

The next stage was the forming of THE STONE (NATION).
The 'UNITED STATES' of America. This is the 'STONE' which was 'cut out' of (or cut itself off from) the Stone Kingdom. This was the 'STONE' referred to by Daniel.

> Then sawest till that a stone was 'cut off' without
> hands, which smote the image upon his feet that
> were of iron and clay, and brake them to
> pieces....
> And the stone that smote the image became a
> great mountain and filled the whole earth.
> Daniel 2:34-35

> For as much as thou sawest that the stone was
> cut out of **the** mountain without hands, and that
> it brake into pieces the iron, the brass, the clay,
> the silver, and the gold; the great God hath made
> known to the king what shall come to pass
> hereafter: and the dream is certain, and the
> interpretation thereof sure.
> Daniel 2:45

The Saviour referred to this STONE **(NATION)** in the Kingdom parable of the Householder MATTHEW 21. Speaking to the JEWS he said:

> Therefore say I unto you, the kingdom of God
> shall be taken from you, and given unto a
> (nation) bringing forth the fruits thereof.
> *And whosoever shall fall on this stone (nation) shall be*
> *broken: But on whomsoever 'it' shall fall 'it' will grind him*
> *to powder.*
>
> *Daniel 2: 43-44*
> *Brackets added*

This small stone **'NATION'** was to develop and grow to become a **'GREAT MOUNTAIN'** or singular 'great **'NATION'** (USA) opposed to the stone **'KINGDOM'** (United Kingdom) which was to develop into a great EMPIRE or **COMMONWEALTH.**

Between them The stone **'KINGDOM'** and the stone **'NATION'** have consumed the continental Empires of Europe and those of Babylon and Persia. The Kingdoms of **SPAIN, FRANCE,** (Napoleon's Empire), **Austria, Hungary, Italy, Germany** and one could even include communist **Russia (1987)**.

It was Karl Marx who is quoted as saying.

> 'England seems to be the '<u>rock</u>' against which all revolutionary
> waves are broken'
>
> The National Message 24 – 6 – 33
> the Rev A. Pritchard M.A

> *And I beheld till the thrones were cast down.*
>
> **Daniel 7:9**

Those of the older generation to-day can remember when the only countries or peoples who were **NOT** ruled by Kings were Switzerland and the U.S.A., yet since then, the thrones of FRANCE, CHINA, PORTUGAL, SPAIN AUSTRIA, HUNGARY, SERBIA, ROMANIA, BULGARIA, GERMANY, RUSSIA, TURKEY, ITALY, EGYPT, GREECE, JAPAN, have fallen.

The prophecy will not be complete until all but one shall have disappeared.

Third stage: The Greater (Stone) Kingdom

This third stage of the 'Stone' Kingdom, is yet future, and is dealt with more fully in chapter 18 of this book, suffice it to say that, prophecy informs us that the United Kingdom of Great Britain and Commonwealth, and the United States of America will eventually come together under one head to form a greater Anglo Saxon, Celtic Federation (A greater United Kingdom). This greater Political and Economic Federation will be 'set up' before the return of the Saviour, and will form the foundation of His Kingdom on Earth.

The First Beast of the Image

Babylon

Wings on the **Lion** represents speed of movement. Babylon rose quickly to power under its first two Kings Nebopolassar and Nebuchdnezzar who conquered Assyria, Palestine, Arabia, Egypt. But later Kings lost interest in conquest i.e. lost its wings.

The Second Beast of the Image

Medo Persia

The *three ribs* in the mouth of the **Bear** represent the three great powers conquered by the Medes and Persians, namely Lydia (645 BC), Babylon (534 BC) and Egypt (525 BC).

The bear like character of the Medo – Persian Empire may be recognized in the great size of its armies and their consequent ponderous movement. When Xerxes attacked Greece he required over four years to organise his mighty army, said by Herotous to number 1,700,000 men.

The Third Beast of the Image

Greece

The four *wings* on the **Leopard**. A leopard is noted for its speed and this feature is given a double measure by the four wings on its back.

Alexander was in all probability the first military leader to invent Blitzkrieg. He moved his armies so quickly that none could prepare for their coming. Alexander's whole campaign lasted only 11 years from 334 to 323 BC. But in that short time he had conquered Asia Minor, Syria, Egypt, Babylon, Persia as well as territories as far as India.

The four **Heads** on the **Leopard** initially represent the 'Greek League' – the states of Athens, Sparta, Thebes, Macedonia. United under the threat of a Persian invasion in 480 BC. Later, after the sudden death of Alexander in 323 BC the Greek Empire was divided up by his four generals, referred to in Daniel 8:21-22.

The Four Generals

Seleuchus	Gained Syria, Babylon, Arabia
Ptolemy	Gained Egypt and part of Palestine
Lysimachus	Gained Asia Minor
Cassander	Gained Greece

These are the "four notable ones" mentioned in Daniel 8:8

They plotted and assassinated Alexander's wife and son in order to gain control. There was also a fith general Antigonus. In turn Seleuchus and Lysimachus plotted against him and had him assassinated. Eventually the Empire was controlled by Seleuchus and Ptolemy. In history they became known as the King of the North (the Selucid Kingdom) and King of the South (Kingdom of Ptolemy). These are so referred to in Daniel 11.

These divisions of the Greek Empire were overthrown by the Romans in 160 BC.

However, these divisions of Alexander's Empire continued in their influence during Roman occupation.

The Fourth Beast of the Image

Rome

> "After this I saw in the night visions, and behold a fourth beast, dreadful and terrible, and strong exceedingly; and it

had great iron teeth: it devoured and brake in pieces, and stamped the residue with the feet of it: and it was diverse from all the beasts that were before it; and it had **ten horns**.

I considered the horns, and, behold, there came up among them another **little horn**, *before whom there were* **three of the first horns plucked up by the roots***: and, behold, in this horn were eyes like the eyes of man, and a mouth speaking great things."*

Daniel 7:7-8
Emphasis added

Daniel was really curious about this beast:

"Then I would know the truth of the fourth beast, which was diverse (different) from all the others, exceeding dreadful, whose teeth were of iron, and his nails of brass; which devoured, brake in pieces, and stamped the residue with his feet;"

Daniel 7:19
Emphasis added

"And of the ten horns that were in his head, and of the other (little horn) which came up, and before whom three fell; even of that horn that had eyes, and a mouth that spake very great things, whose look was more stout than his fellows.

I beheld, and the same horn made war (persecuted) with the saints, and prevailed against them;"

Daniel 7:20-21
Emphasis added

The angel replied:

> *"Thus he said, The fourth beast shall be the fourth kingdom upon earth, which shall be diverse (different) from all kingdoms, and shall devour the whole earth, and shall tread it down, and break it in pieces.*
>
> *And the* **ten horns** *out of this kingdom are* **ten kings** *that shall arise: and another shall rise after them; and he shall be diverse from the first, and he shall subdue* **three kings***.*
>
> *And he shall speak great words against the most High, and shall wear out the saints of the most High, and think to change times and laws: and they shall be given into his hand until* **a time and times and the dividing of time.***"*
>
>

Daniel 7:23-25
Emphasis added

> *"As concerning the rest of the beasts, they had their dominion taken away: yet their lives were prolonged for a season and time."*
>
>

Daniel 7:12

Even though Rome had conquered all, the influence of Babylon, Persia and Greece would continue to live on though their *political, economical* and *religious* systems, even their military system. Rome adopted them all. They established their Empire by:

> The *power* of the **Lion**
> The *strength* of the **Bear**
> And the *speed* of the **Leopard**

And they controlled the Empire with their

> *Political* System
> *Economical* System
> *Religious* System

1. All it needs for us to do now is to identify who represents the ten horns.
2. Who represents the little horn.
3. What were the three horns which were uprooted by the little horn?
4. And how the 'time' prophecy of 1260 years was fulfilled

> *"… and* **they** *(the remaining seven kings) shall be given into his hand until* **a time and times and the dividing of time.***"*
>
> *Daniel 7:25*
> Emphasis added

5. Finally, all we need to do is to determine the date the prophecy commenced.

Heads and Horns are interchangeable. Representing divisions of an Empire.

Horns usually representing a 'Head' of state.

Little Horns represent a prominent *religious leader*. In this case it represents the Pope. The Ten Horns represent the Ten Divisions of the Roman Empire, which lasted until 476 AD. These divisions were made up of the European Tribes at that time. It must be remembered that the Roman Empire was not the Europe we know to day. Europe at that time was occupied by tribes. These are known in history as:

Visigoths	Ostrogoths
Vandals	Heruli
Franks	Burgundians
Lombards	Suevi
Allemanni	Britons

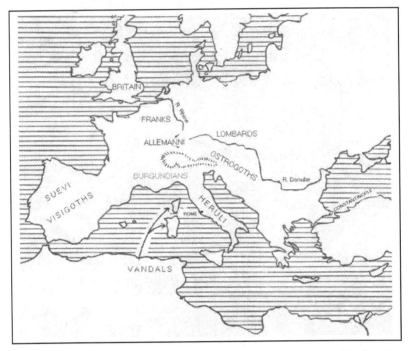

Figure 20. Europe 476 – 508 AD: showing the divisions of Roman Territory into ten Kingdoms

After the death of Constantine the Great (23rd May 337 AD), the Great Empire which he had established began to decay. Theodosius (378 – 395 AD) was the last ruler of a united Roman Empire. At his death the Empire was divided between his two sons Honorus (in the West) and Arcadius (in the East). The separation proves to be permanent.

The Division of the Roman Empire

With Constantinople as the headquarters of the East and Rome as the headquarters of the West.

The Deadly Wound

Division results in weakness and from that time on the city of Rome and the western 'head' of the Empire was continually under threat from the Gothic, Germanic and Barbarian tribes.

Rome was besieged by both the Visgoths and non-Germanic Huns by Attila in 455 AD Geiseric (Genseric) the Vandal King occupies Rome.

By 476 AD Rome is occupied in turn by both the Heruli led by Odoacer. Quickly followed by the Ostrogoths led by Theodoric.

The Western Division (head) has fallen – described in history and scripture as "the deadly wound".

The Transition Period

With the fall of the Western Empire in 476 AD a transitional period follows until 554 AD.

The Three Horns Uprooted

Vandals, Heruli, Ostrogoths

These tribal elements were the three 'Horns' mentioned previously. In 527 AD a new Emperor comes to power in the Eastern Empire. Justinian. He has a burning ambition: The recovery of the western Empire. His dream is to restore the Roman Empire to its full ancient grandeur. Justinian sees himself as the rightful Emperor of the whole Roman Empire. Justinian knows that there cannot be unity of Empire without unity of religion. So he enlists the support of the Pope in Rome. Together they will drive out the barbarian occupiers of Rome and the Western Empire.

In return Justinian was to grant the Bishop of Rome supreme authority over the whole of the Church! And he would receive the title of Pope.

Justinian sends Belisarius the greatest general of his day to do the job.

In **533 – 534 AD** Imperial armies make short work of the Vandals, quickly followed by the Heruli and Ostrogoths.

In **549 AD** Belisarius is recalled to Constantinopole. He is replaced by Narses who quickly finishes the job begun by Belisarius.

By **554 AD** Rome and Italy were firmly in Justinian's hands.

The Deadly Wound is Healed
554 AD

The three barbarian Kingdoms have been uprooted and swept away! The deadly wound of 476 AD is healed! The ancient Roman Empire is revived – Restored under the sceptre of Justinian.

Both "legs" of the Empire East and West are now under his personal control.

The Imperial Restoration
History will memorialise his achievements as the Imperial Restoration. It is a milestone in the history of mankind. However, Justinian's ambitions of gaining supreme power in the West was eventually to fall into the hands of the Pope. After which it became known as the 'Holy' Roman Empire.

The 1,260 Years
We now have a date for the commencement of the time prophecy regarding the remaining Seven Kings.

554 AD------------------------1260 years------------------------1814 AD

> *"... and they (the remaining seven kings) shall be given into his (the pope's) hand **until** (for a period of) a time and times and the dividing of time."*
>
> *Daniel 7:25*
> Emphasis added

The Western Empire

554 AD to 1814 AD	During this period the Western Empire is ruled in turn by the following five 'Heads'
544 AD	The imperial restoration by Justinian
744 AD	The Frankish Kingdom
800 AD	Charlemagne crowned by the Pope
962 AD	Holy Roman Empire – German Head
	Otto the Great crowned by the Pope
1520 AD	Hapsburg dynasty – Austrian Head
	Charles the Great crowned by the Pope
1805 AD	Napoleon's Kingdom – French Head
	Napoleon crowned by the Pope

What happened in 1814?

On the 6th April 1814 Napoleon Bonaparte, Emperor (1804 – 1814) abdicated bringing to and end the Holy Roman Empire. This event is likened in scripture to the 'Beast' going into Perdition – meaning a period of curtailment.

In October 1793 France deliberately broke away from her religious past, then in 1796 Napoleon invaded Italy threatening the Pope who was forced to pay heavily to secure a truce. This lasted only until 1798 when the French army entered Rome. Pope Pius VI refused to renounce his temporal sovereignty and was taken prisoner in March 1799 and sent into exile, where he died.

Relations between Napoleon and the Papacy deteriorated still further. Pope Pius VII refused to co-operate with Napoleon, and again in February 1808 French forces occupied Rome. The Pope is arrested. In 1809 Napoleon decrees the Papal States annexed as part of the French Empire. The Pope is put under close arrest, and imprisoned at Fontainebleau near Paris. He does not return to the Vatican until May 1814, Napoleon had a series of dramatic military victories including Austerlitz (1805), Jena (1806) and Wagram (1809), establishing a French Empire stretching from Spain to Poland.

British sea power frustrated his plans to invade England and resulted in the destruction of the French fleet at Trafalgar, 21st October 1805. Then there followed a disastrous failure in his attack on Russia (1812). In 1814 he was forced to abdicate by a coalition of allied opponents and was banished to the island of Elba off the west coast of Italy. However, he escaped a year later and returned to France to muster another army, but was defeated at Waterloo on 18th June 1815.

He was once again exiled; this time to the island of St. Helena where he died on 5th May 1821 aged 52, allegedly poisoned to death by one of his jailors.

The fall of Napoleon and the French Empire which brought an end to the Holy Roman Empire, was a landmark, in secular and scriptural history fulfilling the 'Time' prophecy of Daniel's vision and as we shall see confirmed by John's 'Time' prophecy in Revelation 13:5.

It will not go unnoticed that this event was the forerunner to the event described by John in Revelation 14:6

> *"And I saw another angel fly in the midst of heaven, having the everlasting gospel to preach unto them that dwell on the earth, and to every nation, and kindred, and tongue, and people,"*
>
> *Revelation 14:6*

This event was fulfilled, when on the evening of 23rd September 1823 the Angel Moroni appeared to the prophet Joseph Smith to reveal unto him the fullness of the Everlasting Gospel.

Figure 21. The Division of the Empire after Constantine

11
THE BEAST AND THE DEADLY WOUND

Revelation chapter 13

1 AND I stood upon the sand of the sea, and saw a beast rise up out of the sea, having seven heads and ten horns, and upon his horns ten crowns, and upon his heads the name of blasphemy.

2 And the beast which I saw was like unto a leopard, and his feet were as the feet of a bear, and his mouth as the mouth of a lion: and the dragon gave him his power, and his seat, and great authority.

3 And I saw one of his heads as it were wounded to death; and his deadly wound was healed: and all the world wondered after the beast.

4 And they worshipped the dragon which gave power unto the beast: and they worshipped the beast, saying, Who is like unto the beast? who is able to make war with him?

5 And there was given unto him a mouth speaking great things and blasphemies; and power was given unto him to continue forty and two months.

6 And he opened his mouth in blasphemy against God, to blaspheme his name, and his tabernacle, and them that dwell in heaven.

7 And it was given unto him to make war with the saints, and to overcome them: and power was given him over all kindreds, and tongues, and nations.

8 And all that dwell upon the earth shall worship him, whose names are not written in the book of life of the Lamb slain from the foundation of the world.

9 If any man have an ear, let him hear.

10 He that leadeth into captivity shall go into captivity: he that killeth with the sword must be killed with the sword. Here is the patience and the faith of the saints.

11 And I beheld another beast coming up out of the earth; and he had two horns like a lamb, and he spake as a dragon.

12 And he exerciseth all the power of the first beast before him, and causeth the earth and them which dwell therein to worship the first beast, whose deadly wound was healed.

13 And he doeth great wonders, so that he maketh fire come down from heaven on the earth in the sight of men,

14 And deceiveth them that dwell on the earth by the means of those miracles which he had power to do in the sight of the beast; saying to them that dwell on the earth, that they should make an image to the beast, which had the wound by a sword, and did live.

15 And he had power to give life unto the image of the beast, that the image of the beast should both speak, and cause that as many as would not worship the image of the beast should be killed.

16 And he causeth all, both small and great, rich and poor, free and bond, to receive a mark in their right hand, or in their foreheads:

17 And that no man might buy or sell, save he that had the mark, or the name of the beast, or the number of his name.

18 Here is wisdom. Let him that hath understanding count the number of the beast: for it is the number of a man; and his number is Six hundred threescore and six.

The Beast Which Suffered the Deadly Wound

Revelation chapter 13 portrays the events in secular history, which took place shortly after the Saviour's first advent, during the 5th and 6th seals commencing with the events of Roman history from about 450 AD to 1814 AD.

The events of this chapter are a follow on to Daniel chapter 7.

In this vision John sees *two* beasts. He portrays the first beast as follows:

> *"And I stood upon the sand of the sea, and saw a beast rise up **out of the sea**, having seven heads and ten horns, and upon his horns **ten crowns**, and upon his heads the name of blasphemy.*
>
> *And the beast which I saw was **like unto** a leopard, and his feet were as the feet of a bear, and his mouth as the mouth of a lion: **and the dragon gave him his power, and his seat, and great authority.**"*
>
> Revelation 13:1-2
> Emphasis added

"Coming up out of the sea" means "like unto" previous Empires.

You will also notice that the 'Horns' now have 'Crowns', showing that the divisions of the Roman Empire had progressed from Tribal status to a Sovereign status. *This was a new development in the progress of the Beast.*

This 'one beast' is described as being "like unto" or "in the likeness of" Daniel's beast!

This 'one beast' was "like unto" a **leopard**, with the feet of a **bear**, and the mouth of a **lion**.

This was portraying that the Roman Empire had received all the territory, power and influence of the previous three beasts: Babylon, Persia and Greece and had adopted their systems of government.

Rome inherited from the previous Empires:

The power of the Lion	Babylon
The Strength of the Bear	Persia
The cunning and speed of the Leopard	Greece

And she controlled the Empire by their:

Military, Political, Economical and Religious Systems.

The Empires of Babylon, Persia and Greece lived on in the Roman system just as Daniel foresaw that they would.

> *"As concerning the rest of the beasts, they had their dominion taken away: yet their lives were prolonged for a season and time."*
>
> *Daniel 7:12*

John describes the beast as having great power:

> *"And they worshipped the dragon which gave power unto the beast: and they worshipped the beast, saying, Who is like unto the beast? who is able to make war with him?"*
>
> *Revelation 13:4*

Well, who or what could make war with Rome? It was the most powerful Empire ever. Possessing the speed and cunning of a Leopard and the power and characteristics of the two other most powerful beasts – the Bear and the Lion.

> *"And it was given unto him to make war with the saints, and to overcome them: and power was given him over all kindreds, and tongues, and nations.*
>
> *And all that dwell upon the earth shall worship him, whose names are **not** written in the book of life of the Lamb slain from the foundation of the world."*
>
> *Revelation 13:7-8*
> Emphasis added

Yes! The Roman Empire wielded great power over all people and did make war (persecute) the early Christian Saints of the true church putting many to death for their faith.

The Second Beast

"Which looked like a Lamb – But Spake as a Dragon"

> *"And I beheld another beast coming up out of the **earth**; and he had two horns **like a lamb**, and he spake as a dragon."*

Revelation 13:11
Emphasis added

John describes this beast as 'he' referring to a man, coming up "out of the **earth**" which means a ruling Empire (see our list of Keys to Symbols). This 'beast man' is described as having "two horns". Men do not have horns – so what does it mean? Since the time of Pope Gregory 590 AD all Roman Catholic bishops have worn a Pallium (cloke) of specially blessed lambs wool. And the Abbots have also worn the two pointed mitres and were known as Goruti or Horned ones. This two horned beast looked like a lamb, but spake as a dragon.

The Lamb is a symbol of Christ John 1:29, Rev 17:14.
The Dragon is a symbol of Satan Rev 12:9, Rev 20:2 2 Thes 2:3-4 and 9-10, Dan 7:25.

Fig 22. Abbot with mitre (Goruti)

This man then is a religious leader. A literal wolf in sheep's clothing! Remember the story of Little Red Riding Hood? Christ warned people against these 'wolves in sheep's clothing'. The reference is obviously apparent.

The two horned lamb/dragon symbolises the Pope. The 'Little horn' of Daniel 7:

> "... *before whom ... three of the* **(10)** *... horns* **(were)** *plucked up by the roots...*"
>
> *Daniel 7:8*
> Emphasis added

> "*And the ten horns out of this kingdom are ten kings that shall arise: and another shall rise after them; and he shall be diverse from the first, and he shall subdue three kings.*"
>
> *Daniel 7:24*

John informs us that "he exercised all the power of the first Beast" (Revelation 13:12).

And 'he' had the power to give 'life' unto 'the image' of the beast, "which suffered the deadly wound and was healed" (see Revelation 13:3, 12, 15).

Therefore before we can discuss the further involvement of this two horned lamb dragon in our story, we must first discover what the "deadly wound" was which the first beast suffered; "which had the wound by a sword and did live" Revelation 13:14. Because the second beast the two horned lamb dragon, did not arise **until after** the deadly wound was healed!

The Deadly Wound

> "*And I saw one of his heads as it were wounded to death; and his deadly wound was healed: and all the world wondered after the beast.*"
>
> *Revelation 13:3*

The beast described by John included seven heads, but the only head existing at the time of John was the fourth beast of Daniel, containing the seventh head and also the 10 horns – the Roman Empire, divided east and west.

So the specific "one of its heads" that was wounded to death was the **western head** of the Roman Empire.

After the death of Constantine the Great, the Empire became divided – divisions cause weakness. The Western 'leg' of the Empire was overran by the Barbarian hordes putting an end to this 'Western Head' in 476 AD.

Notice this scripture does not say the whole beast died only **one** of the heads was "wounded" – and was as though it was dead and finished.

But the deadly wound was healed!

The deadly wound then, was the one administered to the Western division of the Roman Empire, when, in its last decaying stages, the Barbarian hordes overran it, ending its government in 476AD.

The 10 horns now reign one by one.

Referring to our chart 'The Seven Seals of Revelation'. It will be observed that the first 3 horns were the Barbarian hordes, the Vandals, Heruli and Ostrogoths.

The Vandals

With the sacking of Rome in 455 AD by the armies of Gaiseric the Vandal, the weakness of the Western Empire was fully revealed. Thereafter the influence of the Barbarians in the Imperial Court, became supreme.

The Heruli

Then in 476 AD the last Emperor in the West, Romulus Augustulus, was dethroned by Odoacer, King of the Heruli. Odoacer set up his government in Rome but it did not heal the deadly wound, for this was only a government in Rome. It was not a Roman government but of foreign barbarians.

The Ostrogoths

493 AD to 554 AD. The Ostrogoths, the Eastern branch of the Goths, who had formerly been allies of Attila the Hun, made an incursion into Italy at the instigation of the Eastern Emperor, but were eventually driven out to found an independent kingdom.

The historical references being obtained from 'Milestones of History' Volume 2: Readers Digest London and Newsweek Books, New York.

These three kingdoms filled a period in Roman history known as the Transition Age. That is, the transition between the wound and the healing.

The Deadly Wound Healed

554 AD the Emperor Justinian of the Eastern Empire set up his government through an Imperial Legate at Ravenna, Italy, and brought about what is known in history as the Imperial Restoration.

Justinian agreed to share power with the Pope, thinking that he, as a ruling Emperor, would be the supreme authority over all the Empire – east and west – in all aspects of life: Militarily, politically, economically and religiously. But it was not to be. Eventually it was the Pope(s) who gained supreme authority over the Restored Empire.

Of the 'little horn', Daniel says his "look was more stout than his fellows" (Daniel 7:20). The papacy dominated completely all the horns to follow.

The first three horns – Vandals, Heruli, Ostrogoths – were plucked up "by their roots" by this alliance of Pope and Emperor.

The expression "plucked up by their roots" means that they were never to rise again.

The Healed Beast

Once healed John informs us that power was given to this healed beast to continue for 42 months.

> *"And there was given unto him a mouth speaking great things and blasphemies; and power was given unto him to continue **forty and two months**."*
>
> Revelation 13:5
> Emphasis added

In prophetical time measures we have discovered that 42 months is 42 x 30 = 1,260 days or years.

Following the healing in 554 AD the following 'heads' or 'horns' ruled the Holy Roman Empire in succession.

544 AD	The imperial restoration by Justinian
744 AD	The Frankish Kingdom
800 AD	Charlemagne crowned by the Pope
962 AD	Holy Roman Empire – German Head
	Otto the Great crowned by the Pope
1520 AD	Hapsburg dynasty – Austrian Head
	Charles the Great crowned by the Pope
1805 AD	Napoleon's Kingdom – French Head
	Napoleon crowned by the Pope

The Imperial power would therefore remain with the Pope(s) for a period of 1,260 years from 554 AD and terminate in 1814 AD with the defeat of Napoleon.

554 AD------------------------1260 years--------------------------1814 AD

This is confirmed by Daniel:

> *"... and they shall be given into his hand until a time and times and the dividing of time."*
>
> Daniel 7:25
> Emphasis added

Time	360	360
Times	360 x 2	720
Dividing (Half) of Time		180
		1,260

'They' referring to the remaining seven horns which the Little Horn was to have power over for a period of 1,260 years.

Therefore both Daniel and John confirm that the Imperial power would be with this 'Little Horn' for a period of 1,260 years.

> *"And he exerciseth all the power of the first beast before him, and causeth the earth and them which dwell therein to worship the first beast, whose deadly wound was healed."*
>
> *Revelation 13:12*

The Pope(s) received both temporal and spiritual power over the Empire. They wielded all the power of the Imperial Emperors which had gone before them, in addition to having the Ecclesiastical power – claiming to be God's Vicar upon the earth.

> *"And he had power to give life unto the **image** of the beast, that the **image** of the beast should both speak, and cause that as many as would not worship the **image** of the beast should be killed."*
>
> *Revelation 13:15*
>
> Emphasis added

The Pope(s) wielded greater power than the Emperors. The second beast was only an "image" of the first beast. The Pope(s) however, patterned their 'Holy' Roman Empire on the Pagan Empire which they had replaced.

It is said that during the early centuries millions of people were put to death during the inquisition period. *Especially those who printed bibles!*

The Pope(s) and the church had control over all aspects of life:

> *"And that no man might buy or sell, save he that had the mark, or the name of the beast, or the number of his name."*
>
> *Revelation 13:17*

The Pope(s) controlled the Empire even more ruthlessly than the Emperors. No man or woman could 'buy or sell' – that is, conduct any business without their approval.

Even the kings and rulers in Europe became subject to their authority.

The Papal Throne

> *"And the beast which I saw was like unto a leopard, and his feet were as the feet of a bear, and his mouth as the mouth of a lion: and the dragon gave him his power, and his seat, and great authority."*
>
> *Revelation 13:2*

There is a literal throne (seat) in the Vatican upon which all the Popes have been enthroned, upon which they receive a ***triple crown!***

John makes no bones about who it is that is the power behind this throne. This throne has been in conflict with the throne of the Lord in England since 1558 AD.

> *"And **the dragon** was wroth with **the woman**, and went to make war with the remnant of her seed..."*
>
> *Revelation 12:17*
>
> Emphasis added

That conflict is still in its progressive stages even to this day!

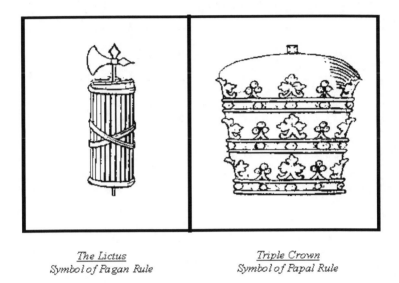

The Lictus
Symbol of Pagan Rule

Triple Crown
Symbol of Papal Rule

Figure 23. Picture of Lictus and the Triple Crown

The Beast in the Bottomless Pit

By 1814 AD *8 horns* of both Daniel's vision and John's vision had come and gone (see chart).

And the beast (Roman Empire) seems to have died. John symbolised the condition in Revelation 17:8 as the "bottomless pit", which simply means a period of curtailment.

Other references to this period of curtailment are found in Revelation 11:7 and 20:1-3.

The Gospel Restored

During the period 1814 to 1870 the period in which the beast was curtailed – the Gospel was restored:

> *"And I saw another angel fly in the midst of heaven, having the everlasting gospel to preach unto them that*

*dwell on the earth, and to every nation, and kindred, and
tongue, and people,"*

Revelation 14:6

This event was fulfilled when on the evening of 23rd September 1823 the
angel Moroni appeared to the prophet Joseph Smith to reveal unto him
the fullness of the Everlasting Gospel. Which places this chapter and
verse in the correct chronological and historical order!

The Remaining Horns

What of the remaining two horns (refer to fig 24)?

The 9th and 10th horns of Daniel's beast (Daniel 7) or the remaining 6th
and 7th horns of John's beast (Revelation 13).

THE KINGDOM OF GARIBALDI AND MUSSOLINI

The 9th Horn

By the year 1870 Giuseppe Garibaldi (1807 – 1882), Italian patriot and
military leader, one of the heroes of the Risorgimento. After involvement
in early struggles against Austrian rule in the 1830's and 1840's
commanded a volunteer force on the Sardinian side in the campaign of
1859, and successfully led his 'Red Shirts' to victory in Sicily and
southern Italy in 1860 – 1861 thus playing a vital part in uniting the
fragmented divisions of Italy into one state.

A biscuit made in Britain was named after him for this achievement!
These biscuits are still popular today. Garibaldi biscuits! The kingdom
thus established the 9th horn of Daniel 7 and the 6th horn of the
remaining seven horns of Revelation 13 which culminated in the fascist
rule of Mussolini in 1945 (refer to chart).

A CHART SHOWING PROPHECIES OF REIGN OF GENTILE KINGDOMS							
Dan 2 The IMAGE	Dan. 7 The FOUR BEASTS		Dan. 8 The RAM and GOAT	Rev 13 The BEAST and IMAGE		Rev. 17 BABYLON and BEAST	EXPLANATION of Symbols	The EVENTS Fulfilled in HISTORY
	(State)	(Church)		(State)	(Church)			
Head of GOLD v. 32, 39	1st BEAST like LION v. 4						1st HEAD of prophetic BABYLON	The CHALDEAN EMPIRE (Babylon) 625 - 538 B.C.
Breast and arms of SILVER v. 32, 39	2nd BEAST (BEAR) v. 5		RAM with 2 horns v. 3, 4, 20				2nd HEAD of prophetic BABYLON	The PERSIAN EMPIRE (Medo-Persia) 558 - 330 B.C.
Belly and thighs of BRASS v. 32, 39	3rd BEAST (LEOPARD) 4 heads v. 6		HE GOAT with great horn and 4 notable ones v. 5-8, 21, 22				3rd, 4th, 5th, 6th HEAD of prophetic BABYLON	GREECE, under Alexander the Great and four divisions began 333 B.C.
Legs as IRON v. 33, 40-43	4th BEAST strong like IRON with 10 HORNS v. 7, 23, 24			The BEAST with 7 HEADS and 10 HORNS V. 1, 2			7th HEAD of prophetic BABYLON	The ROMAN EMPIRE 31 B.C. - 476 A.D. in 2 divisions, West and East
				The DEADLY WOUND v. 3				Fall of the ROMAN EMPIRE 476 A.D.
	1st HORN (plucked by roots)			1st HORN			These three horns, destroyed at behest of Pope, fill the "Transition Age"	The VANDALS 429 - 533 A.D.
	2nd HORN (rooted up)			2nd HORN				The HERULI, Odoacer's government 476 - 493 A.D
	3rd HORN (rooted up)			3rd HORN				The OSTROGOTHS 493 - 554 A.D.
		LITTLE HORN among ten v. 8, 20-22, 24-27			2 horned "LAMB DRAGON" and "IMAGE" v. 11-18	SCARLET WOMAN who rode the BEAST v. 1, 2	Ruled the beast, so called BABYLON the GREAT	ROMAN CATHOLIC CHURCH and PAPACY, "image" of Roman Empire government
	4th HORN			1st of remaining 7 horns- DEADLY WOUNDED (to continue 1260 years) v. 5		1st HEAD of BEAST (healed) ridden by scarlet-clothed woman	Since the "Great Whore" never rode any of the 7 heads of the 1st 4 beasts, but did mount and ride the last 7 horns of Daniel's 4th beast, it follows that the last 7 horns of Dan. 7 and Rev. 13 are the 7 HEADS of Rev. 17 (5 fallen at collapse of Napoleon).	"IMPERIAL RESTORATION" of empire by Justinian, 554 A.D. He recognized supremacy of the Pope in the West.
	5th HORN			2nd of remaining 7 HORNS		2nd HEAD ridden by woman		FRANKISH KINGDOM Began 774 A.D. Charlemange crowned by Pope 800 A.D.
	6th HORN			3rd of remaining 7 HORNS		3rd HEAD ridden by woman		HOLY ROMAN EMPIRE (German head). Otto the Great crowned by Pope 962 A.D.
	7th HORN			4th of remaining 7 HORNS		4th HEAD ridden by woman		HAPSBURG dynasty (Austrian head), Charles the Great crowned by Pope 1520.
	8th HORN			5th of remaining 7 HORNS		5th HEAD ridden by woman		NAPOLEON'S KINGDOM (French head), crowned by Pope, 1805

554 - 1814 = 1260 Years Beast Continued

In 1814, just 1260 years after "deadly wound" was healed, the "HOLY ROMAN EMPIRE" was dissolved.
"So closed a government that dated from Augustus Caesar"

	9th HORN			6th of remaining 7 HORNS		6th HEAD ridden by woman	(One IS) Rev. 17:10	ITALY united by Garibaldi 1870 to 1945
The Ten Toes	10th HORN			7th and last HORN	Beast ascends out of pit	7th HEAD and ten HORNS	(One YET TO COME)	Revived ROMAN EMPIRE, by 10 rulers under one leader.

Fig 24: A chart showing prophecies of reign of Gentile kingdoms

12
THE FINAL ROMAN EMPIRE

Revelation chapter 17

AND there came one of the seven angels which had the seven vials, and talked with me, saying unto me, Come hither; I will shew unto thee the judgment of the great whore that sitteth upon many waters:

With whom the kings of the earth have committed fornication, and the inhabitants of the earth have been made drunk with the wine of her fornication.

So he carried me away in the spirit into the wilderness: and I saw a woman sit upon a scarlet coloured beast, full of names of blasphemy, having seven heads and ten horns.

And the woman was arrayed in purple and scarlet colour, and decked with gold and precious stones and pearls, having a golden cup in her hand full of abominations and filthiness of her fornication:

And upon her forehead was a name written, MYSTERY, BABYLON THE GREAT, THE MOTHER OF HARLOTS AND ABOMINATIONS OF THE EARTH.

And I saw the woman drunken with the blood of the saints, and with the blood of the martyrs of Jesus: and when I saw her, I wondered with great admiration.

And the angel said unto me, Wherefore didst thou marvel? I will tell thee the mystery of the woman, and of the beast that carrieth her, which hath the seven heads and ten horns.

The beast that thou sawest was, and is not; and shall ascend out of the bottomless pit, and go into perdition: and they that dwell on the earth shall wonder, whose names were not written in the book of life from the foundation of the world, when they behold the beast that was, and is not, and yet is.

And here is the mind which hath wisdom. The seven heads are seven mountains, on which the woman sitteth.

And there are seven kings: five are fallen, and one is, and the other is not yet come; and when he cometh, he must continue a short space.

And the beast that was, and is not, even he is the eighth, and is of the seven, and goeth into perdition.

And the ten horns which thou sawest are ten kings, which have received no kingdom as yet; but receive power as kings one hour with the beast.

These have one mind, and shall give their power and strength unto the beast.

These shall make war with the Lamb, and the Lamb shall overcome them: for he is Lord of lords, and King of kings: and they that are with him are called, and chosen, and faithful.

And he saith unto me, The waters which thou sawest, where the whore sitteth, are peoples, and multitudes, and nations, and tongues.

And the ten horns which thou sawest upon the beast, these shall hate the whore, and shall make her desolate and naked, and shall eat her flesh, and burn her with fire.

For God hath put in their hearts to fulfil his will, and to agree, and give their kingdom unto the beast, until the words of God shall be fulfilled.

And the woman which thou sawest is that great city, which reigneth over the kings of the earth.

Revelation Chapter 17 – The Symbols

The Great Whore	Roman apostate church
The Waters	Nations and people of the earth. Verses 1 and 5.
The Woman	Rome: The City which rules over the kings of the earth. Verses 4 and 8. Drunken with the blood of the saints. Verse 6.
The Seven Heads	The seven last horns of Daniel's 4th beast. Seven mountains upon which Rome is built. Verses 3 and 9.
The Ten Horns of the 7th Head	Ten nations united together giving power to the beast. Verses 3, 12 and 13.
The Scarlet Coloured Beast	"That Was, And Is Not, And Yet Is." This is a clear indication of an empire THAT WAS – THEN DECLINED. Then finally to be resurrected in a Federation in the Treaty of Rome over ten nations. Eventually to extend itself into a common religion – presided over by the Pope.

Let us note in passing that the 'woman' mentioned in this chapter never rode on any part of the beast of Revelation 13 **except its last seven horns**.

That is the remaining seven horns of the 'healed beast' form 554 AD.

This 'woman' is the little horn of Daniel 7 and the two horned Lamb/Dragon of Revelation 13. And since this woman rode on all seven heads of the beast in Revelation 17, it is obviously then – that the seven heads of Revelation 17:3 and the seven horns of the 'healed' beast of Revelation 13:3 **are one and the same!**

Notice, at the time John saw this scarlet coloured beast of Revelation 17 he declares:

> *"And there are seven kings: five are fallen, and one is, and the other is not yet come; and when he cometh, he must continue a short space."*
>
> *Revelation 17:10*

What a teaser – if we were not aware of the connection between Daniels vision in chapter 7 – John's vision in Revelation 13 and the woman who rides the beast of Revelation 17.

The seven kings are the seven heads of the beast.

The five that are fallen are the 5 heads ruling during the 1,260 year period from 554 AD to 1814 AD in which power was given, by Papal authority for the beast to continue.

"The one that is" the 6th head: The kingdom that extended from Garibaldi to Mussolini 1870 – 1945.

"And one is yet to come" this 7th head then is yet to come! This head is yet future to our day.

John explains this as:

*"The beast that ... was, and is not; and shall ascend out
of the bottomless pit ...*

And

...the beast that was, and is not, and yet is."

Revelation 17:8

He goes on to explain further:

*"And the beast that was, and is not, even he is the eighth,
and is of the seven..."*

Revelation 17:11

What a puzzler! Well it would be – but I suspect our readers have already
worked it out.

The 'head' that was, and is not, was the 5th head ridden by the woman –
Napoleon's Kingdom. "Even he is the eighth". Napoleon's Kingdom
was the 8th of the 10 horns of Daniel 7.

"And is of the seven".

Napoleon's Kingdom was also the 5th horn of the remaining seven horns
of Revelation 13 which extended from the Imperial Restoration.

And one yet remains.

The 10th horn of Daniel chapter 7
The 7th horn of Revelation chapter 13
And the 7th head of Revelation chapter 17.

We have discovered that six of the 'heads', i.e. Dynasties of Emperor,
since the Imperial Restoration have come and gone.

The 7th head is yet future!

The Final Ten Horns

John was puzzled by all this – and of the 10 horns on the head of the scarlet coloured beast.

He may have asked the question – what of the ten horns? These have not yet been accounted for?

> *"And the ten horns which thou sawest are ten kings,* **which have received no kingdom as yet;** *but* **receive power as kings one hour** *with the beast."*
> *Revelation 17:12*
> Emphasis added

These 10 horns then are yet future.

> *Note*
> These future 10 horns – have no connection and are not to be confused with the 'Horns' mentioned in Daniel 7 *or* Revelation 13.

These ten horns grow out of the seventh head of the scarlet coloured beast of Revelation 17.

These ten horns only apply to this seventh and last head – and it will be noted that these ten horns – have no crowns. **Denoting a political federation – that receive power "as kings"**

(Revelation 17:12).

The Final Roman Empire

These final 10 Kingdoms will emerge as a future resurrected Roman Empire. These 10 Kingdoms are symbolised by the 10 toes of Nebuchadnezzar's Great Image.

And the fourth kingdom shall be strong as iron: forasmuch as iron breaketh in pieces and subdueth all things: and as iron that breaketh all these, shall it break in pieces and bruise.

And whereas thou sawest the feet and toes, part of potters' clay, and part of iron, the kingdom shall be divided; but there shall be in it of the strength of the iron, forasmuch as thou sawest the iron mixed with miry clay.

And as the toes of the feet were part of iron, and part of clay, so the kingdom shall be partly strong, and partly broken.

And whereas thou sawest iron mixed with miry clay, they shall mingle themselves with the seed of men: but they shall not cleave one to another, even as iron is not mixed with clay.

And in the days of these kings shall the God of heaven set up a kingdom, which shall never be destroyed: and the kingdom shall not be left to other people, but it shall break in pieces and consume all these kingdoms, and it shall stand for ever.

Forasmuch as thou sawest that the stone was cut out of the mountain without hands, and that it brake in pieces the iron, the brass, the clay, the silver, and the gold; the great God hath made known to the king what shall come to pass hereafter: and the dream is certain, and the interpretation thereof sure.

Daniel 2:33, 40-45

And it is in the days of 'these kings' – this future federation of 10 nations in the forthcoming Federal United States of Europe – that Christ will 'set up' His Kingdom. That is the world wide political Kingdom.

This future – Resurrected Empire – will be composed of ten or more nations

> *"These have* **one mind**, *and shall give their power and strength unto the beast."*
> > Revelation 17:13
> > Emphasis added

> *"These (federation of 10 nations) shall make war with the Lamb, and the Lamb shall overcome them: for he is Lord of lords, and King of kings: and they that are with him are called, and chosen, and faithful."*
> > Revelation 17:14
> > Emphasis added

This Empire or Union of ten modern nations will become a great political, economical and military power. These will give their power to a central overall leader.

But this Union of nations will, it is predicted, inherit the weakness symbolised by Daniel as "iron mixed with mire clay".

This union will endure for "one hour" with the Beast (a period of 15 years) – dealt with in greater detail in chapter 15.

> *"And he saith unto me, The waters which thou sawest, where the whore sitteth, are peoples, and multitudes, and nations, and tongues.*
>
> *And the ten horns which thou sawest upon the beast, these shall hate the whore, and shall make her desolate and naked, and shall eat her flesh, and burn her with fire.*
>
> *For God hath put in their hearts to fulfil his will, and to agree, and give their kingdom unto the beast,* **until the words of God shall be fulfilled."**
> > Revelation 17:15-17
> > Emphasis added

It is evident from these verses that this confederation will last but 15 years and eventually turn upon "The Whore" – political, ecclesiastical power, "making her desolate", bringing about her death. The confederacy will break up, but will **remain "until the words of God shall be fulfilled"**.

13
THE WOMAN THAT RIDES THE BEAST

The False Woman

The 'woman' mentioned in Revelation chapter 17 has no connection with the woman of Revelation chapter 12. The woman in chapter 12 is the true Israel woman.

The 'woman' of chapter 17 is the false woman posing as the true woman. Satan has his civil government on earth and we are informed that it was Satan who gave the Beast "his power – and his seat – and great authority". His seat? This means his throne – the Papal throne.

The Counterfeit Church

Satan has organised religion as his instrument deceiving the whole world. Paul was warning the Corinthian saints about these false teachers and Apostles:

> *"For such are false apostles, deceitful workers, transforming themselves into the apostles of Christ.*
>
> *And no marvel; for Satan himself is transformed into an angel of light.*
>
> *Therefore it is no great thing if his ministers also be transformed as the ministers of righteousness; whose end shall be according to their works."*
> *2 Corinthians 11:13-15*
>
> *"In whom the god of this world hath blinded the minds of them which believe not, lest the flight of the glorious gospel of Christ, who is the image of God, should shine unto them."*
> *2 Corinthians 4:4*

Here we are informed that Satan – the god of this world – can transform himself as an angel of light and his workers can also transform (make people believe they are true apostles or ministers of righteousness!). Revelation 12:9 and 20:3.

"Let no man deceive you by any means: for that day shall not come, except there come a falling away first, and that man of sin be revealed, the son of perdition;

Who opposeth and exalteth himself above all that is called God, or that is worshipped; so that he as God sitteth in the temple of God, shewing himself that he is God.

Even him, whose coming is after the working of Satan with all power and signs and lying wonders,

And with all deceivableness of unrighteousness in them that perish; because they received not the love of the truth, that they might be saved."

2 Thessalonians 2:3,4,9,10

The Image of the Beast

"And he had power to give life unto the image of the beast, that the image of the beast should both speak, and cause that as many as would not worship the image of the beast should be killed."

Revelation 13:15

What is an image? The dictionary says: A likeness, a copy, model or counterpart.

So here we have a church making itself a model or counterpart of the civil government. This counterpart of civil government was originated by Leo I (440 – 461 AD) on the imperial model. This church government is the Image of the Beast.

The Encyclopaedia Britannica calls it an "Ecclesiastical world Empire"!

The Mother of Harlots

This imperial world wide church became the Mother Church and John describes her as:

> *"...THE MOTHER OF HARLOTS..."*
>
> *Revelation 17:5*

Her daughters are called Harlots, therefore she represents the Madame.

By 1100 AD this counterfeit church or false woman had gained great power.

The Holy Roman Empire

The old pagan Empire was then referred to as the Holy Roman Empire and proclaimed as the Kingdom of God on earth (see Encyclopaedia Britannica: Millennium). They claimed the Millennium had arrived!

An Empire controlled by the church or Papacy with civil and military authority. Even today the Vatican is recognised as a State. An independent sovereign state with its own ambassadors – and to which other states send their representatives!

By 1179 AD this Church Empire proclaimed that there was to be 'no traffic with heretics'. Those who opposed the Bishops could not buy or sell or even receive a decent burial (Revelation 13:17).

Emperors and kings of all the European nations were subject unto this organisation, which had the power to make or break: Kings, Emperors or any others who opposed it's authority.

The only kingdom which eventually opposed this tyranny was the British Monarchy and Kingdom in 1554 AD, during the reign of Henry VIII.

But Rome mustered the help of Spain and France and other nations in an attempt to bring Britain into subjugation to its rule; in the attempted invasion by the Spanish Armada and Napoleonic wars. But through Divine intervention these attempts failed because Britain had a Divine calling to fulfil. Here in these islands the Lord also fulfilled his sworn oath to King David of Israel that his throne would endure throughout all generations, Jeremiah 33:17-26, Psalm 89:20-37

The False Prophet

> *"And I saw the beast, and the kings of the earth, and their armies, gathered together to make war against him that sat on the horse, and against his army.*
>
> *And the beast was taken, and with him the false prophet that wrought miracles before him, with which he deceived them that had received the mark of the beast, and them that worshipped his image. These both were cast alive into a lake of fire burning with brimstone."*
>
> *Revelation 19:19 - 20*

Here is pictured the beast, and the false prophet that wrought miracles, with which he deceived them that had received the 'mark' of the beast and those that worshipped the image of the beast.

Compare this description with the two horned lamb/dragon (see Revelation 13:11-17).

1. Both perform 'miracles' and great wonders.
2. Both deceive them that dwell on earth by means of the 'miracles'.
3. With them ('miracles') both the false prophet and the two horned lamb/dragon deceive them which have the 'mark' of the beast, or have caused them to receive his mark, and with those who worship the image of the beast.

Certainly then – there is only one conclusion!

1	The Little Horn	Daniel 7:8, 24-25
2	The Two Horned Lamb/Dragon Beast	Revelation 13:11-18
3	The False Prophet	Revelation 19:19-20
4	The Man of Sin	2 Thessalonians 2:3-4
5	The Woman that Rides the Scarlet Beast	Revelation 17:3

| 6 | The Great Whore that Sitteth upon many Waters | Revelation 17:1 |
| 7 | The Mother of Harlots | Revelation 17:5 |

Are all one and the same: The Pope and Rome!

The Three Unclean Spirits Of Babylon the Great

> *"And I saw three unclean spirits like frogs come out of the mouth of the dragon, and out of the mouth of the beast, and out of the mouth of the false prophet."*
>
> *Revelation 16:13*

This counterfeit religious/political Empire and its policies are described by John as three unclean spirits, **like frogs**, which come out of the mouths of

1. The Dragon,
2. The Beast
3. and the false Prophet

This organisation will continue clear down to **Armageddon** and the Second Coming of Christ.

These are the spirits of devils, which seem to be working miracles.

> *"For they are the spirits of the devil, working miracles, which go forth unto the kings of the earth and of the whole world, to gather them to the battle of that great day of God Almighty."*
>
> *Revelation 16:14*

> *"And he gathered them together into a place called in the Hebrew tongue Armageddon."*
>
> *Revelation 16:16*

Notice that the last battle of "that great day of God Almighty", is described in Revelation 19:19 - 20.

The Roman Empire or its modern counterpart again restored along with a religious leader described as "The false prophet" – all in the power and influence of Satan! It really is too frightening to think about.

Frogs? Frogs are considered by most people to be ugly slimy creatures, which make loud croaking noises – mostly at night. Who are the people today that make loud croaking noises? Yes, of course: Politicians, Financiers, Businessmen and Traders. They are always croaking about something (or nothing).

It is a sad fact that in our modern society most of these men are insincere, unscrupulous, devious and, in some cases, dishonest. Even in the Banking world this is an unfortunate fact; proven by the collapse of BCCI (Bank of Commerce and Credit International) where it has been disclosed that billions upon billions of dollars have been 'laundered' for the underworld and syphoned off into the private accounts of its directors, leaving thousands of people facing bankruptcy.

Honest Sincere Men in a Minority

Of course there are a few sincere, honest and trustworthy politicians, bankers and businessmen, but these are in the minority today.

As each day passes more and more corruption is disclosed in high places – no wonder the people feel insecure – no wonder the world is in such a mess.

And what would the false prophet be croaking about? Yes, of course, religious matters, false religious matters.

- Men's political organisations and ideologies
- Men's finance and monetary systems
- Men's apostate religions

These are the three unclean spirits which have been and still are the cause of all the worlds problems, unrest, and the cause of all wars, and will be according to John the Revelator the cause that leads up to the Battle of Armageddon.

Figure 25. The Three Unclean Spirits

Babylon the Great Identified

Men's political system
Men's economical system
Men's counterfeit religious system

Together they are called 'Babylon the Great' – These are its three divisions.

One division is ecclesiastical Babylon.

This three fold Babylon the Great is doomed to collapse. Error and falsehood mixed with some truth are the tools of the great deceiver. This false system will give way to truth and the divine laws of Almighty God when Christ establishes His Kingdom on earth.

> *"And there followed another angel, saying, Babylon is fallen, is fallen, that great city, because she made all nations drink of the wine of the wrath of her fornication."*
> *Revelation 14:8*

> *"And he cried mightily with a strong voice, saying, Babylon the great is fallen, is fallen...*
>
> *And I heard another voice from heaven, saying, Come out of her, my people, that ye be not partakers of her sins, and that ye receive not of her plagues."*
> *Revelation 18:2 - 4*

Some of the 'Daughters' did come out of her in *protest* – calling themselves *protestant* churches and *protestant* nations. But all have worldly forms of government as opposed to the divine laws contained in the Commandments, Statutes and Judgements given to God's people Israel at Sinai.

The Mark of the Beast

> *"And he causeth all, both small and great, rich and poor, free and bond, to receive a mark in their right hand, or in their foreheads:*
>
> *And that no man might buy or sell, save he that had the mark, or the name of the beast, or the number of his name."*
>
> *Revelation 13:16 - 17*

The 'mark' is something that will be very popular, in fact an absolute necessity, something that the majority of all people will be in favour of, and will seek for.

For without it no man will be able to buy or sell.

Everyone wants to – needs to – buy and sell.

Anyone refusing to accept the 'mark' would actually not be able to earn a living, or engage in any kind of business.

It will be noticed that the 'mark' is to be found in the *forehead* **or** in the *hand*. Notice not both.

The forehead symbolises the part of your body which contains the seat of intellect – knowledge, learning, thinking, the part which influences and directs your life.

The hand or hands symbolise the part of your body by which you earn a living.

What are the mediums which influence our thinking and our working life today?

Yes, of course: Politics – Economics – Money – Religion.

This then is the 'mark'.

And the two horned Lamb/Dragon 'causes' them, all people, to receive the mark. Both in their way of thinking and in their working life.

> *"… and cause that as many as would not worship the image of the beast should be killed."*
>
> *Revelation 13:15*
> Emphasis added

Note

This two horned Lamb/Dragon – the counterfeit church does not actually kill these martyrs – she merely 'causes' them to be killed.

It is a fact of history that the Roman Church through the Inquisition during the early and middle ages, had millions put to death for opposing its rule and doctrines.

This persecution of the 'Saints' began after the death of the Saviour and continued without respite through the 5th Seal and into the 6th Seal, almost into the 20th Century.

The First Tribulation

History informs us that in the middle ages more than 50 million people were put to death, many for their faith obedience to God and the true church, refusing to accept the authority and doctrines of this Beast and his church.

These martyrs – 'Saints' of the Church of Jesus Christ are heard by John as saying:

> *"And when he had opened the fifth seal, I saw under the altar the souls of them that were slain for the word of God, and for the testimony which they held:*
>
> *And they cried with a loud voice, saying, How long, O Lord, holy and true, dost thou not judge and avenge our blood on them that dwell on the earth?"*
>
> *Revelation 6:9, 10*

This 'mark' of the beast then existed almost 2,000 years ago. It was being enforced in the 5th Millennium!

These 'Saints' refused to be identified with this Empire and church.

This dreaded condition is once again going to be enforced. Soon it will be an offence to preach the true gospel.

The Second Great Tribulation

> *"And I saw the woman drunken with the blood of the saints, and with the blood of the martyrs of Jesus: and when I saw her, I wondered with great admiration."*
>
> *Revelation 17:6*

> *"And I saw thrones, and they sat upon them, and judgment was given unto them: and I saw the souls of them that were beheaded for the witness of Jesus, and for the word of God, and which had not worshipped the beast, neither his image, neither had received his mark upon their foreheads, or in their hands; and they lived and reigned with Christ a thousand years."*
>
> *Revelation 20:4*

> *"For then shall be great tribulation, such as was not since the beginning of the world to this time, no, nor ever shall be."*
>
> *Matthew 24:21*

This tribulation is the wrath of Satan, "because he knoweth that he hath but a short time" (Revelation 12:11).

This second great tribulation will be inflicted by the influence of the Apostate Church.
The political power of Babylon, with the economic power of Babylon – united as one with the ecclesiastical power of Babylon!

14
THE FEDERAL UNITED STATES OF EUROPE

The Emblem

Do you know what the emblem of this federation is? Yes, a *crown of twelve golden stars on a blue background!*

What does that remind you of? Yes, it was the emblem seen by John the Revelator in chapter 12. The Israel woman – God's true kingdom on earth – was seen to have upon her 'Head' a crown of twelve stars.

The Counterfeit Kingdom

And true to character the emblem of Satan's counterfeit kingdom is exactly the same.

This federation represents the final 10th horn and 7th head with its 10 horns (see chart Seven Seals of Revelation).

This is the beast that ascends "out of the bottomless pit". The beast "that was, and is not, and yet is" Revelation 17:8.

This community has its roots in the 'Treaty of Rome' signed in March 1957. Originally it began as an Economic Union.

Today we are facing a political and monetary addition to this union, called the Single European Act.

The Single European Act was signed in February 1986 and came into force in July 1987. It endorses member states commitment to the legislative programme needed to create a single European market by the end of 1992.

The final decision to complete majority voting on all issues is soon to be taken. This is one of the areas where Britain is at odds with her European partners. It would mean that member states would have to abide by the majority decision and would be unable to Veto anything that they judge to be against their own national interests. The S.E.A (Single European

Act) became fully and finally effective at midnight 31st December 1992. It will effect all our lives. All nations are trying to obtain membership of this Federation – it will be the most powerful federation of states ever seen. *A mighty economic and political colossus!*

The nations outside of this federation will stand no chance. This colossus will call the shots. Is this "the beast" that both John and Daniel predicted as "coming out of the sea" i.e. **S**ingle **E**uropean **A**ct (SEA)? Surely the reference cannot be just a coincidence!

A Trading Colossus

It will be a greater economic power than the United States of America, Japan and all the rest *put together!*

It will be composed of as many as 25 nations, but according to prophecy will have an 'inner council' of *ten* nations.

Even Russia has recognised this fact in so much that she has been prepared to abandon communism for a Market Economy. And give up all her Eastern European Empire, to prepare herself for application to join this Federation, she sees as does the USA, Japan and others that they are 'dead' outside of this federation.

Vital Ingredient Missing

But there is still one vital ingredient missing to complete the 'power' of this federation.

Yes, it is the religious authority and power.

Politics – Economics – Religion. This is the final and most powerful ingredient.

The Woman That Rides the Beast

The Church of Rome will impose her power and influence upon this great federation. All people will be required to become subject to this Ecclesiastical Beast. All the 'Protestant' churches will be 'persuaded' to accept her power or face great persecution.

Everyone will have to make a choice.

But the Lord instructs his people to "come out of her" (Revelation 18:4). The term 'my people' in this text was given to the House of Israel (Deut 14:2, 26:18; Ex 33:13; 1 Chron 17:22; Gen 48:19; Hosea 1:9 - 10, 2:23).

Therefore, it is the modern Israel nations which are told to "come out of her". That the Israel nations of Britain and Denmark will either withdraw or be expelled because they will refuse to give up their sovereignty.

The British are in the main staunch Royalists. They are also a fiercely independent people, fearing subjection or slavery to any form of government or power.

This fear of suspicion is born of their slavery in Egypt! This is reflected in the national 'anthems' *Land of Hope and Glory* and *Rule Britannia.*

It Will Last One Hour
However, scripture informs us that this Beast will be short lived.

From the year in which it is fully organised as a political, economical, monetary and ecclesiastical power, which has its beginnings in 1992/3, we are informed that it will last for "one hour" (Revelation 17:12; 18:10,19).

One hour of prophetic time is 15 years.

The 15 years will apply to its three separate influences and will be effective at different 15 year periods. Commencing in 1987 when the Single European Act came into force.

1987 AD-----------------------15 years----------------------------2002 AD

1992 AD-----------------------15 years----------------------------2007 AD

All we wait for now is the date (year) for the ecclesiastical factor to be added to conclude that terminal date of the prophecy.

15
THE FALL OF BABYLON THE GREAT

AND after these things I saw another angel come down from heaven, having great power; and the earth was lightened with his glory.

And he cried mightily with a strong voice, saying, Babylon the great is fallen, is fallen, and is become the habitation of devils, and the hold of every foul spirit, and a cage of every unclean and hateful bird.

For all nations have drunk of the wine of the wrath of her fornication, and the kings of the earth have committed fornication with her, and the merchants of the earth are waxed rich through the abundance of her delicacies.

And I heard another voice from heaven, saying, Come bout of her, my people, that ye be not partakers of her sins, and that ye receive not of her plagues.

For her sin have reached unto heaven, and God hath remembered her iniquities.

Reward her even as she rewarded you, and double unto her double according to her works: in the cup which she hath filled fill to her double.

How much she hath glorified herself, and lived deliciously, so much torment and sorrow give her: for she saith in her heart, I sit a queen, and am no widow, and shall see no sorrow.

Therefore shall her plagues come in one day, death, and mourning, and famine; and she shall be utterly burned with fire: for strong is the Lord God who judgeth her.

And the kings of the earth, who have committed fornication and lived deliciously with her, shall bewail her, and lament for her, when they shall see the smoke of her burning,

Standing afar off for the fear of her torment, saying, Alas, alas, that great city Babylon, that mighty city! for in one hour is thy judgment come.

And the merchants of the earth shall weep and mourn over her; for no man buyeth their merchandise any more:

The merchandise of gold, and silver, and precious stones, and of pearls, and fine linen, and purple, and silk, and scarlet, and all thyine wood, and all manner of vessels of ivory, and all manner of vessels of most precious wood, and of brass, and iron, and marble,

And cinnamon, and odours, and ointments, and frankincense, and wine, and oil, and fine flour, and wheat, and beasts, and sheep, and horses, and chariots, and slaves, and souls of men.

And the fruits that thy soul lusted after are departed from thee, and all things which were dainty and goodly are departed from thee, and thou shalt find them no more at all.

The merchants of these things, which were made rich by her, shall stand afar off for the fear of her torment, weeping and wailing,

And saying, Alas, alas, that great city, that was clothed in fine linen, and purple, and scarlet, and decked with gold, and precious stones, and pearls!

For in one hour so great riches is come to nought. And every shipmaster, and all the company in ships, and sailors, and as many as trade by sea, stood afar off,

*And cried when they saw the smoke of her burning, saying,
What city is like unto this great city!*

*And they cast dust on their heads, and cried, weeping and
wailing, saying, Alas, alas, that great city, wherein were
made rich all that had ships in the sea by reason of her
costliness! for in one hour is she made desolate.*

*Rejoice over her, thou heaven, and ye holy apostles and
prophets; for God hath avenged you on her.*

*And a mighty angel took up a stone like a great millstone,
and cast it into the sea, saying, Thus with violence shall that
great city Babylon be thrown down, and shall be found no
more at all.*

*And the voice of harpers, and musicians, and of pipers, and
trumpeters, shall be heard no more at all in thee; and no
craftsman, of whatsoever craft he be, shall be found any more
in thee; and the sound of a millstone shall be heard no more
at all in thee;*

*And the light of a candle shall shine no more at all in thee;
and the voice of the bridegroom and of the bride shall be
heard no more at all in thee: for thy merchants were the great
men of the earth; for by thy sorceries were all nations
deceived.*

*And in her was found the blood of prophets, and of saints,
and of all that were slain upon the earth.*

Revelation 18

Why Babylon?

We now move to chapter 18 – once again we request or readers to read
the whole chapter before continuing.

Babylon: Why Babylon? What has the ancient city and Empire of
Babylon got in connection with our modern society?

To answer this it will be necessary to return again to the book of Daniel and investigate the meaning of an incident recorded in chapter 3, a dream recorded in chapter 4 and a vision know as the Writing Upon The Wall in chapter 5.

The city of Babylon was situated about 50 miles north of where the modern city of Baghdad is today. It was built by the Great Shah *Nebuchadnezzar*. The city was four square and the river Euphrates ran through the middle of it. According to Herodutus the walls were 56 miles in circumference, 335 feet high and 85 feet wide, almost as high as the post office tower in London, and, as high as some modern skyscrapers! A large part of the city consisted of beautiful parks and gardens. The chief building was the famous temple of Bel or Baal – the Babylonian God: In this city and over the Empire *Nebuchadnezzar* reigned supreme. To control such a vast empire would have meant the upkeep of a great army, but Nebuchadnezzar thought of a better idea, he realised that he who controlled the medium of exchange, that is, the money supply, controlled men's lives and the means of their livelihood. Nebuchadnezzar had build up a vast horde of gold, plundered from the vaults and temples of countries he had conquered, including all of the vessels from Gods temple build by Solomon.

Nebuchadnezzar set up the beginnings of our modern banking system, he made all transactions subject to the value of gold (the gold standard), therefore everyone who traded in goods or commerce of any kind had to borrow from him on the strength of gold *and pay interest on the loan to boot!*

Just like the banking system today! Except that today banks loan money which they don't have – called Bank Credit, which comes out of the end of a Bank Managers pen. Modern banks can loan up to 90 times their capital, 90 times more than they hold in 'real' cash, and its very survival based upon the continued creation of debt, no wonder the world is in such a state of chaos.

The Pillar of Gold

In Daniel chapter 3 Daniel informs us that Nebuchadnezzar made an image (standing Pillar or Monolith) of gold sixty cubits high and six cubits wide, in modern terms this would be 120 feet high and 12 feet square at the base in solid gold, and "set it up" on the plains of Dura in the province of Babylon. At the dedication ceremony, Nebuchadnezzar called all ranks of government officials from every province of his empire to the ceremony and commanded that, when summoned by the sound of musical instruments, they were to fall down and worship the gold standard. The penalty for failing to do so was to be 'cast into a burning fiery furnace'.

Daniel and his companions, Shadrach, Meshach and Abed-nego, refused to fall down and worship the image. Nebuchadnezzar had great respect for Daniel and his companions, but he warned them that the punishment would be carried out if they failed to bow down and worship the pillar. Daniel and his companions continued to refuse:

> *"Then was Nebuchadnezzar full of fury, and the form of his visage was changed against Shadrach, Meshach, and Abed-nego: therefore he spake, and commanded that they should heat the furnace one seven times more than it was wont to be heated."*
>
> *Daniel 3:19*

The furnace was heated '**Seven Times**' more than normal, and he commanded that Daniel and his companions be thrown into the furnace. The furnace was so hot that the heat of the fire slew those who threw them in, however, the furnace had no effect upon the three Hebrew youths. The king was surprised to see them walking about unharmed in the midst of the fire, as well as a fourth person whom he described as 'like the son of God'. He called them to 'come out', which they did, quite unharmed and in consequence of this miraculous deliverance, Nebuchadnezzar made a decree that anyone who said a word against the God of Daniel, Meshach, Shadrach and Abed-nego was to be put to death: "Because there is no other God that can deliver in this way" (Daniel 3:29).

Can we not see that this experience of Daniel and his companions seems to represent Israel's 'Seven Times' of being tempered in the fiery furnace of trial and testing in a hostile world, being subject to men's laws – political, economical, monetary and religious systems and yet in the moment of need those who refuse to bow down to these systems, the God of Israel is able to deliver them!

The Great Tree
Daniel Chapter 4

The story of Nebuchadnezzar continues with the king having a second dream which troubled him greatly. He called together all the magicians, astrologers and soothsayers and told them the dream, but they could not make known the meaning of it.

> *"But at the last Daniel came in before me, whose name was Belteshazzar, according to the name of my god, and in whom is the spirit of the holy gods: and before him I told the dream…,"*
>
> Daniel 4:8

Nebuchadnezzar explained the dream:

> *"Thus were the visions of mine head in my bed; I saw, and behold a tree in the midst of the earth, and the height thereof was great.*
>
> *The tree grew, and was strong, and the height thereof reached unto heaven, and the sight thereof to the end of all the earth:*
>
> *The leaves thereof were fair, and the fruit thereof much, and in it was meat for all: the beasts of the field had shadow under it, and the fowls of the heaven dwelt in the boughs thereof, and all flesh was fed of it.*
>
> *I saw in the visions of my head upon my bed, and, behold, a watcher and an holy one came down from heaven;*
>
> *He cried aloud, and said thus, Hew down the tree, and cut off his branches, shake off his leaves, and scatter his fruit: let the beasts get away from under it, and the fowls from his branches:*
>
> *Nevertheless leave the stump of his roots in the earth, even with a band of iron and brass, in the tender grass of the*

field; and let it be wet with the dew of heaven, and let his portion be with the beasts in the grass of the earth:

*Let his heart be changed from man's, and let a beast's heart be given unto him; and let **seven times** pass over him.*

This matter is by the decree of the watchers, and the demand by the word of the holy ones: to the intent that the living may know that the most High ruleth in the kingdom of men, and giveth it to whomsoever he will, and setteth up over it the basest of men."

Daniel 4:10 - 17
Emphasis added

Daniel informed the king that the tree which he had seen:

"It is thou, O king, that art grown and become strong: for thy greatness is grown, and reacheth unto heaven, and thy dominion to the end of the earth."

Daniel 4:22

Babylon's influence to Continue

And as for the tree being hewn down to a stump with a band of iron and brass: This represents the eventual collapse of the Babylonian Empire but *its influence would continue* in the two Empires represented by the bands of brass and iron – that is the Greek and Roman Empires, which were to follow it.

The Seven Times of Madness

The 'Seven Times' of madness which Nebuchadnezzar was to suffer was a mental condition called 'Lycanthropy' in which a person suffers from the delusion that he is a wolf or some other beast. Daniel warned Nebuchadnezzar that this condition would come upon him if he continued in his pride, and his sins, and did not show compassion on the poor, but Nebuchadnezzar forgot this warning.

At the end of twelve months, one day whilst walking upon the walls of the city of Babylon, he boasted:

> *"... Is not this great Babylon, that I have built for the house of the kingdom by **the might of my power**, and for the honour of **my** majesty?"*
>
> *Daniel 4:30*
> Emphasis added

And the moment this boastful declaration was made he began to suffer the 'Seven Times of madness".

> *"The same hour was the thing fulfilled upon Nebuchadnezzar: and he was driven from men, and did eat grass as oxen, and his body was wet with the dew of heaven, till his hairs were grown like eagles' feathers, and his nails like birds' claws."*
>
> *Daniel 4:33*

After the seven times (seven years) had elapsed Nebuchadnezzar's sanity returned unto him:

> *"And at the end of the days I Nebuchadnezzar lifted up mine eyes unto heaven, and mine understanding returned unto me, and I blessed the most High, and I praised and honoured him that liveth for ever..."*
>
> *Daniel 4:34*

> *"Now I Nebuchadnezzar praise and extol and honour the King of heaven, all whose works are truth, and his ways judgment: **and those that walk in pride he is able to abase.**"*
>
> *Daniel 4:37*
> Emphasis added

Nebuchadnezzar learned the hard way that all our blessings, wealth and achievements are gifts of the God of Heaven.

It seems that the 'Seven Times of madness' which was to pass upon Nebuchadnezzar represented 2,520 years of economic madness which would stem from Babylon's monetary system based upon the gold standard and which has influenced the worlds economy since that time. But after seven times or 2,520 years the world would return to the sanity of the Lords divine economic and monetary system, which was revealed to Moses and which will be re-introduced under the rule of Jesus Christ in the Seventh Millennium.

The bands of brass and iron which were around the stump of the tree represents the gentile powers which would adopt the Babylonian monetary system, which continues in our modern banking and monetary systems to this day.

We are all suffering the madness of this system, but one day soon the world will regain its sanity. This man-made system will collapse, and mankind will acknowledge the God of Heaven and His laws.

The Writing on the Wall

Daniel Chapter 5
The fifth chapter of Daniel tells of a great festival held in the royal palace in the city of Babylon, the night in which Babylon fell to the armies of the Medes and Persians led by the great general Cyrus in 534 BC.

King Belshazzar, grandson of Nebuchadnezzar, made a great feast for a thousand of his Lords, and while he tasted the wine, commanded that the vessels of Gold and Silver which had been taken out of the temple in Jerusalem be brought, that he and his lords, his wives and concubines might drink from them. They drank the wine, "and praised the gods of *Gold* and of *Silver*, of brass, iron, wood and stone".

These blasphemous revelries were suddenly cut short when, "In the same hour came forth fingers of a man's hand, and wrote over against the candlestick upon the plaister of the wall of the king's palace: and the king saw the part of the hand that wrote." (Daniel 5:5).

The apparition terrified the king so much "that his limbs gave way and his knees knocked together".

This feasting and drinking by Belshazzar and his lords, just before the fall of ancient Babylon, has its counterpart in our Lord's prophecy:

> *"For as in the days that were before the flood they were eating and drinking, marrying and giving in marriage, until the day that Noe entered into the ark,*
>
> *And knew not until the flood came, and took them all away; so shall also the coming of the Son of man be."*
> *Matthew 24:38, 39*

We notice that Belshazzar called for the holy vessels plundered from the Lords temple, so that he and his revellers could drink from them, after which they praised the gods of gold, silver, brass, iron. This could foreshadow the modern contempt for the true church, and the rejection of spiritual values in favour of the god of money and worldly pleasures.

With regard to the writing on the wall, God always speaks to men in a language they understand. The Babylonians understood money. The inscription was in Chaldean, their own language, so the Lord was making sure they would understand the message.

Mene, Mene, Tekel, Upharsin

> *"And this is the writing that was written, MENE, MENE, TEKEL, UPHARSIN.*
>
> *This is the interpretation of the thing: MENE; God hath numbered thy kingdom, and finished it.*

TEKEL; Thou art weighed in the balances, and art found wanting.

PERES; Thy kingdom is divided, and given to the Medes and Persians."

Daniel 5:25 - 28

For interpreting the inscription Belshazzar clothed Daniel in scarlet and placed a chain of gold about his neck, and proclaimed him to be the third ruler in the kingdom.

Nabonidus the father of Belshazzar had relinquished the throne and made his son co-regent in his place, therefore Daniel was proclaimed to be the 3rd ruler in the kingdom of Babylon, but Daniel knew it was to be short lived for,

*"In that night was Belshazzar the king of the Chaldeans slain.
And Darius the Median took the kingdom, being about threescore and two years old."*

Daniel 5:30 – 31

The Interpretation

The inscription actually contains a string of weight names; from the JST Bible Dictionary under *Mene mene tekel upharsin* we are informed: "It can be literally translated" numbered, weighted and divisions. Possibly the words are names of weights, "a mina, a mina, a shekel and a half" (mina).

The last word in the inscription is given as *upharsin* which is a make up of the Aramaic conjunction U- and Pharsin, the plural of Paras, and since only the consonants were written in ancient Hebrew and Aramaic, the Word Paras could also be written Peres which means divided.

"The *gerah* was the smallest weight used among the Hebrews and amounted to the twentieth part of a Shekel". This statement is taken out of the authorised Kings James translation of the Holy Bible under Weights, Measures, Coinage and references to its value can be found in Exodus 30:31, Leviticus 27:25, Num 3:47 and Numbers 18:16.

The **Shekel** was valued at twenty Gerahs.

The **Mene** (sometimes called Maneh) was an Aramaic word and the equivalent in Hebrew is Mina and according to the JST Bible Dictionary page 789 this is valued at a fixed fifty Shekels, and sometimes referred to as a Pound, in the New Testament. "From the Phoenicians the word Mina passed on to the Greeks who pronounced it MNA, and to the Italians who pronounced it MINA" (AV Concordance).

1 Shekel = 20 Gerahs
1 Mina = 50 Shekels or 1000 Gerahs

Therefore the total value in Gerahs is signified by the writing was:

Mina	=	1000	Gerahs
Mina	=	1000	Gerahs
Shekel	=	20	Gerahs
Half Mina	=	500	Gerahs
Total		2520	Gerahs

It can hardly be coincidental that this figure of 2,520 is the same as the number given in dozens of other illustrations of Biblical prophecy of 'Seven Times' and the same number denoted by the 'Seven Times' of Nebuchadnezzar's madness in Daniel chapter 4. its significance is obvious; it suggests that we are to reckon this same number of years from the fall of Babylon 539 BC Ushers Dating – Bible dictionary.

However, information in the British museum, has been cited by chronologists as confirming the date of 536 BC as the first year of Cyrus, King of Persia, and the fall of Babylon as 534 BC. This is also confirmed by modern revelation (D&C 20:1), which makes the birth of Christ 1 BC as opposed to Usher's reckoning of 5 BC. Babylon fell to the Medes and Persians in the week 10th – 19th October 534 BC.

This is a fixed terminal date for Biblical time prophecy and is connected to the Babylonian monetary system.

19 October 534 BC------------2520 years-------------19 October 1987 AD

It is significant that just as ancient Babylon fell 2,520 years ago so would its influence begin to collapse in 1987 AD.

It is also significant that on the 19th October 1987 there was a great collapse of the world stock markets. The Seven Times prophecy fulfilled to the very day!

This event was preceded by a great wind, which caused the destruction of 50 million trees in Britain and Europe beside other damage caused by floods and to property. These events commenced on Friday 16th October 1987.

These events were seen by Ezekiel 2,500 years ago (Ezekiel 13:1 - 15)!

¹AND the word of the LORD came unto me, saying,

²Son of man, prophesy against the prophets of Israel that prophesy, and say thou unto them that prophesy out of their own hearts, Hear ye the word of the LORD;

³Thus saith the Lord GOD; Woe unto the foolish prophets, that follow their own spirit, and have seen nothing!

⁴O Israel, thy prophets are like the foxes in the deserts.

⁵Ye have not gone up into the gaps, neither made up the hedge for the house of Israel to stand in the battle in the day of the LORD.

⁶They have seen vanity and lying divination, saying, The LORD saith: and the LORD hath not sent them: and they have made others to hope that they would confirm the word.

⁷Have ye not seen a vain vision, and have ye not spoken a lying divination, whereas ye say, The LORD saith it; albeit I have not spoken?

[8]Therefore thus saith the Lord GOD; Because ye have spoken vanity, and seen lies, therefore, behold, I am against you, saith the Lord GOD.

[9]And mine hand shall be upon the prophets that see vanity, and that divine lies: they shall not be in the assembly of my people, neither

shall they be written in the writing of the house of Israel, neither shall they benter into the land of Israel; and ye shall know that I am the Lord GOD.

[10]Because, even because they have seduced my people, saying, Peace; and there was no peace; **and one built up a wall, and, lo, others daubed it with untempered mortar.**

[11]Say unto them which daub it with untempered morter, that it shall fall: there shall be an overflowing shower; and ye, O great hailstones, shall fall; **and a stormy wind shall rend it.**

[12]Lo, when the wall is fallen, shall it not be said unto you, Where is the daubing wherewith ye have daubed it?

[13]Therefore thus saith the Lord GOD; **I will even rend it with a stormy wind in my fury;** *and there shall be an overflowing shower in mine anger, and great hailstones in my fury to consume it.*

[14]So will I break down the wall that ye have daubed with untempered mortar, **and bring it down to the ground, so that the foundation thereof shall be discovered, and it shall fall,** *and ye shall be consumed in the midst thereof: and ye shall know that I am the LORD.*

[15]Thus will I accomplish my wrath upon the wall, and upon them that have daubed it with untempered mortar, and will

say unto you, The wall is no more, neither they that daubed it.

Ezekiel 13:1 - 15
Emphasis added

The Wall of Untempered Mortar

The 'foolish prophets' mentioned in this chapter are those who in our own day – politicians, bankers, world financiers and false religious leaders who have seduced the people into thinking the crisis is over; giving the world a false sense of security.

> *"...and they have made others to hope that they would confirm the word."*
>
> *Ezekiel 13:6*

> *"...and one built up a wall, and, lo, others daubed it with untempered mortar..."*
>
> *Ezekiel 13:10*

Untempered mortar has no adhesion – therefore no matter how much they plaster up the cracks of this banking and monetary system it won't last.

> *"Say unto them which daub it with untempered morter, that it shall fall: there shall be an overflowing shower; and ye, O great hailstones, shall fall; and a stormy wind shall rend it."*
>
> *Ezekiel 13:11*

The 'wall' shall fall and be accompanied with a mighty wind and storm, and overflowing shower and great hailstones (see Jeremiah 25:31 - 33)!

> *"Therefore thus saith the Lord GOD; I will even rend it with a stormy wind in my fury; and there shall be an overflowing shower in mine anger, and great hailstones in my fury to consume it.*
>
> *So will I break down the wall that ye have daubed with untempered morter, and bring it down to the ground, so*

> *that the foundation thereof shall be
> discovered,* *and it shall fall, and ye shall be consumed
> in the midst thereof: and ye shall know that I am the*
> LORD.
>
> *... and will say unto you, The wall is no more, neither
> they that daubed it;"*
>
>

Ezekiel 13:13 - 15
Emphasis added
>

Wall Street

Well, the interpretation is clear. The Wall represents Wall Street the
'control centre' of world finance and stock markets.

The events of 19th October 1987 was just the beginning! The Lord has
said that not only the wall will go but that he will seek out and destroy
the very foundations of the wall (or system). And when 'wall street'
finally falls all the other world finance and stock markets will fall with it.

It is not yet also another coincidence that the centre for finance in Britain
is found in Threadneedle Street! The Lord said it would be easier for a
camel to go through the eye of a needle than for a rich man to enter into
the Kingdom of Heaven (Matthew 16:24).

The fall of 'Babylon the Great' in Revelation chapter 18 begins with an
angel calling with a mighty voice:

> *"Babylon the great is fallen, is fallen!"*

And declares the kings of the earth shall mourn saying, "Alas! Alas! Thou
great city, thou mighty city of Babylon! **In one hour** is thy judgement
come, and the merchants of the earth weep and mourn for her, since no
one buys her cargo anymore."

God declares that this 'modern' Babylon is full of devils 'foul spirits' of
all kinds, and a cage full of every unclean thing. **All** nations have
participated in her fornication. The merchants of the earth have waxed
rich through the use of this ungodly system. Only the rich and merchants
of the earth will mourn when this Babylonian monetary and finance

system collapses. God's people are told not to be involved with it or if they are involved to "come out of her" (Revelation 18:4.

> *"Go ye out from Babylon. Be ye clean that bear the vessels*
> *of the Lord.*
> *Go ye out from among the nations, even from Babylon,*
> *from the midst of wickedness, which is spiritual Babylon."*
> D&C 133:5, 14

> **"…for in one hour is thy judgment come."**
> *Revelation 18:10*
> Emphasis added

In particular, the prophecy appears to deal with 'economic Babylon' which is still flourishing; a system of the giving and taking of usury (interest); a system where the cost of goods increases and the value of money 'decreases' a system where international financiers can make millions, even billions of pounds/dollars for the cost of a telephone call' a system which flourishes on debt, and requires a war every generation to create 'new debt' a system which makes the 'poor poorer and the rich richer' a system totally opposed to the Divine laws of God given to Israel at Sinai.

"One hour", using our prophetical time principal represents 15 years. And 15 years from 1987 brings us to 2002 AD! The Babylonian monetary system cannot survive, a world banking collapse has many times been predicted' is it possible that we shall live to witness the fall of economic Babylon the Great after that year?

We are living in the transitory period of 15 years. For many years now modern prophets have been warning us to prepare ourselves both physically (in our food storage programme) and spiritually for these great events predicted by John, which are to come upon this earth, and may already be here.

1987 AD----------------------15 years----------------------------2002 AD

11th September 2001

Since then of course we have witnessed the terrible events of 11th September 2001 when the twin towers of the World Trade Center were destroyed by terrorist action.

Since then the area which was occupied by the Twin Towers has become to be known as 'Ground Zero'!

"So that the foundation thereof shall be discovered". Did Ezekiel foresee this all those years ago? I wonder if this event is a 'harbinger' of things to come?

One hour of prophetical time from 11th September 2001 brings us to 2015/6.

2001 AD------------------------15 years--------------------------2015/6 AD

The years 2015/6 coincides with the year of Israel's **490th Sabbatical** and **70th Jubilee** from the year of the Exodus in 1486 BC.

The Jubilee took place every 50th year. It was a Pentecostal Sabbath following the seventh Sabbatical year. The laws relating to the Sabbaths can be found in Leviticus 25. Also in the Bible Dictionary under Sabbatical Year and Jubilee Year.

16
THE ASTOUNDING PROPHECY OF MATTHEW 18

"Then came Peter to him, and said, Lord, how oft shall my brother sin against me, and I forgive him? **till seven times?***

Jesus saith unto him, I say not unto thee, **Until** *seven times: but,* **Until seventy times seven.***

Matthew 18:21 - 22
Emphasis added

This sounds like an innocent statement and answer to Peter's question. But the Saviour never made any statement that did not have a significant meaning.

Peter referred to 'Seven Times' because he knew that, that period of 'time' was the period allocated for one to work out his repentance, and acknowledge his sins in order to receive forgiveness, and be reconciled to God and his brother.

So what was the real meaning?

70 x 7 = 490 Times

"Unto" or until, means exactly **to, not** beyond. But why stop at 490 times – why not forgive 500 times or 690 times?

Why didn't the Saviour say 90 times 7 or 80 times 5 or 100 times 9?

70 times 7 wasn't a number He just picked out of a hat.

A Period Of Perfection
490 Times is a period of preparation. This period was given in a revelation to the prophet Daniel as a preparation for the Jews to receive

their Messiah (see Daniel 9:24). In this prophecy 490 Times was given as 70 weeks (70 x 7 = 490).

We also find this same period used in Genesis 4:24 and in the Book of Jasher (Jasher 2:26 - 37).

A Period of Correction

490 was also a period of correction. It was due to the House of Israel and Judah failing to keep the law of the Sabbaths that they were taken captive into Babylon for 70 years, "so that the land could enjoy its Sabbaths".

> *"And them that had escaped from the sword carried he away to Babylon; where they were servants to him and his sons until the reign of the kingdom of Persia:*
>
> *To fulfil the word of the LORD by the mouth of Jeremiah, until the land had enjoyed her sabbaths: for as long as she lay desolate she kept sabbath, to fulfil threescore and ten years."*
>
> 2 Chronicles 36:20 - 21
> See also Jeremiah 25:12 and Daniel 9:2

This, of course, was referring to the Land Sabbaths which occurred every seventh year – followed by a Jubilee every 50ᵗʰ year.

If they were to be punished for 70 years so that the land could enjoy its Sabbaths – *for how long had they neglected to keep the law of the land Sabbaths and Jubilees?*

Yes, for 490 years (70 x 7 years) since the days of King David 1080 BC!

But What Is The Point?

What has all this got to do with the Saviour's reply to Peter regarding forgiveness?

That's a good question. And I must admit it puzzled me for a long time. I knew the reply had a deeper symbolic meaning. I also decided it was related to the Sabbaths. But how?

The Number of Spiritual Perfection Intensified

It meant nothing to me – until one day I mused to myself – what would happen if I intensified 490 by 7 again? I wrote it down.

490 x 7 = 3,430 years!

Even that meant nothing to me for a while until I discovered that 3,430 years *consisted of 490 Sabbaticals!* Thereby giving the Saviour's statement of forgiveness its greater spiritual meaning.

The Four Perfect Numbers

These are 3, 7, 10 and 12.

3 is the number of the Godhead – meaning completeness.

7 is the number of Spiritual Perfection.

10 is the number of Ordinal Perfection.

12 is the number of Governmental Perfection.

490 is a combination of 10 and 7.

7 x 10 = 70
70 x 7 = 490

We find these same four perfect numbers used in the order of Heaven.

3 x 7 x 10 x 12 = 2,520

And the number 2,520 is in itself a number of completeness.

In His statement the Saviour intensified both the numbers 10 and 7.

The Order of Heaven

The Heavens

Now for astronomical proof that God's Times are periods of 360 years.

This shows a pathway round the heavens passing through 12 constellations en route.

The hands of the great clock are the Sun – Moon – Stars which appear to move slowly though the heavenly clock occasionally eclipsing each other on route.

On this giant clock there is one period formed by solar eclipses which create a cycle of 360 days (36 x 10) and another also formed by solar eclipses, which produce a cycle of 360 years.

Hence we see that these facts not only produce an astronomical time of 360 years, but demonstrate that a day for a year is both astronomical as well as a scriptural computation planned by an all-wise creator.

The number 2,520 is the lowest common multiple of all the numbers:

$$1 - 2 - 3 - 4 - 5 - 6 - 7 - 8 - 9 - 10$$

It is a fundamental and astronomical number and also a prophetical number of great importance in all God's creative design and works. The zodiac displays numbers in a remarkable fashion:

12 signs with 3 constellations = 36 plus the 12 signs = 48
12 is the one of the perfect numbers.
3 signifies completeness
7 spiritual perfection
10 perfection of divine order
12 perfection in government (12 tribes – 12 apostles – 12 patriarchs)

360 degrees arises out of 4 numbers: 3 x 4 x 5 x 6 = 360 and 360 x 7 = 2,520.

No one can tell us why the number of degrees were fixed at 360. However, it is accepted universally without question and is the year, which is used in all prophecies of the Bible.

Law of the Sabbaths

The numbers 7 – 10 – 70 – 49 (7 x 7) figure prominently in the Law of Sabbaths. The Sabbaths were organized in sevens.

1). **The 7th Day**
Deuteronomy 5:12 - 14
Exodus 31:14 - 15
Exodus 35:2

2). **The 7th Week** (or 7 x 7) = 49 days
Leviticus 25

During the first sacred calendar month of *Abib* or *Nisan* this 49th day from Passover was followed by Pentecost or Feast of First Fruits the 50th day.
Both 49th and 50th day were Sabbaths.

3). **The 7th Month**

Which contained three sacred festivals

4). **The 7th Year** (Land Sabbath and the Year of Release) Deuteronomy 15:1-10

A one year sabbatical also a land and financial Sabbath
Leviticus 25:2 - 7, 18 - 22
Exodus 23:10,11

5). **The 7th x 7th Year or 49th Year** Leviticus 25:35 - 38
Deuteronomy 15:1 - 11

Followed by a Jubilee Year.

6). **The 50th Year – A Jubilee Sabbath**

Leviticus 25:8 - 16

A Pentecostal Sabbath. A year of Liberty

The Jubilee
A year of reconciliation between all people in Israel. Between man and man, and also between man and State.

Men released all slaves.
The State released all prisoners.
ALL property returned to its proper owner.
ALL debts were released.
It was a year of liberty – a new beginning.

Then the 49-year cycle started all over again.

What a wonderful law!

Can you imagine a wonderful world this would be if we were keeping this law today?

At first (for many years) I was influenced by the 'experts' (scholars) who concluded that the 50th year of the Jubilee was the first year in the count for a new 49-year cycle. *But this is entirely wrong.* The 50th year of Jubilee was the **end** of a 49-year cycle and *the year after* the Jubilee was the *beginning* of a new 49-year cycle.

Therefore there are 70 Sabbaticals and 10 Jubilees to each cycle of 500 years.

70 x 7 = 490 years plus 10 Jubilees = 500 years
7 x 490 = 3,430 years plus 70 Jubilees = 3,500 years

And in those 3,500 years there are 490 Sabbaticals and 70 Jubilees (70 x 7)!

The count for the 3,500 years began when the law of the Sabbaths were given at Sinai (Exodus 31). And the dates for the exodus are given as:

Year of Exodus	490th Sabbatical	70th Jubilee
1491 BC	2009 AD	2010 AD
1490 BC	2010 AD	2011 AD
1498 BC	2011 AD	2012 AD
1488 BC	2012 AD	2013 AD
1487 BC	2013 AD	2014 AD
1486 BC	2014 AD	2015 AD

Due to the Jubilee years being counted in **addition** to the Sabbatical years. This would make the year 2014 AD the 490th Sabbatical and 2015 AD the 70th Jubilee, counting from 1486 BC as the exodus year.

By adding one year to the count for crossing of BC years to AD years will make the year 2015 AD the 490th Sabbatical and 2016 AD the 70th Jubilee.

I have good reasons for selecting the year 1486 BC as the year of the Exodus, as shown on the chart *Biblical Time Prophecies*.

The 3,500 year period expiring with the 70th Jubilee in the year 2016 AD coinciding with the Seven Times period of 2,520 years from 506 BC – the year in which the Jews rebuild the Temple in Jerusalem.

Could the 490th Sabbatical and 70th Jubilee also be a year of liberty and reconciliation between Jews and Palestinians?

Could we also see the re-building of the ancient Temple in Jerusalem?

The Great Prophetic Week of Years

Year of Exodus

1486 BC
> 500 years **Day 1** of 70 Sabbaticals and 10 Jubilees

986 BC
> 500 years **Day 2** of 70 Sabbaticals and 10 Jubilees

486 BC
> 500 years **Day 3** of 70 Sabbaticals and 10 Jubilees

14 AD
> 500 years **Day 4** of 70 Sabbaticals and 10 Jubilees

514 AD
> 50 years **Day 5** of 70 Sabbaticals and 10 Jubilees

1014 AD
> 500 years **Day 6** of 70 Sabbaticals and 10 Jubilees

1514 AD
> 500 years **Day 7** of 70 Sabbaticals and 10 Jubilees

2014 AD

490th Sabbatical	70th Jubilee
2015 AD	2016 AD

Adding one year to the count for crossing of BC years to AD years

Fig 26. The Great Prophetic Week of Years

Now, if these are all unrelated events. Then the exercise has not done us any harm. On the other hand, if these events and conclusions are related then they have a significant meaning for us today.

And should alert us into action!

It has been said:

If something happens once it is an accident,
If twice it may be a coincidence,
If three times **or more it is a fact**.

And the fact is – That the 7th Millennium Sabbath of 1000 years is with us now. We are approaching the climax of the age.

Have we reached a point of time when a new beginning – a true year of liberty – a year of reconciliation with Israel's God is to take place?

Figure 27. Biblical Time Prophecy

Section 4:

Jesus Christ Triumphant

17
THE STORY OF SNOW WHITE

The 19th chapter of the Book of Revelation is the climax to our story.

As in most folklore tales the beautiful princess is captured by the dragon and taken captive to his lair, she is kept there for many years and is despaired of ever being rescued, but eventually a handsome prince on a white horse comes along, slays the dragon, and rescues the princess, whisking her up on his horse they ride away into the sunset to his castle in the sky, are married, and live happily ever after.

The originator of the folklore stories captured the whole story of the Book of Revelation in his tale Snow White and the Seven Dwarfs, although the same story is told with a different flavour in many others.

Snow White and the Seven Dwarfs

Within the fabric of this tale is a Queen's daughter (Snow White) who was turned out of her palace by a jealous stepmother and left to wander in the 'forest' or woods, is woven the story of the Lost House of Israel. This 'fairy tale' does indeed carry a profound message, and a familiar one to those who make a thorough study of the Bible and the wanderings of the House of Israel.

This simple story tells us in vibrant imagery the adventures of the woman – Israel (Snow White) and her migration out of Assyria across the 'wilderness' of northern Europe – through Germany and on to England. It is the prophecies of Hosea, Isaiah, Amos, Micah, Jeremiah, Daniel, Ezekiel and John the Revelator. *All wrapped into one!*

The Saxon seer who first related the story should stand next to these prophets – more especially John the Revelator, so intimate is his theme with that contained in the Book of Revelation. It is the story of Israel and her ultimate destiny. The story delights the ears of children, yet for those who have "ears to hear" and "eyes to see", there is an inner and deeper meaning. In Snow White we recognise Israel. A clue to her name is found in Isaiah 1:18:

> *"Come now, and let us reason together, saith the LORD: though your sins be as scarlet, they shall be as **white as snow**; though they be red like crimson, they shall be as wool."*
>
> *Isaiah 1:18*

For those of our readers who wish to read the story the rest of the characters are identified as follows:

The wicked stepmother	Babylon, Mother of Harlots and its counterpart of Rome
The forest	Israel's Wilderness period of correction
The little cottage in the forest which Snow White discovered	England or the Island of Britain
The seven dwarfs	The Seven Angels
The seven candlesticks used by the dwarfs to light the cottage	The true church of Jesus Christ
The seven beds in the cottage which Snow White tried	The Seven Times of Israel's punishment or Period of Correction for breaking her 'vows' to her husband. A period of 2,520 years from 721 BC to 1800 AD
The last of the seven beds which suited Snow White	Seven is the number of Spiritual Perfection. Israel's redemption and reconciliation with her God in her island cottage home after her period of correction was completed in 1800 AD
The Queen: Who disguised herself as an old peddler woman	Rome: Disguised as the true church. Who sold Snow White some laces

	for her stay? And who assisted Snow White to lace up her stay, and pulled it so tight Snow White passed out and was left for dead. But was *'revived'* by the Seven Dwarfs (Hosea 6:1 - 2)
The Queen: Who disguised herself as a farmers wife and sold Snow White a poisoned comb and a poisoned apple	Rome: Ecclesiastical Babylon the Great full of poison and false doctrines
The poisoned Comb	Snow White's hair represents Israel's spiritual strength, which Rome attempted to destroy though its power and doctrines. And the attempted subjugation by the use of force by Spain's Armada and Napoleon. These attempts failed, so a third attempt was made
The piece of poisoned apple which stuck in Snow White's throat	Again Rome: And its doctrines which seemed to cause the death of Snow White (Israel Britain), for which the Seven Dwarfs could find no cure, and Snow White was placed in a glass coffin and taken to a hilltop, where she lay for years and years, until the piece of poisoned apple was jolted out when she was found by her prince
The prince: Who fell in love with and was betrothed to Snow White	The Saviour Jesus Christ

In the story Snow White succumbs three times to the whiles of the jealous Queen. The Queen is thrice angry when she looks into her magic mirror and discovers Snow White is still alive and living in the forest with the dwarfs.

The First Attempt

The dwarfs were able to 'revive' the stricken princess, loosening the laces, which had caused her to lapse into unconsciousness. The awakening of Snow White is dramatised in English History as the Acts of Reformation and the Act of Supremacy, which made Henry VIII of England himself the head of the Church of England, rather than the Pope (1509 AD). The Acts of Reformation passed by parliament stopped the flow of money form the Churches out of England into the pockets of the Pope. That problems within the church should be settled in English courts, and gave the King power to appoint his own Bishops. In 1547 AD under Edward VI, England became even more Protestant abandoning crucifixes, images and the worship of relics. A new prayer book was written in English instead of Latin.

The Second Attempt

The princess is overcome by the scheming Queen through the use of a poisoned comb. The comb is associated with Spain being an important part of hair dress of the women of Spain. This then relates to England's history with Spain.

In 1553 AD Edward VI died and his sister Mary Tudor, known as Bloody Mary, took the throne. Mary was a 'die in the wool' Catholic. Mary made parliament agree to repeal the Act of Supremacy and England again came under the influence of Rome.

In order to strengthen the cause of Rome she married Philip II of Spain, also a Roman Catholic, and began to change the ritual of the church back to the Roman pattern: Hugh Latimer, Bishop of Worcester and Nicholas Ridley, Bishop of Rochester, were burned at the stake for refusing to accept the Pope's authority, also many thousands of Protestants gave their lives during this period as martyrs of the faith. However, England was saved form this second malady by the sudden death of Mary Tudor, and the ascension to the throne by Elizabeth I.

Elizabeth defied the Pope, refused to wed Philip who sought her hand (for political purposes), and returned England to the Protestant faith. In response Philip sent a huge Armada to subjugate and punish her, but by the mighty Hand of the God of Israel the attempt failed. After the second attempt with the poisoned comb, when the Queen arrived home she went home to her mirror and said:

> "Mirror, mirror, here I stand
> Who is the fairest in the land?"

And the mirror answered as before:

> "You Oh Queen, are the fairest here,
> But Snow White, who has gone to stay
> With the Seven Dwarfs far, far away,
> Is a thousand times more fair."

When she heard the mirror say that, she trembled and shook with rage. "Snow White must die!" she cried.

"Even if it costs me my own life". It was then that she went to a secret room and made a very poisonous apple. It looked so nice on the outside, white with red cheeks, that anyone who saw it would want it. When the apple was ready, she stained her face and disguised herself as a peasant woman. And again she made her way across the *'Seven Mountains'* to the cottage of the dwarfs.

The Third Attempt

The dwarfs had admonished Snow White to stay indoors, and not to have anything to do with people who came knocking on the cottage door selling things. Had she heeded the warning, Snow White might have avoided the third malady, which was more deadly than any that had preceded it. This was the 'poisoned apple' for which the dwarfs could find no cure. No sooner had Snow White taken a bite she fell to the floor as if dead. Though the apple looked a good apple and was very tempting, it proved itself to be a poisoned apple. So do lies and deceptions take the form of truth?

> *"Having a form of godliness, but denying the power thereof..."*
>
> *2 Timothy 3:5*

The Symbolism

The poisoned apple which Israel Britain will die of and which the Seven Angels cannot cure will prove to be her involvement in the newly formed federation of Europe under the Treaty of Rome. It all looks so very tempting just now.

This will represent the third time the wicked Queen disguised in various ways has crossed the Seven Mountains of Rome (and Rome is literally surrounded by seven mountains) in an attempt to subjugate Israel Britain, its throne and monarchy.

Ancient Israel was warned long ago by an all-wise God not to make any pacts, vows or treaties with foreign nations, as this would lead them into slavery again (Exodus 23:32, 33).

Of course it is because the Anglo-Saxon-Celtic nations are blind to their identity that they heed not this warning. But that blindness is about to be removed; in the meantime it seems we shall have to learn the hard way!

And so in our story we find Snow White being placed in a coffin made of glass by the seven dwarfs, beautiful but inanimate, asleep to await the coming of the Prince.

But the Prince does come. The Prince loves the Princess, *even in her sleep*!

The final story, which captures the heart and imagination of every child who hears it, is the wondrous love of the Prince for the Princess, and his determination to take her with him at whatever cost *even though she is unaware of His love*. But by a miracle, as the Prince's servants were carrying the glass coffin down the mountain, they stumbled over a root. The jolt dislodged the piece of poisoned apple out of Snow White's throat, and Snow White revives, and a great marriage feast is prepared. They are married and live happily ever after.

Here we see the similarity of the story with that contained in the 19th chapter of Revelation, which describes the coming of the Prince on a white horse.

> *"... and behold a white horse; and he that sat upon him*
> *was called Faithful and True..."*
> Revelation 19:11

And we read there also of the rejoicing at the marriage feast.

> *"Let us be glad and rejoice, and give honour to him: for*
> *the marriage of the Lamb is come, and his wife hath made*
> *herself ready.*
>
> *And to her was granted that she should be arrayed in fine*
> *linen, clean and white: for the fine linen is the*
> *righteousness of saints.*
>
> *And he saith unto me, Write, Blessed are they which are*
> *called unto the marriage supper of the Lamb. And he*
> *saith unto me, these are the true sayings of God."*
> Revelation 19:7 - 9

Before this joyous event can happen it seems that it will only be Jesus Christ and His servants who can dislodge Israel's trance like condition of seemingly hypnotic blindness. It is going to require that the Anglo-Saxon-Celtic nations receive some kind of jolt for this to happen – some kind of shock treatment before she is able to come to her senses!

God does move in mysterious ways His wonders to perform. He has a gentle hand fixed upon Israel's destiny and upon all the Overcomers.

Israel is being prepared for the coming marriage ceremony when the glorious prince shall come and claim His bride.

18
THE GREAT AWAKENING

Nearly thirty five hundred years ago the nation of Israel gathered at the foot of Mount Sinai where they were organised into a kingdom. There they received laws that they were enjoined to administer – laws covering every phase of human activity. The moral code contained in the Ten Commandments has been the standard of personal conduct among civilised people: likewise the laws of national administration contained in the Statutes and Judgements given to them by almighty God are just as perfect, and the day is near when nations must recognise these laws if they would establish righteousness and peace.

Summary of Laws Contained in the Statutes and Judgements

The Law contained in the Statutes
These were the laws governing the civil administration of the nation of Israel. Briefly they applied to the following:

1 Economics
2 Finance
3 Interest
4 Debt
5 Inflation
6 Revenue
7 Taxation and Tax Exemption
8 Government Organisation
9 Education
10 Home, Property and land Ownership
11 Laws pertaining to Land, Agriculture, Husbandry, Cattle
12. Laws governing War, Defence, Conscription
13. Health, Sanitation and Food (Dietary) Holy Festivals (Holidays)
14 Social Security Offerings
15 Laws governing Weights and measures
16 Management and Labour

17 Servants and Slaves
18 Laws governing the Individual and Family
19 Marriage and Divorce
20 Business Transactions
21 Compensation for Injuries (Law of Restitution)
22 Courts of Appeal
23 Witnesses
24 Naturalisation of Foreigners
25 Wills and Inheritance
26 Views, Pacts, Treaties
27 Laws governing the Sabbaths, Annual Holy Festivals (Holidays) and Offerings
28 Retirement
29 Capital Punishment
30 All other penalties for Law Breaking

The Laws Contained in the Judgements

These were the Judicial Laws dealing with offenders, such as broke the Statutes and Laws governing the people.

1. Murder
2. Manslaughter.
3. Rape
4. Kidnapping
5. Witchcraft
6. Idolatry
7. Disobedience to parents
8. Adultery
9. Homosexuality
10. Incest – Bestiality
11. Blasphemy, Talebearers, Gossip
12. Theft, Robbery, Muggings
13. Embezzlement, Fraud, Bribery
14. Rioting, Lawlessness
15. Compensation of injuries
16. Sabbath Breaking
17. Disobeying Decisions of Courts

The Carnal Law

The Laws Contained in the Ordinances

Consisted of the sacrificial ordinance of the blood sacrifices and ritualistic ceremonies performed by the Aaronic Priesthood. To teach and install into the people the habit of obedience. This 'law' was the schoolmaster which would bring them to Christ (Galatians 3: 19-21)

These are therefore five divisions of Law.

1. The Law of the Gospel:
   Ecclesiastical laws and ordinances administered by the Melchizedec Priesthood

2. The Ten Commandments:
   Constitutional and moral laws

3. The Statutes
   The Civil Laws

4. The Judgements:
   The Judicial Laws

5. The Ordinances and Performances:
   Ordinances and Performances of the Aaronic and Levitical Priesthoods pertaining to blood sacrifice and offerings.

This brief summary has been given to acquaint the readers in the scope of the Laws given to the Israel nation at Sinai. The usual reaction to this is: Do you mean to say that all the items mentioned here in the Statutes and Judgements are all covered in the Old Testament law?

The answer is yes, and the scope of the law was even more comprehensive, but it is not the object of this book to examine these laws, to do so would take many volumes, but the reader must be aware of the divisions of law given at Sinai, the scope of them covering every facet of national and individual conduct.

God requires modern Israel to awaken to her identity and restore these fundamental laws and thus demonstrate their perfection through their operation.

Men are accepting a false philosophy when they teach that they can make law. No one would dream of applying such a doctrine to laws governing the physical universe.

Experience has taught man that he cannot legislate contrary to the God given moral code and hope to escape suffering, it is because man is lacking in such a real understanding of the facts that he thinks he can with immunity to himself, change economic and administrative policies regardless of the fundamental laws governing their operation. The very fact that man suffers is evidence that he has legislated contrary to those principals. The laws given at Sinai are as fixed and rigid as the laws governing the physical manifestations of nature, and the full benefit of the law accrues to man when he complies with its requirements, while their violation brings confusion and trouble.

We have here an axiom of truth. Where there is confusion, suffering, poverty and trouble, these fundamental principles of righteousness have been violated.

The Lord knew that men would attempt to change or tamper with His divine laws, therefore He instructed:

> *Ye shall not add unto the word which I command you, neither shall ye diminish ought from it..."*
>
> Deuteronomy 4:2

Men were forbidden to alter, change, add to, or amend these laws.

These laws deal with every aspect of man's relationship to God and fellow man, they set forth the only perfect and equitable method of administrating national affairs: that give the only rules that will enable people to be prosperous and happy, that lay down the only method that will establish justice, equity and judgement on the earth. Moses codified these laws, which code is set forth in the book of Deuteronomy. It cannot be too strongly urged upon all to read this book again and again to digest these laws.

Only in these laws will the earth obtain the peace, prosperity, and happiness it seeks.

The Law of the Gospel Restored

With the restoration of the Gospel in the spring of 1823 and the restoration of the Melchizedec Priesthood the Law of the Gospel was restored in its fullness. Today we have all the ordinances revealed which are necessary for the salvation and exaltation of mankind. The Church of Jesus Christ of Latter-day Saints has full authority for the administration of this Law – the Law of the Gospel, which applies only to Ecclesiastical Law and ordinances.

The Statutes and Judgements to be Restored

The Church does not have any civil authority to administer the civil and judicial laws of the nation. Laws contained in the Statutes and Judgements. However, it seems that in the not too distant future our nation, in fact all nations, are going to be ruled by these Divine Laws.

When the great restoration of the House of Jacob is completed then the Lord will have to restore these Laws upon a world of chaos, and at that time He will cleanse the whole House of Israel – this the Almighty God declares in no uncertain terms.

> *"For I will take you from among the heathen, and gather you out of all countries, and will bring you into your own hand.*
>
> *Then will I sprinkle clean water upon you, and ye shall be clean: From all your filthiness, and from all your idols, will I cleanse you.*
>
> *A new heart also will I give you, and a new spirit will I put within you: and I will take away the* **stony heart** *out of your flesh, and I will give you an heart of flesh.*
>
> **And I will put my spirit within you, and cause you to walk in my Statutes, and ye shall keep my judgments, and do them**"
>
> Ezekiel 36:24-27
> (Emphasis added)

Yes! The Statutes and Judgements are to be restored. Could any statement be clearer than that quoted above? The Statutes and Judgements – **Not some others, but the same ones that God gave to Moses at Mount Sinai.**

Modern Israel's Awakening

A study of Ezekiel chapter 34 through 39 depict a story of Israel's disobedience, scattering and future restoration which is followed by great tribulations and warfare (chapter 39).

At this time of restoration the Lord says:

> Then will I sprinkle clean water upon you, and ye
> shall be clean: from all our filthiness, and from
> all your idols, will I cleanse you.
>
> *Ezekiel 36:25*

This appears to be a sudden change from the old ways – the beginning of a new life.

This change to a new life will **not** be a gradual process, it seems it will come suddenly upon our nation – Great Britain, USA and all the related Anglo-Saxon-Celtic nations.

The process of repentance may require many years to acquire and build up, but when the time comes it can all be fulfilled in a moment.

> *"Moreover the word of the LORD came unto me, saying,*
>
> *Son of man, when the house of Israel dwelt in their own land, they defiled it by their own way and by their doings: their way was before me as the uncleanness of a removed woman.*
>
> *Wherefore I poured my fury upon them for the blood that they had shed upon the land, and for their idols wherewith they had polluted it:*

And I scattered them among the heathen, and they were dispersed through the countries: according to their way and according to their doings I judged them.

And when they entered unto the heathen, whither they went, they profaned my holy name, when they said to them, These are the people of the LORD, and are gone forth out of his land.

But I had pity for mine holy name, which the house of Israel had profaned among the heathen, whither they went.

Therefore say unto the house of Israel, Thus saith the Lord GOD; I do not this for your sakes, O house of Israel, but for mine holy name's sake, which ye have profaned among the heathen, whither ye went.

And I will sanctify my great name, which was profaned among the heathen, which ye have profaned in the midst of them; and the heathen shall know that I am the LORD, saith the Lord GOD, when I shall be sanctified in you before their eyes.

For I will take you from among the heathen, and gather you out of all countries, and will bring you into your own land.

Then will I sprinkle clean water upon you, and ye shall be clean: from all your filthiness, and from all your idols, will I cleanse you.

A new heart also will I give you, and a new spirit will I put within you: and I will take away the stony heart out of your flesh, and I will give you an heart of flesh.

And I will put my spirit within you, and cause you to walk in my statutes, and ye shall keep my judgments, and do them.

And ye shall dwell in the land that I gave to your fathers;
and ye shall be my people, and I will be your God."
Ezekiel 36:16 - 28

In this work the author has proved that the British people and those related nations of the Anglo-Saxon-Celtic Commonwealth including the USA are the modern nations of Israel – and the tremendous things which arise therefrom will be shown, not secret things, for they are revealed, but most assuredly unknown things, world wide in their effect, and which closely concern every man and woman in Anglo- Saxondom.

The news that we are Israel falls upon the ears of some as a glad evangel, they accept it the first time they hear it: But as for others, no amount of proof is sufficient for them: They do not want to know it. And the great revealing will come to them as an overwhelming surprise!

The Lord says He will take away our stony hearts – hearts which have stubbornly resisted His love and His laws – and place in them His Spirit – a spiritual heart – one that is willing – receptive and obedient – a heart willing to keep His laws and apply them.

> *"And I will put my spirit within you, and cause you to walk in **my statutes**, and ye shall keep **my judgments**, and do them."*
>
> *Ezekiel 36:27*
> Emphasis added

We will no longer be saying God's laws are "done away" or "barbaric" – we will be willing to learn that law contained in the Statutes, and just as importantly to *keep my judgements*, and do them! That is a full restoration of **all** the Judgements – **and penalties**, including capital and corporal punishment and laws of Restitution.

How long does it take for the Spirit of God to come to a man? One moment! These are New Men, with new hearts, walking before God, possessing His spirit; keeping His Judgements, dwelling in the land which He set aside for them (verse 24 and 2 Sam 7:10 and Jer 31:10).

These divine laws are going to be written in "our hearts" and "in our minds" and we are going to ask the Lord to do this for us, which indicates a *national* period of repentance and reconciliation.

> *"But this shall be the covenant that I will make with the house of Israel; After those days, saith the LORD, I will put my law in their inward parts, and write it in their hearts; and will be their God, and they shall be my people.*
>
> *And they shall teach no more every man his neighbour, and every man his brother, saying, Know the LORD: for they shall all know me, from the least of them unto the greatest of them, saith the LORD: for I will forgive their iniquity, and I will remember their sin no more."*
>
> *Jeremiah 31:33, 34*

Right in the very centre of verse 33 is a point where one age ends and another begins. It is described in the words *"after those days"*. Those are vital words marking off one age from another. They are like the finger post at the crossroads, one arm pointing backwards to the way we have come and the other pointing forward and marked *the millennium* "after those days" – days of obstinacy, stubbornness, disobedience, resistant, blindness to our true identity and refusal to recognise God's law. There shall come a New Era, a reign of truth and righteousness; for God says: *"I will put my law in their inward parts (minds) and write it in their hearts"* – that is, - God will enforce His law.

Man has failed. His people have failed. His Son however has not failed; and the redemption wrought out by Him is now seen at work mightily accomplishing the work He set out to do.

God takes the disobedient Israel nation in hand, and brings her to her senses (this particular passage however does not tell us how – we shall see how shortly) writing the Law in their inward parts – in their minds and in their hearts, till every man and woman in the whole of Anglo-Saxondom shall know the Lord and His Laws from the least to the greatest of them.

Paul says this will require a "renewing of the mind".

> *"And be not conformed to this world: but be ye transformed by the renewing of your mind, that ye may prove what is that good, and acceptable, and perfect, will of God."*
>
> *Romans 12:2*

All the old pre-conceived ideas must be erased, man's ways – and his laws must be buried and forgotten – a renewing of the mind means a completely new change of direction – a new way of thinking, for all that the Lord requires of us is

> *Behold, the Lord requireth the heart and a willing mind; and the willing and obedient shall eat the good of the land of Zion in these last days.*
>
> *And the rebellious shall be cut off out of the land of Zion, and shall be sent away, and shall not inherit the land.*
>
> *D&C 64:34, 35; Ezekiel 20:38*

The price for the redemption of Israel was paid and continues **now** at this very moment: But the other renewing, revitalising and changing of the heart of Israel in actual deed and fact, **is then** i.e. *"after those days"*: And will be so deep and thorough, so extensive, so national, that there shall be no exception, "they shall all know me"…"I will remember their sin no more".

We have in Acts 3:20,21 a direct New Testament reference by the Apostle Peter to this restoration:

> *And he shall send Jesus Christ, which before was preached unto you:*
>
> *Whom the heaven must receive until the times of restitution of all things, which God hath spoken by the mouth of all his holy prophets since the world began.*
>
> *Acts 3:20, 21*

The great plan of the restoration commenced in the spring of 1820 and will continue until the second advent of the Lord Jesus Christ – and include in the '*all things*' must be a full restoration of the Divine Laws contained in the Statutes and Judgements.

The scriptures plainly show that there is a time to come in the very near future when God abandons all secrecy, and arises out of His place publicly to acknowledge in the eyes of <u>all</u> the nations the identity of His people 'Israel'.

Now, is it possible to ascertain from the predictions of scripture how God will reveal Himself; and what methods He will use to tear aside the veil, and open the blind eyes of Israel herself? This is a very serious question, and one of intrinsic importance.

Most assuredly God will reveal Himself to Israel, fully unreservedly, and before all the nations, and in such a manner that the world will know it!

> *"The LORD hath made bare his holy arm in the eyes of all the nations; and all the ends of the earth shall see the salvation of our God."*
>
> *Isaiah 52:10*

> *"And the heathen shall know that I the LORD do sanctify Israel, when my sanctuary shall be in the midst of them for evermore."*
>
> *Ezekiel 37:28*

The Seven Events of Israel's National and Spiritual Awakening

Ezekiel chapters 34 to 39 record in particular the events of modern Israel's national and spiritual awakening <u>after 1800 AD</u>.

The events of these chapters were to be *"in the last days"*. The introduction to chapters 34 and 36 begin with *"in the last days"* and chapters 37, 38, 39 are a continuity of those events.
The terms *"in the last days"*, *"after those days"*, *"in the end time"* or *"time of the end"*, *"the fullness of time"*, *"in that day"*, *"from that day"* – all refer to the

period after 1800 AD – when Israel's Seven Times punishment ended. First let us summarise chapters 34 and 36.

Chapter 34

The introduction to the chapter commences IN THE LAST DAYS (after 1800 AD).

Ezekiel speaks to scattered Israel and condemns the false shepherds (both <u>political</u> and <u>religious</u>) who have misled **and still are** misleading the modern Israel nations today. In this chapter the Lord promises to re-gather His people and raise up His throne among them of the royal line of David.

Chapter 36: Verses 16 – 20

The Lord refers to Israel's sins as "the uncleanness of a removed woman". Divorced for her idolatry and human sacrifices. For this Israel was scattered (removed) for a period of 7 Times (2,520 years).

Verses 21 – 23

But the Lord had pity on Israel because he had given 'her' 'His name' (!) just as a human wife receives her husband's name in marriage, the husband then being responsible for his wife, and the wife being responsible to honour his name. The Lord says he had pity on her (Israel) *not for their sake – but – for my holy name's sake.* Because he had sworn an oath and covenant to Abraham which Israel had inherited. He had given His word, and because of this oath He would stand by her – and sanctify His 'Great' name.

Verses 24 – 27

Israel was to be gathered to their 'own land' – a land specially selected and reserved for them. There he would commence the sanctification of His people. Eventually modern Israel will return to keeping His Statues, Judgements and Laws under a 'New Constitution'! See also Jeremiah 30:7 - 11 and 31:33, 34. The events of these chapters are also introduced as 'In the last days'. A study of Isaiah chapters 40 – 66 is also advisable, as all these chapters are related.

We are now prepared to examine the content of Ezekiel chapter 37.

Ezekiel Chapter 37: The First Six Events

This chapter records the <u>first six events</u> related to Israel's national and spiritual awakening. The <u>seventh event</u> is recorded in chapters 38 and 39.

It must be kept in mind that, when reading these chapters of Ezekiel and those of Jeremiah and Isaiah just mentioned, that the Lord is speaking to Israel the nation **NOT** the Church or individuals.

By 'Israel' the nation we mean the modern nations of Israel; in particular Great Britain and the United States of America.

The First Event

> *THE hand of the LORD was upon me, and carried me out in the spirit of the LORD, and set me down in the midst of the valley which was full of bones,*

> *And caused me to pass by them round about: and, behold, there were very many in the open valley; and, lo, they were very dry.*

> *And he said unto me, Son of man, can these bones live? And I answered, O Lord GOD, thou knowest.*

> *Again he said unto me, Prophesy upon these bones, and say unto them, O ye dry bones, hear the word of the LORD.*

> *Thus saith the Lord GOD unto these bones; Behold, I will cause breath to enter into you, and ye shall live:*

> *And I will lay sinews upon you, and will bring up flesh upon you, and cover you with skin, and put breath in you, and ye shall live; and ye shall know that I am the LORD.*

> *So I prophesied as I was commanded: and as I prophesied, there was a noise, and behold a shaking, and the bones came together, bone to his bone.*

> *And when I beheld, lo, the sinews and the flesh came up upon them, and the skin covered them above: but there was no breath in them.*

Then said he unto me, Prophesy unto the wind, prophesy, son of man, and say to the wind, Thus saith the Lord GOD; Come from the four winds, O breath, and breathe upon these slain, that they may live.

So I prophesied as he commanded me, and the breath came into them, and they lived, and stood up upon their feet, an exceeding great army.

Then he said unto me, Son of man, these bones are the whole house of Israel: behold, they say, Our bones are dried, and our hope is lost: we are cut off for our parts.

Therefore prophesy and say unto them, Thus saith the Lord GOD; Behold, O my people, I will open your graves, and cause you to come up out of your graves, and bring you into the land of Israel.

And ye shall know that I am the LORD, when I have opened your graves, O my people, and brought you up out of your graves,

And shall put my spirit in you, and ye shall live, and I shall place you in your own land: then shall ye know that I the LORD have spoken it, and performed it, saith the LORD.

Ezekiel 37:1-14

Israel's National Awakening

The parable of the 'wilderness' of dry bones. Firstly, let it be made clear that this parable or vision has nothing whatever to do with the resurrection of mankind – but Israel's national restoration.

These bones are the *whole* house of Israel (verse 11).
If it were referring to the resurrection of mankind then, the parable suggests it will only apply to the nation of Israel. *Secondly*, the resurrection of mankind would have taken place before the joining together of 'Stick

of Judah' and 'Stick of Joseph'. And *thirdly* before the event of the Battle of Armageddon, recorded in chapters 38 and 39.

It is a fact that these chapters under consideration are in their correct chronological order, so then the events contained within them are also in the correct order.

We have discovered that the House of Israel – the Ten Tribes – were taken into the 'Graveyard' of captivity in BC 721 (Hosea 13:14). Then after their escape from Assyrian captivity they would migrate across Europe in a north westerly direction. This period in their history is referred to as the **'Wilderness'** period. (Hosea 2:14, Jeremiah 31:1-3).

> *And I will bring you into the wilderness of the people, and there will I plead with you face to face Like as I pleaded with your fathers in the wilderness of the land of Egypt, so will I plead with you, saith the Lord GOD.*
>
> **Ezekiel 20:35, 36**

They were then to occupy their new home 'in the isles of the sea' – the islands of Britain, and there from AD 540 to AD 1300 they would experience a **'Nourishing'** period. From AD 1300 to AD 1800 they would experience a **'Revival'** period and after AD 1800 a **'Restoration'** period.

This parable portrays Israel's emancipation and national awakening commencing with the **'Revival'** period (AD 1300) and her Restoration to become a 'Great' Empire after her Seven Times period of correction, which ended in AD 1800.

The **full** effect of Christ's atonement and redemption of His 'wife' did not take effect IN A NATIONAL SENSE until this period was completed.

It is interesting to note that the United Kingdom of Great Britain did not come into effect until AD 1801(!) when Ireland became united with England, Scotland and Wales – giving rise to a Union Flag called the "Union Jack" (meaning Union of Jacob). Many people are unaware that America was *born* as a nation **before** the United Kingdom was formed!

That this was also in keeping with prophecy to Jacob. 'A nation' and 'a company of nations' shall be of thee (Genesis 35:10, 11).

In this blessing given to Jacob the singular 'Great Nation' came first, followed by the 'Company' or 'Commonwealth' of nations, and was fulfilled exactly in that order!

The year AD 1800 commenced Israel's national awakening. Paul explained that before there could be a spiritual awakening there must of necessity be a natural or national awakening (1 Corinthians 15:46).

At first Ezekiel saw the bones had sinews of flesh come upon them – "But there was no breath in them" (verse 8) or in other words: No spirit in them. But the breath of God (the Holy Spirit) gave life to the bones (nation).

It will be noted in these verses that the Lord uses the term "O my people" not "O my nation". This expression is also used when referring to the United States of America: Of the people, by the people, for the people, the people of America.

The Second Event

The word of the LORD came again unto me, saying,

Moreover, thou son of man, take thee one stick, and write upon it, For Judah, and for the children of Israel his companions: then take another stick, and write upon it, For Joseph, the stick of Ephraim, and for all the house of Israel his companions:

And join them one to another into one stick; and they shall become one in thine hand.

And when the children of thy people shall speak unto thee, saying, Wilt thou not shew us what thou meanest by these? Say unto them, Thus saith the Lord GOD; Behold, I will take the stick of Joseph, which is in the hand of Ephraim, and the tribes of Israel his fellows, and will put them with him, even with the stick of Judah, and make them one stick, and they shall be one in mine hand.

And the sticks whereon thou writest shall be in thine hand before their eyes.

And say unto them, Thus saith the Lord GOD; Behold, I will take the children of Israel from among the heathen, whither they be gone, and will gather them on every side, and bring them into their own land:

Ezekiel 37:15-21

Israel's Spiritual Awakening

Following Israel's 'national' emancipation in AD 1800, the next event was to be Israel's spiritual awakening.

The method and cause was the coming forth of the Book of Mormon, i.e. 'Stick of Joseph', which was to be joined to the Holy Bible, i.e. 'Stick of Judah'. This event took place in AD 1820 at the commencement of the Lunar Millennium, after which the Lord restored His true church in AD 1830 and the 'keys' of the Holy Priesthood in AD 1836, which were necessary for mankind's salvation and exaltation.

This restoration commenced in the 13th century with what is called the Reformation, which John Wycliffe began with his first translation of the Holy Bible into the English language, opening the way for all men to read and seek the truth. For this great gift to mankind John Wycliffe paid the ultimate price. He was called the 'Morning Star' of the Reformation.

The Reformation and early reformers being but forerunners to "prepare the way" for the "Greater light" of the Restoration. It is also to be noted that preceding the year AD 1800 man's emancipation seems to have been at a standstill. The progress of man had been in the grip of the 'Dark Ages'. But just prior to and following the year AD 1800 there began an explosion of knowledge, with almost all the inventions coming from either Britain or America – a list of which follows:

Invention	Year	Inventor	Country
Steam locomotive (experiment)	1801	Trevithick	England
Steamboat, practical	1802	Symington	Scotland

Steam locomotive	1821	Stephenson	England
Electromagnet	1824	Sturgeon	England
Matches, phosphorescent	1827	John Walker	England
Photography	1835	Talbot	England
Telegraph	1837	Morse	USA
Cement, Portland	1846	Aspdin	England
Printing Press, rotary	1846	Hoe	England
Steel	1856	Bessemer	England
Telephone	1876	Bell	USA
Electric light	1878	Edison	USA
Steam turbine	1884	Parsons	England
Radio, transatlantic signals	1901	Marconi	Italy
Flight, power driven	1903	Wright	USA
Radio amplifier	1907	De Forest	USA
X-ray tube	1913	Coolidge	USA
Jet engine	1926	Whittle	England
Movies, talking	1927	Warner	USA

The Lord released this knowledge in engineering, science and medicine because they were important to Israel's national and spiritual greatness. This 'Time' represented a period of growth, discovery, and greatness both for America into a singular Great Nation and Great Britain (United Kingdom) into an Empire.

The Third Event

Moreover I will make a covenant of peace with them; it shall be an everlasting covenant with them: and I will place them, and multiply them, and will set my sanctuary in the midst of them for evermore.

My tabernacle also shall be with them: yea, I will be their God, and they shall be my people.

And the heathen shall know that I the LORD do sanctify Israel, when my sanctuary shall be in the midst of them for evermore.

Ezekiel 37:26-28

A New And Everlasting Covenant

With the ending of Israel's Seven Times punishment and the restoration of the gospel, the Lord was able to make a *new* and *everlasting covenant* with His people.

The "constitution" of this covenant is given in section 132 of the Doctrine and Covenants and elsewhere.

My Tabernacle Shall Also Be With Them

Following the events of the restoration in 1820, the Lord commanded a Temple to be built that He might reveal those ordinances of the Priesthood which had been hid from before the world was (D&C 124:38).

'Tabernacle' is another word for temple.

You will notice that in the introduction to verse 26 the Lord uses the word "***moreover***" which means ***in addition to*** that event which preceded it. This means that the events recorded in verses 22 – 25 could in fact take place <u>after</u> the events of verses 26 – 27. and this is exactly the case.

Forth Event

> *And I will make them one nation in the land upon the mountains of Israel; and one king shall be king to them all: and they shall be no more two nations, neither shall they be divided into two kingdoms any more at all:*
>
> *Neither shall they defile themselves any more with their idols, nor with their detestable things, nor with any of their transgressions: but I will save them out of all their dwellingplaces, wherein they have sinned, and will cleanse them: so shall they be my people, and I will be their God.*
>
> *And David my servant shall be king over them; and they all shall have one shepherd: they shall also walk in my judgments, and observe my statutes, and do them.*

And they shall dwell in the land that I have given unto Jacob my servant, wherein your fathers have dwelt; and they shall dwell therein, even they, and their children, and their children's children for ever: and my servant David shall be their prince for ever.

Ezekiel 37:22 – 25

A New and Greater United Kingdom of Israel

These verses record a future time to our day but not too distant future when, the modern nations of Israel – representing Ephraim and Manasseh (Britain and America) will be **United into One Nation in a New Enlarged (Greater) United Kingdom of Israel.**

I know that most of our readers will have accepted the chronological events of the previous verses, but for some scholars this may be too unbelievable.

But God's word will be vindicated, as sure as the sun rises in the morning and the moon and the stars at night.

In order to get to the truth we must accept scripture, especially prophecy, at face value. Who would have thought that the great mighty Socialist Republic of Russia is no more – and how gently and speedily God brought that about!

And we wish to remind our readers that these events were to happen 'after' the restoration of the Gospel and 'before' the Battle of Armageddon. Consequently therefore 'before' our Lord's appearance to the Jews at that time, and *before* His second advent in glory during the Millennium.

I believe that this situation will be forced upon our nations. Today as I write, 2002, both Britain and America are facing political, economic and civil problems of greater magnitude than any other generation. It certainly is a time of "Jacob's trouble" (Jeremiah 30:7)

What Is The Event To Bring This Union About?

On the 31 December 1992 the 12 nations of the European Union signed the S.E.A (Single European Act) at Maastricht, The Netherlands. It is my opinion that both Britain and Denmark will eventually be expelled from the Federal European Union because the terms will be unacceptable to them. Not being able to surrender their sovereignty to this super state. The economic, monetary and political power of Federal Europe led by Germany and France will become so great that it will force the nations of Britain and America together into an economic and political union. This will most possibly include Denmark, Norway, Sweden, Canada, Australia and New Zealand – in fact it will be literally an Anglo Saxon Federation of Nations – 'The United (Anglo Saxon) States'.

The Fifth Event

The new United Anglo Saxon Federation Will Have One Supreme Monarch

Verse 24

> *"…and David my servant shall be king over them…"*

The term "David my servant" does not refer to an individual called David, *but* to the Royal House of David, the continuation of which is to be found in the British monarchy, the Royal House of Windsor, this family being the present custodians of the Throne of David – until "He who comes whose right it is" (Geneses 49:10). See also J.S.T Bible footnotes under Shiloh and Ezekiel 21:25 – 27. This is both scriptural and prophetical, we must not allow our prejudices to cloud our logic.

But someone will point out that in the Book of Mormon it states that no kings will reign in this land (America). We therefore quote the scripture referred to:

> *"And this land shall be a land of liberty unto the* Gentiles, **and there shall be no kings upon the land**, *who shall raise up unto the Gentiles."*
>
> 2. Nephi 10:11
> Emphasis added

There it states that no kings would rule in America – No it does not! It states that no kings *'of the Gentiles'* would rule in that land. Gentile kings – **not** the Royal House of Israel, the Royal House of David.

When Nephi said "in this land" he meant the whole of North America – including Canada, of which Queen Elizabeth II and her predecessors were head of state; and still are. And what about George III, who ruled America for many years in the late 1700s and early 1800s?

Nephi was careful to distinguish between a 'Gentile' king and one of the Royal House of David. It seems therefore that at that time the Royal House of Windsor will be elected 'Head of State' of this Greater United Anglo Saxon States.

Jeremiah clarifies the situation:

> *But they shall serve the LORD their God, and David*
> *their king, whom I will raise up unto them."*
>
> *Jeremiah 30:9*

As we have already pointed out the events of this chapter were to be *in the last days*. Here modern Israel was to serve – the Lord their God *and* David their King – whom I (the Lord) will raise up unto them.

If we are to accept that the 37, 38, and 39 chapters of Ezekiel are in their correct chronological and historic order, then these things cannot be dismissed – to do so would cause our vision of prophetical things to be blurred.

Sherlock Holmes was always quoted as saying: "Eliminate the impossible and what you have left must be the truth". And in this day and age anything seems possible.

The Sixth Event

> *And David my servant shall be king over them; and they all*
> *shall have one shepherd: they shall also walk in my judgments,*
> *and observe my statutes, and do them.*
>
> *Ezekiel 37:24*

A New Constitution

This new and Greater United Kingdom of Israel will have a new constitution:

> *They shall also walk in My Judgements, and observe My Statutes and do them.*

Yes, men's political, economic, monetary and judicial orders will be abolished. This Federation of Anglo Saxon States will be rebuilt upon God's Divine Laws, contained in Jehovah's Statutes and Judgements delivered to Moses at Sinai, the most complete and equitable laws ever given to mankind.

Israel's blindness will be removed; that is, her national and spiritual blindness, and we shall come to recognise Christ *in a national sense.*

> *...So will I make my holy name known in the midst of my people Israel; ... and the heathen shall know that I am the LORD, the Holy One in Israel...*
>
> *So the house of Israel shall know that I am the LORD their God from that day and forward*
>
> *Ezekiel 39:6 - 8, 22*

How and when will these things be? And what will be the cause of modern Israel reawakening?

These are most vital questions which will now be answered for they bring us to the final and seventh event, which may follow shortly after the events just mentioned. It seems the success and wealth created by this new United Anglo Saxon Federation of States will be the envy of the Gentile nations.

The Seventh Event

AND the word of the LORD came unto me, saying,

Son of man, set thy face against Gog, the land of Magog, the chief prince of Meshech and Tubal, and prophesy against him,

And say, Thus saith the Lord GOD; Behold, I am against thee, O Gog, the chief prince of Meshech and Tubal:

And I will turn thee back, and put hooks into thy jaws, and I will bring thee forth, and all thine army, horses and horsemen, all of them clothed with all sorts of armour, even a great company with bucklers and shields, all of them handling swords:

Persia, Ethiopia, and Libya with them; all of them with shield and helmet:

Gomer, and all his bands; the house of Togarmah of the north quarters, and all his bands: and many people with thee.

Be thou prepared, and prepare for thyself, thou, and all thy company that are assembled unto thee, and be thou a guard unto them.

After many days thou shalt be visited: in the latter years thou shalt come into the land that is brought back from the sword, and is gathered out of many people, people, against the mountains of Israel, which have been always waste: but it is brought forth out of the nations, and they shall dwell safely all of them.

Thou shalt ascend and come like a storm, thou shalt be like a cloud to cover the land, thou, and all thy bands, and many people with thee.

*Thus saith the Lord GOD; It shall also come to pass, that
at the same time shall things come into thy mind, and thou
shalt think an evil thought:*

And thou shalt say, I will go up to the land of
unwalled villages; I will go to them that are at
rest, that dwell safely, all of them dwelling
without walls, and having neither bars nor gates,

*To take a spoil, and to take a prey; to turn thine hand upon
the desolate places that are now inhabited, and upon the
people that are gathered out of the nations, which have gotten
cattle and goods, that dwell in the midst of the land.*

*Sheba, and Dedan, and the merchants of Tarshish, with all the
young lions thereof, shall say unto thee, Art thou come to take
a spoil? hast thou gathered thy company to take a prey? to
carry away silver and gold, to take away cattle and goods, to
take a great spoil?*

*Therefore, son of man, prophesy and say unto Gog, Thus
saith the Lord GOD; In that day when my people of Israel
dwelleth safely, shalt thou not know it?*

*And thou shalt come from thy place out of the north parts,
thou, and many people with thee, all of them riding upon
horses, a great company, and a mighty army*

*And thou shalt come up against my people of Israel, as a
cloud to cover the land; it shall be in the latter days, and I
will bring thee against my land, that the heathen may know
me, when I shall be sanctified in thee, O Gog, before their
eyes.*

*Thus saith the Lord GOD; Art thou he of whom I have
spoken in old time by my servants the prophets of Israel,
which prophesied in those days many years that I would bring
thee against them?*

And it shall come to pass at the same time when Gog shall come against the land of Israel, saith the Lord GOD, that my fury shall come up in my face.

For in my jealousy and in the fire of my wrath have I spoken, Surely in that day there shall be a great shaking in the land of Israel;

So that the fishes of the sea, and the fowls of the heaven, and the beasts of the field, and all creeping things that creep upon the earth, and all the men that are upon the face of the earth, shall shake at my presence, and the mountains shall be thrown down, and the steep places shall fall, and every wall shall fall to the ground.

And I will call for a sword against him throughout all my mountains, saith the Lord GOD: every man's sword shall be against his brother.

And I will plead against him with pestilence and with blood; and I will rain upon him, and upon his bands, and upon the many people that are with him, an overflowing rain, and great hailstones, fire, and brimstone.

Thus will I magnify myself, and sanctify myself; and I will be known in the eyes of many nations, and they shall know that I am the LORD.

Ezekiel 38

THEREFORE, thou son of man, prophesy against Gog, and say, Thus saith the Lord GOD; Behold, I am against thee, O Gog, the chief prince of Meshech and Tubal:

And I will turn thee back, and leave but the sixth part of thee, and will cause thee to come up from the north parts, and will bring thee upon the mountains of Israel:

And I will smite thy bow out of thy left hand, and will cause thine arrows to fall out of thy right hand.

Thou shalt fall upon the mountains of Israel, thou, and all thy bands, and the people that is with thee: I will give thee unto the ravenous birds of every sort, and to the beasts of the field to be devoured.

Thou shalt fall upon the open field: for I have spoken it, saith the Lord GOD.

And I will send a fire on Magog, and among them that dwell carelessly in the isles: and they shall know that I am the LORD.

So will I make my holy name known in the midst of my people Israel; and I will not let them pollute my holy name any more: and the heathen shall know that I am the LORD, the Holy One in Israel.

Behold, it is come, and it is done, saith the Lord GOD; THIS IS THE DAY WHEREOF I HAVE SPOKEN.

And they that dwell in the cities of Israel shall go forth, and shall set on fire and burn the weapons, both the shields and the bucklers, the bows and the arrows, and the handstaves, and the spears, and they shall burn them with fire seven years:

So that they shall take no wood out of the field, neither cut down any out of the forests; for they shall burn the weapons with fire: and they shall spoil those that spoiled them, and rob those that robbed them, saith the Lord GOD.

And it shall come to pass in that day, that I will give unto Gog a place there of graves in Israel, the valley of the passengers on the east of the sea: and it shall stop the noses of the passengers: and there shall they bury Gog and all his multitude: and they shall call it The valley of Hamon-gog.

And seven months shall the house of Israel be burying of them, that they may cleanse the land.

Yea, all the people of the land shall bury them; and it shall be to them a renown the day that I shall be glorified, saith the Lord GOD.

And they shall sever out men of continual employment, passing through the land to bury with the passengers those that remain upon the face of the earth, to cleanse it: after the end of seven months shall they search.

And the passengers that pass through the land, when any seeth a man's bone, then shall he set up a sign by it, till the buriers have buried it in the valley of Hamon-gog.

And also the name of the city shall be Hamonah. Thus shall they cleanse the land.

And, thou son of man, thus saith the Lord GOD; Speak unto every feathered fowl, and to every beast of the field, Assemble yourselves, and come; gather yourselves on every side to my sacrifice that I do sacrifice for you, even a great sacrifice upon the mountains of Israel, that ye may eat flesh, and drink blood.

Ye shall eat the flesh of the mighty, and drink the blood of the princes of the earth, of rams, of lambs, and of goats, of bullocks, all of them fatlings of Bashan.

And ye shall eat fat till ye be full, and drink blood till ye be drunken, of my sacrifice which I have sacrificed for you.

Thus ye shall be filled at my table with horses and chariots, with mighty men, and with all men of war, saith the Lord GOD.

And I will set my glory among the heathen, and all the heathen shall see my judgment that I have executed, and my hand that I have laid upon them.

So the house of Israel shall know that I am the LORD their God from that day and forward.

And the heathen shall know that the house of Israel went into captivity for their iniquity: because they trespassed against me, therefore hid I my face from them, and gave them into the hand of their enemies: so fell they all by the sword.

According to their uncleanness and according to their transgressions have I done unto them, and hid my face from them.

Therefore thus saith the Lord GOD; Now will I bring again the captivity of Jacob, and have mercy upon the whole house of Israel, and will be jealous for my holy name;

After that they have borne their shame, and all their trespasses whereby they have trespassed against me, when they dwelt safely in their land, and none made them afraid.

When I have brought them again from the people, and gathered them out of their enemies' lands, and am sanctified in them in the sight of many nations;

Then shall they know that I am the LORD their God, which caused them to be led into captivity among the heathen: but I have gathered them unto their own land, and have left none of them any more there.

Neither will I hide my face any more from them: for I have poured out my spirit upon the house of Israel, saith the Lord GOD.

Ezekiel 39

The Battle of Armageddon

And he gathered them together into a place called in the Hebrew tongue Armageddon."

Revelation 16:16

In Ezekiel chapters 38 and 39 are recorded a future time of great tribulation for the Israel nations – a time which Jeremiah calls "Jacob's trouble".

> *Alas! for that day is great, so that none is like it: it is even the time of Jacob's trouble; but he shall be saved out of it."*
>
> *Jeremiah 30:7*

A reading of this Jeremiah chapter 30 and also chapter 31 reveals the Lord's great love for His people and His protection at this future time of great tribulation – But Israel is going to be saved out of it!

> *For I am with thee, saith the LORD, to save thee: though I make a full end of all nations whither I have scattered thee, yet will I not make a full end of thee: but I will correct thee in measure, and will not leave thee altogether unpunished.*
>
> *Jeremiah 30:11*

Daniel records these events thus:

> *AND at that time shall Michael stand up, the great prince which standeth for the children of thy people: and there shall be a time of trouble, such as never was since there was a nation even to that same time: and at that time thy people shall be delivered, every one that shall be found written in the book.*
>
> *Daniel 12:1*

It is evident that the Anglo Saxon nations of modern Israel are to be punished or receive some kind of corrective training for their disobedience, to bring them to their senses, but their God will be there to "save them out of it".

It seems that the Lord will use many nations to perform this work of sanctification of His people. And even identifies the nations involved.
Ezekiel gives a full description of the events of these days. Chapters 38 and 39 of Ezekiel have been known for many years as the 'Russians chapters of Ezekiel' (these chapters should be read before continuing).

Students of prophecy are in agreement with this. Meshech and Tubal are now known as Moscow and Tobolsk, and today Russia is responsible for bringing into being the great confederacy of nations that will precipitate the final conflict the prophets describe as the "Battle of That Great Day of God Almighty" (Revelation 16:14 – 16).

Magog, Meshech, and Tubal are all identified as the descendants of Japheth (1 Chronicles 1:5, Genesis 10:2).
The descendants of Tubal my be identified with the Balkan nations (TU-BAL-CAN). All confederate with Russia today.

In his book 'The Russian Chapters of Ezekiel', W. M. H. Milner provides information identifying GOG with Russia.

> *GOG – is a long o, both in the Hebrew and in the Greek – is made from the old world word root 'GG', which in the early language, implied something 'g-i-g-antic'. Russia has long been the 'COLOSSUS' of the north. A potentate of Bible history and prophecy as A-g-a-g. That name, or rather title, comes from the same root. He was (in his own estimation) A, Aleph, + GG = No. 1 Great! 'The Agagites', we are told in Young's Analytical Concordance, were an AMALEK-ITE tribe, and AGAG was a poetic name of Amalek.*

Ezekiel's Gog is thrice described in the Authorised English Version as, Chief Prince of Mesheck (Ezekiel 38:2, 3 and 39:1). However, in the Revised Version of 1885, he is described more correctly as Prince of Rosh – the learned Hebrew linguist Gesenius remarks it is a proper name – undoubtedly answering to the name of ROSH-IA and in our day to RUSS-IA.

And Russia today is the chief of the Amelekite nations upon the earth – a nation or people which the Almighty God predicted He would be at war with from generation to generation (Exodus 17:16)

This clearly identifies Russia as the nation which is to engineer the formation of a great 'GOG' confederacy consisting of Persia (modern Iran), Ethiopia, Libya, Gomer, Togarmah (Turkoman). *And Ezekiel names them all* (Ezekiel 38:5, 6)!

We are being shown that the time of Divine assessment has arrived for the Israel nations. *The winds of change in the Kremlin fit into the chronological pattern remarkably.*

In one sense, it is a relief to see this picture of Divine Judgement, which reveals that the Lord is about to deal with the question of His people's transgression of His law. Weighed in the balance and found wanting, perhaps the scales may tip in our favour by true national repentance, when events begin to break upon us.

The total pattern of time cycles is amazing in its consistency.

The climax of the age is reached when the King of the North (Daniel 11) invades the Holy Land.

> *Thus saith the Lord GOD; Art thou he of whom I have spoken in old time by my servants the prophets of Israel, which prophesied in those days many years that I would bring thee against them?"*
>
> *Ezekiel 38:17*

The prophecy through Ezekiel makes it clear that there is a **fixed time** in the Divine purpose for specified accomplishments to come to pass. This godless confederacy is of the opinion that they are making careful plans of their own for world conquest, completely unaware that actually they are being held in reserve for the day when the Lord will use them to demonstrate His mighty power before all nations.

Ezekiel sets the specific time when this great confederacy of nations under Russian leadership is to move

> *After many days thou shalt be visited: in the latter years thou shalt come into the land that is brought back from the sword, and is gathered out of many people, against the mountains of Israel, which have been always waste: but it is brought forth out of the nations, and they shall dwell safely all of them'*
>
> *Ezekiel 38:8*

The description of this coming invasion fixes the time of its commencement as after the airplane becomes a major factor in aggressive warfare:

> *Thou shalt ascend and come like a storm, thou shalt be like a cloud to cover the land, thou, and all thy bands, and many people with thee.*
>
> *Ezekiel 38:9*

When the great air armada of Russia ascends for the attack upon the Holy Land the security of the people dwelling there will be gone. However, at the time this attack is planned to occur in the Middle East, a land other than Palestine – modern <u>Jewish</u> state of Israel – becomes the object of Russian aggression:

> *Thus saith the Lord GOD; It shall also come to pass, that at the same time shall things come into thy mind, and thou shalt think an evil thought:*
>
> *And thou shalt say, I will go up to the land of unwalled villages; I will go to them that are at rest, that dwell safely, all of them dwelling without walls, and having neither bars nor gates,*
>
> *To take a spoil, and to take a prey; to turn thine hand upon the desolate places that are now inhabited, and upon the people that are gathered out of the nations, which have gotten cattle and goods, that dwell in the midst of the land.*
>
> *Ezekiel 38:10 – 12*

Ferrar Fenton translates the last paragraph "…and residing on top of the earth".

This second description is not that of Palestine (Jewish Israel State) but of another territory that had once been a wilderness and then had become inhabited with villages and cities without walls, bars or gates – an identifying feature of newly settled countries far removed from the ancient lands – residing "on the top of the earth". This description perfectly describes the United States, with Alaska and Canada, whose land extends to the Arctic, having neither bars nor gates referring to the free borders which exist between these nations!

At the time of the instigation of these aggressive moves on the part of Gog, two questions are posed <u>by those who are threatened</u> by these despoilers, who are designated by Ezekiel as "Sheba and Dedan and the merchants of Tarshish, with *all the young lions thereof*". They ask:

> *Art thou come to take a spoil? hast thou gathered thy company to take a prey? to carry away silver and gold, to take away cattle and goods, to take a great spoil?*
>
> *Ezekiel 38:13*

Who are *these* nations?

Sheba and Dedan represent certain tribal segments of the Arabs – Jokshan, a son of Abraham by Keturah, had two sons named Sheba and Dedan.

Ezekiel states further that there is also another people against whom the enemy is confederated – and are identified by the designation 'Tarshish'.

An ancient map in the British Museum, London, shows that the isles of Great Britain were anciently known as the Isles of Tarshish. The 'Young lions thereof' would be the nations which have sprung from the 'mother country'.

Thus we see that it is the Anglo-Saxon and kindred people, with their allies, against whom Russia and her confederate nations – as Gog, is planning their depredations, beside the Holy Land and Middle East.

> *And thou shalt come from thy place out of the north parts, thou, and many people with thee, all of them riding upon horses (tanks), a great company, and a mighty army:*
>
> *And thou shalt come up against my people of Israel, as a cloud to cover the land; it shall be in the latter days, and I will bring thee against my land, **that the heathen may know me,***

> *when I shall be sanctified in thee, O Gog, before*
> *their eyes."*
>
> *Ezekiel 38:15, 16*
> Emphasis added

Russia has declared war upon God and God has accepted the challenge. This decisive test of strength is timed to occur in the 'latter days', which are the days in which we are now living! God states what He will do and why He will do it.

> *And it shall come to pass at the same time when Gog shall*
> *come against the land of Israel, saith the Lord GOD, that my*
> *fury shall come up in my face.*
>
> *For in my jealousy and in the fire of my wrath have I spoken,*
> *Surely in that day there shall be a great shaking in the land of*
> *Israel;*
>
> *Ezekiel 38:18, 19*

George Washington's Vision

Many thoughtful folk in the United States must be wondering in these days whether, after all, the remarkable vision that George Washington was reputed to have received during the War of Independence in 1775 – 1781 has special application to America in her present renewed prosperity.

According to the testimony of Wesley Bradshaw, he heard from the lips of Anthony Sherman an account of the amazing vision that Washington had one winter's afternoon. God-fearing Sherman declared that he heard the story from Washington himself.

In brief, the vision told of three great perils which would descend upon the United States. The first was the War of Independence which brought bloodshed and anguish to the American people. During the darkest period of that war, when Washington suffered several reverses, the praying Commander retreated to Valley Forge, where he resolved to spend the Winter of 1777. Often Washington would pray in secret for aid and comfort from God. Sherman told Bradshaw that he had often seen the tears coursing down the careworn cheeks of the great warrior as he enquired about the condition of his soldiers.

In his vision Washington saw a dark cloud enveloping, and then passing away eastward from America. The second great peril told of an ill-omened spectre which approached the Republic from Africa. "It flitted slowly and heavily over every town and city. The inhabitants set themselves in battle array against each other". This second great peril was, of course, the Civil War of 1861 – 1865. Washington died many years before this sore trial beset the Republic (his death was on 14th December 1799).

The third peril seen by Washington in his vision was of an appalling nature. It told of thick, black clouds which, coming from Europe, Asia and Africa, soon joined into one. "And throughout this mass there gleamed a dark red light by which I saw hordes of armed men who, moving with the cloud, marched by land and sailed by sea to America, which country was enveloped in the volume of the cloud. I dimly saw these vast armies devastate the whole country and burn the villages, towns and cities that I had beheld springing up". According to the vision, the inhabitants of America, when well-nigh overcome by the godless hordes arrayed against them, were miraculously delivered by Divine intervention (doubtless, a deep national repentance occurs).

Whatever we may think of that amazing revelation to Washington – the earliest publication of the reputed vision was in 1859 – the fact remains that the prophecy concerning the nature and outcome of the first two perils was fulfilled in the War of Independence and the Civil War. Has the third peril against America and indeed against all the Israel nations commenced – if so, when will the climax be reached? This question needs to be asked, for the present nation-wide outbreak of rebellion against law and order, with its rioting, killings and looting, may well be the forerunner of something far more terrible, even by the present threat of terrorism.

As we have stated before, the predicted "time of Jacob's trouble" (Jeremiah 30:7) is upon all His nations and is speaking to us in ways that can no longer be avoided or denied. The obscene language, the vulgar behaviour and wanton destructiveness of milling mobs of demonstrators clearly prove that more than one privileged Israel nation is ripe for the climax of judgement. Surely God himself is speaking loudly to His servant people in America, Britain, Canada and indeed, to the whole family of Jacob spread forth in the western world, to prepare themselves for judgement on a vast scale.

It was the late Russian leader, Brezhnev, who, on the eve of the centenary of Lenin's birth, on 21st April 1970, said: "Imperialism will not collapse by itself, automatically. No, it is still strong. Active and determined action by all the revolutionary forces is needed to overthrow it".

If Washington's vision of the third peril is true, then America may be faced with a mighty onslaught of Russian forces which will devastate much of her country and bring that great republic to its knees in agonising prayer and deep repentance before God.

On the very day that the forces of Gog make this fateful move, God will be aroused in the full fury of His anger. He will take action against *His enemy* – and the enemy of *His kingdom* – bringing forth the weapons of His indignation: Cosmic disturbances, destructive Earthquakes, tempests, hailstone and pestilence (Ezekiel 38:18 – 23)

Modern Israel's Blindness Removed.
In chapter 39 Ezekiel tells of the tremendous slaughter of the foes of God and His kingdom people, and the months required to bury the dead and cleanse the land after the carnage.

This is not going to be achieved without tremendous cost to our peoples in lives and goods, destruction of our cities, and destruction and pollution of our lands. There will be a great mourning in our nations at that time. However there is a special result which will be the outcome of all this carnage. The purpose is threefold:

1 To make Himself known to the heathen nations as Almighty God (Ezekiel 39:7).

2 To make Himself known as the Holy One in the midst of His people (Ezekiel 39:22 and 34:30).

3 and to make the identity of His people known to themselves and to **all** nations (Jeremiah 31:1 and Isaiah 49:26).

Thus, all the Anglo-Saxon-Celtic people *will awaken* to the recognition of their identity as the true Israel people of God – **and it will happen in one day!** That's how long it will take for Israel's blindness to be removed – and for her to receive a new heart and a new spirit – a spiritual re-birth.

> *So the house of Israel shall know that I am the LORD their God from **that day** and forward.*
>
> *Ezekiel 39:22*

> ***Thus** shall they know that I the LORD their God am with them, and that they, even the house of Israel, are **my people**, saith the Lord GOD.*
>
> *Ezekiel 34:30*
> Emphasis added
> (See also Hosea 1:10)

There is the *recognition* – the *discovery of* who they are!

That word 'thus' indicates that through the happenings of these events recorded by Ezekiel there should come to the British and American people the knowledge that they are "**my people**" the people of Israel.

What a revelation that will be!
They do not know this now: They stand today ignorant of the fact that God is their God, for only on that future day, "that day", will that overwhelming knowledge be arrived at!

> *Neither will I hide my face any more from them: for I have poured out my spirit upon the house of Israel, saith the Lord GOD.*
>
> *Ezekiel 39:29*

Therefore, and indisputably, this cannot refer to the Jews wherever they are, or even the Jewish (so called State of Israel) they know themselves as the people of God, even we commonly call them such; but this marvellous thrilling knowledge is to come to a people who are ignorant –

blinded to their identity today – and they are called "The House of Israel". Paul states the people of Israel will be blinded to their identity, until the fullness of the gentiles is come in. A period which is now at hand (Romans 11:25).

So then this House of Israel – are at this present moment blinded to their identity and knowledge that God is *their* God!

Neither can this prophecy refer to the true Church. The true Church knows that God is their God. But this House of Israel does not, and will not till the end of Armageddon when this divine revealing comes to her.

Jesus Christ King of Kings

Not only will all the people of our nations recognise Jesus Christ as their God in a special and national sense – they will also recognise His true Church – His laws – even all the Holy Festivals.

> *And David my servant shall be king over them; and they all shall have one shepherd: they shall also walk in my judgments, and observe my statutes, and do them.*
>
> *Ezekiel 37:24*

The term in this verse "David my servant" means the House of David, upon whose throne Jesus Christ will reign upon the earth. He is the one and only Shepherd whom the people will recognise as the true and rightful heir to the throne of David, and their King – in fulfilment of the angels announcement to Mary, His mother:

> *He shall be great, and shall be called the Son of the Highest: and the Lord God shall give unto him the throne of his father David:*
>
> *And he shall reign over the house of Jacob for ever; and of his kingdom there shall be no end.*
>
> *Luke 1:32, 33*
> See also Isaiah 9:6, 7

That throne exists today upon the earth in fulfilment of Divine prophecy. *And the word of the LORD came unto Jeremiah, saying,*

Thus saith the LORD; If ye can break my covenant of the day, and my covenant of the night, and that there should not be day and night in their season;

Then may also my covenant be broken with David my servant, that he should not have a son to reign upon his throne; and with the Levites the priests, my ministers.

As the host of heaven cannot be numbered, neither the sand of the sea measured: so will I multiply the seed of David my servant, and the Levites that minister unto me.

Moreover the word of the LORD came to Jeremiah, saying,

Considerest thou not what this people have spoken, saying, The two families which the LORD hath chosen, he hath even cast them off? thus they have despised my people, that they should be no more a nation before them.

Thus saith the LORD; If my covenant be not with day and night, and if I have not appointed the ordinances of heaven and earth;

Then will I cast away the seed of Jacob, and David my servant, so that I will not take any of his seed to be rulers over the seed of Abraham, Isaac, and Jacob: for I will cause their captivity to return, and have mercy on them.

Jeremiah 33:19-26

Here the Lord, speaking through Jeremiah, states that as long as the ordinances of heaven and earth exist, that is the sun, moon, stars, heavens, earth, sea, day and night, whilst ever these exist, then the throne of David will exist somewhere upon the earth. The custodians upon that throne today are the British Royal Family and there it will remain secure – until He who comes whose right it is – meaning Jesus Christ (Ezekiel 21:27).

*In those days, and at that time, will I cause the Branch of
righteousness to grow up unto David; and he shall execute
judgment and righteousness in the land.
In those days shall Judah be saved, and Jerusalem shall dwell
safely: and this is the name wherewith she shall be called, The
LORD our righteousness.*

*Jeremiah 33:15, 16
See also Zechariah 6:12, 13
Zechariah 14:9*

Christ will indeed be the King of Kings upon the earth ruling upon the
throne of His Father (descendant) David administering the Divine laws
contained in the Statutes and Judgements. The author believes with all
his heart and soul that the only effective rule for humanity is an absolute
monarchy. For a little while the heavens have received Christ, the only
one worthy of unlimited rule; but the King of men is coming back, in
infinite compassion for the World which drove Him out. For He is
coming, not only to the Church, but all creation waits.

*Whom the heaven must receive until the times of restitution of
all things.*

Acts 3:21

That is the Golden Age. The new order of ages – coming soon under the
rule of Jesus Christ – may the time be hastened.

When the Towers Fall the Countdown Begins

*And there shall be upon every high mountain, and upon every
high hill, rivers and streams of waters in the day of the great
slaughter, **when the towers fall.***

Isaiah 30:25

This amazing prophecy by Isaiah indicates, that the terrorist attack on the
twin towers of the World Trade Centre, of the 11th September 2001
would be the trigger, to the sequence of events leading up to the events
now under discussion.

Coincident with these events it distinctly states in scripture, in quite a number of places that a terrible literal punishment will come upon the wicked commencing at that time.

This terrible time is referred to in Isaiah.

> *For the stars of heaven and the constellations thereof shall not give their light: the sun shall be darkened in his going forth, and the moon shall not cause her light to shine.*
>
> *And I will punish the world for their evil, and the wicked for their iniquity; and I will cause the arrogancy of the proud to cease, and will lay low the haughtiness of the terrible.*
>
> *I will make a man more precious than fine gold; even a man than the golden wedge of Ophir.*
>
> *Therefore I will shake the heavens, and the earth shall remove out of her place, in the wrath of the LORD of hosts, and in the day of his fierce anger.*
>
> *Isaiah 13:10 – 13*

Giving the reason:

> *The earth also is defiled under the inhabitants thereof; because they have transgressed the laws, changed the ordinance, broken the everlasting covenant.*
>
> *Therefore hath the curse devoured the earth, and they that dwell therein are desolate: therefore the inhabitants of the earth are burned, and few men left.*
>
> *Isaiah 24:5*

Confirming this:

> *And it shall come to pass, that he who fleeth from the noise of the fear shall fall into the pit; and he that cometh up out of the midst of the pit shall be taken in the snare: for the windows from on high are open, and the foundations of the earth do shake.*

> *The earth is utterly broken down, the earth is clean dissolved, the earth is moved exceedingly.*
> *The earth shall reel to and fro like a drunkard, and shall be removed like a cottage; and the transgression thereof shall be heavy upon it; and it shall fall, and not rise again.*

> *And it shall come to pass in that day, that the LORD shall punish the host of the high ones that are on high, and the kings of the earth upon the earth.*

> *And they shall be gathered together, as prisoners are gathered in the pit, and shall be shut up in the prison, and after many days shall they be visited.*

> *Then the moon shall be confounded, and the sun ashamed, when the LORD of hosts shall reign in mount Zion, and in Jerusalem, and before his ancients gloriously.*
> *Isaiah 24:18 – 23*

Read again Isaiah 30 where it is speaking of the restoration and redemption of Israel, and God's punishment for her enemies.

> *Moreover the light of the moon shall be as the light of the sun, and the light of the sun shall be sevenfold, as the light of seven days, in the day that the LORD bindeth up the breach of his people, and healeth the stroke of their wound.*

> *Behold, the name of the LORD cometh from far, burning with his anger, and the burden thereof is heavy: his lips are full of indignation, and his tongue as a devouring fire:*

And his breath, as an overflowing stream, shall reach to the midst of the neck, to sift the nations with the sieve of vanity: and there shall be a bridle in the jaws of the people, causing them to err.

verses 26 – 28

And I will turn thee back, and put hooks into thy jaws, and I will bring thee forth, and all thine army, horses and horsemen, all of them clothed with all sorts of armour, even a great

company with bucklers and shields, all of them handling swords:

Ezekiel 38:4

Mark in the next verse the contrast treatment which falls on 'Israel'. For in connection with this punishment of Gog's confederacy nations, there is associated a great and miraculous deliverance for the Israel nations:

Ye shall have a song, as in the night when a holy solemnity is kept; and gladness of heart, as when one goeth with a pipe to come into the mountain of the LORD, to the mighty One of Israel.

Isaiah 30:29

That is modern Israel's portion: Great Britain and America and contrasts very significantly with the punishment of the heathen nations who are confederated against His people for the following verses read:

And the LORD shall cause his glorious voice to be heard, and shall shew the lighting down of his arm, with the indignation of his anger, and with the flame of a devouring fire, with scattering, and tempest, and hailstones.

verse 30

This is not the end of the world; for Israel is preserved in safety through it all, "Ye shall have a song, as in the night … and gladness of heart". But the heathen conspirators, "The flame of favouring fire, and scattering, and tempest, and hailstones".

The Jews Recognise Their God

The prophets Joel and Zechariah foresaw the events of the latter days and confirm the events spoken of by Ezekiel; only their accounts are more descriptive and detailed and are mainly concerned with the events surrounding the Holy Land and in particular the city of Jerusalem. Joel describes these events most vividly:

> *BLOW ye the trumpet in Zion, and sound an alarm in my holy mountain: let all the inhabitants of the land tremble: for the day of the LORD cometh, for it is nigh at hand;*
>
> *Joel 2:1*

Then Joel continues to describe the events of that day in great detail.

At that time there will be a great mourning in the Holy Land because of the power and destruction of the great hordes of Gog. Great fear will be upon the people.

> *And rend your heart, and not your garments, and turn unto the LORD your God: for he is gracious and merciful, slow to anger, and of great kindness, and repenteth him of the evil.*
>
> *verse 13*

> *Let the priests, the ministers of the LORD, weep between the porch and the altar, and let them say, Spare thy people, O LORD, and give not thine heritage to reproach, that the heathen should rule over them: wherefore should they say among the people, Where is their God?*
>
> *verse 17*

> *Then will the LORD be jealous for his land, and pity his people.*

> *Yea, the LORD will answer and say unto his people, Behold, I will send you corn, and wine, and oil, and ye shall be satisfied*

therewith: and I will no more make you a reproach among the heathen:

But I will remove far off from you the northern army, and will drive him into a land barren and desolate, with his face toward the east sea, and his hinder part toward the utmost sea, and his stink shall come up, and his ill savour shall come up, because he hath done great things.

Joel 2:18 - 20

The prophet Zechariah continues the order of events of that day:

In that day shall the LORD defend the inhabitants of Jerusalem; and he that is feeble among them at that day shall be as David; and the house of David shall be as God, as the angel of the LORD before them.

And it shall come to pass in that day, that I will seek to destroy all the nations that come against Jerusalem.

In that day, saith the LORD, I will smite every horse with astonishment, and his rider with madness: and I will open mine eyes upon the house of Judah, and will smite every horse of the people with blindness."

Zechariah 12:8, 9
Zechariah 12:4

And his feet shall stand in that day upon the mount of Olives, *which is before Jerusalem on the east, and the mount of Olives shall cleave in the midst thereof toward the east and toward the west, and there shall be a very great valley; and half of the mountain shall remove toward the north, and half of it toward the south.*

Zechariah 14:4

"And I will pour upon the house of David, and upon the inhabitants of Jerusalem, the spirit of grace and of supplications: **and they shall look upon me whom they have pierced,** *and they shall mourn for him, as one*

mourneth for his only son, and shall be in bitterness for him, as one that is in bitterness for his firstborn."

Zechariah 12:10

And one shall say unto him, What are these wounds in thine hands? Then he shall answer, Those with which I was wounded in the house of my friends.

Zechariah 13:6

And I will bring the third part through the fire, and will refine them as silver is refined, and will try them as gold is tried: they shall call on my name, and I will hear them: I will say, It is my people: **and they shall say, The LORD is my God.**

Zechariah 13:9

There is the recognition – the Jewish people will recognise Jesus Christ as their God. What a day that will be!

And the LORD shall be king over all the earth: in that day shall there be one LORD, and his name one.

And this shall be the plague wherewith the LORD will smite all the people that have fought against Jerusalem; Their flesh shall consume away while they stand upon their feet, and their eyes shall consume away in their holes, and their tongue shall consume away in their mouth.

Zechariah 14:9
Zechariah 14:12

These great events are about to happen. Every day that passes brings that great day nearer when the Lord will arise out of His place publicly to acknowledge in the sight of *all* the nations – His long lost people Israel and the Jews, to reveal Himself to be their God and they to be His people.

The author is only able to touch upon these matters briefly. But one thing is certain, there has yet to come to the Anglo-Saxon-Celtic nations – the House of Israel – and to the 'Jews' – the House of Judah – and

Jerusalem the greatest surprise and the greatest deliverance ever experienced in their long chequered history.

The Holy Festivals to be Restored

> *And it shall come to pass, that every one that is left of all the nations which came against Jerusalem shall even go up from year to year to worship the King the LORD of hosts,* **and to keep the feast of tabernacles.**
> *And it shall be, that whoso will not come up of all the families of the earth unto Jerusalem to worship the King, the LORD of hosts, even upon them shall be no rain.*
>
> *And if the family of Egypt go not up, and come not, that have no rain; there shall be the plague, wherewith the LORD will smite the heathen that come not up to keep the feast of tabernacles.*
>
> *This shall be the punishment of Egypt, and the punishment of all nations that come not up to keep the feast of tabernacles.*
>
> *In that day shall there be upon the bells of the horses,* HOLINESS UNTO THE LORD; *and the pots in the* LORD's *house shall be like the bowls before the altar.*
> *Zechariah 14:16 – 20*

This passage depicts a continuation of the events mentioned previously. It will be a time when Jesus Christ is reigning upon the throne of His father David as King of Kings. *All* nations will recognise Him as such and will also be required to recognise Him as "The Lord of Hosts" – The God of *All* the families upon the earth (Revelation 19:11 – 21).

We are also informed that "all nations" will be required to keep the Feast of Tabernacles! It stands to reason that if *all nations* are to keep this feast then this commandment would also apply to all the other festivals; including the Feast of Unleavened Bread, the Feast of Firstfruits, the Feast of Trumpets and the Day of Atonement. Remember the Passover was not done away, only the symbols were changed when the Law of Sacrifice was fulfilled (Articles of Faith, p. 490. James Talmage).

No longer will the people be saying that the festivals are "all done away", it will be **mandatory** upon all nations on earth to observe and keep these festivals!

In modern revelation we are told that the Lord will restore all His laws contained in the Statutes and Judgements and according to Zechariah these will include obedience and observance of the Holy Festivals.

> *But, verily I say unto you that in time ye shall have no king nor ruler, for I will be your king and watch over you.*
>
> *Wherefore, hear my voice and follow me, and you shall be a free people, and ye shall have no laws but my laws when I come, for I am your lawgiver, and what can stay my hand?*
> D&C 38:21, 22

Great tribulations are predicted upon those nations – even individuals and families – who then refuse to obey and keep His Law and Holy Festivals. They will suffer drought, pestilence, famine and disease. By this admonition it seems that there will be, even then people and nations who will be stubborn and obstinate to accept the universal Law of God.

Oh, if we could let these mighty words seize our souls with the tremendous meaning they bear.

> *In that day shall there be upon the bells of the horses, HOLINESS UNTO THE LORD; and the pots in the LORD's house shall be like the bowls before the altar.*
> Zechariah 14:20

And

> *And if any man will hurt them, fire proceedeth out of their mouth, and devoureth their enemies: and if any man will hurt them, he must in this manner be killed.*
> Revelation 11:5

That is the day of great Revealing!
That is the day of the great Restoration of "all things"!

That is the day of Israel's and Judah's marvellous deliverance!
That is the day on which the Lord takes up again His active
governor-ship over Israel and the world!

That is the day for the restoration of His Divine Laws. From that day
there will never be a hungry man unsatisfied. From that day there will
never be a poorly clad child or a drunken father!
From that day unswerving justice will be meted out to every man!
From that day robbery and violence will be things of the past!

From that day every man will have work to do, and he will not have to
wring out from a reluctant earth a mean and pitiful existence; but the
whole earth, freed from the curse, becoming bountiful and productive
beyond imagination, shall then give back to man its abounding increase.

What a marvellous day that will be!

**Can you understand the intensity of meaning there is in that last
statement? A New World Government under the rule of the Saviour
Jesus Christ and administered by His Priesthood! No wars,
pestilence, disease, hunger, poverty or strife. A glorious age of
peace, prosperity and happiness.**

It will be the fulfilment of the prayer taught by our Lord to His disciples
and used by thousands every day perhaps without knowledge of its
meaning:

> *Thy kingdom come. Thy will be done in earth, as it is in
> heaven.*
> > *Matthew 6:10*

Therefore, let us *unseal the book, the time has come!* Truth demands it, and
God's word demands it! It is the great need of the nation to prepare itself
for the marvellous events close at hand.

The author touches these vital and sacred things with the deepest
reverence; venturing to assert them positively, and offering for the
patient consideration of readers the strange discovery which has been
forced upon him by the earnest and prayerful study of the word.

It is hoped that he has laid some seeds which others will bring to fruition and declare as did Paul

> *I have planted, Apollos watered; but God gave the increase.*
> *1 Corinthians 3:6*

Bibliography

Holy Bible	Authorised Version
Holy Bible	Joseph Smith Translation (JST)
Holy Bible	Ferrar Fenton Translation
Book of Mormon	
Doctrine and Covenants (D&C)	
Books of Moses and Abraham	Pearl of Great Price
Apocrypha	
Josephus – Complete Works	Translation by William Whiston
Documentary History of The Church of Jesus Christ Of Latter-day Saints	
Jewish Encyclopaedia	
Encyclopaedia Britannica	11th edition
Young's Analytical Concordance of the Holy Bible	8th edition
Grimm's Fairy Tales for Young and Old	Translated by Ralph Manheim, Published by Victor Gollancz, London
The Oxford Nursery Rhyme Book	By Iona and Peter Opie, Pub 1980 by Book Club Associates and Oxford University Press
The Two Babylons	Alexander Hislop, Pub Loizeaux Brothes, New Jersey, USA
Milestones of History (9 volumes)	Readers Digest Association Ltd, London in association with Newsweek Books, N.Y.
The Penguin Atlas (4 volumes)	1967 Colin McEvedy, Pub Penguin Books Ltd, Harmondsworth, Middx, England
Pre-Historic London It's Mounds And Circles (1914)	E.O. Gordon, Published by Covenant Publishing Co. Ltd., London
Chronicles of Eri (Ireland) (2 volumes)	by Dr. Roger O'Connor. Translated from the original manuscripts in the Phoenician dialect of the Scythian language, 1822. (British Library Rare Documents Centre, Boston Spa, Weatherby, West Yorkshire, England)
The Incredible Nordic Origins (1981)	S. Gusten Olsen, Published by Nordica S.F. Ltd, Sevenoaks, Kent, England
Articles of Faith	James E. Talmage
The Way to Perfection	Joseph Fielding Smith
Doctrines of Salvation (3 volumes)	Joseph Fielding Smith
Teachings of the Prophet Joseph Smith	Joseph Fielding Smith